CENTER BOOKS ON
CONTEMPORARY LANDSCAPE DESIGN

Frederick R. Steiner
Consulting Editor

George F. Thompson
Series Founder and Director

Published in cooperation with
the Center for American Places,
Santa Fe, New Mexico, and
Harrisonburg, Virginia

PUBLISHING FOR THE WORLD
125 Years
THE JOHNS HOPKINS UNIVERSITY PRESS

BIG

"Sorely throb my feet, a-tramping city pavements (Ah, the springy sod upon an upland moor!)"

R. Stoll

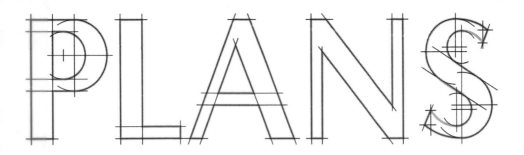

PLANS

The Allure and Folly of Urban Design

KENNETH
KOLSON

The
Johns Hopkins
University Press
*Baltimore
and London*

FRONTISPIECE
*Advertisement showing
the mansions of Shaker
Heights floating on
clouds above Terminal
Tower and Public
Square, Cleveland, 1927.*

Johns Hopkins Paperbacks edition, 2003
9 8 7 6 5 4 3 2 1

The Johns Hopkins University Press
2715 North Charles Street
Baltimore, Maryland 21218-4363
www.press.jhu.edu

*The Library of Congress has cataloged the hardcover
edition of this book as follows:*

Kolson, Kenneth L., 1945–
    Big plans : the allure and folly of urban design /
Kenneth Kolson.
        p. cm. — (Center books on contemporary
landscape design)
Includes bibliographical references (p.) and index.
    ISBN 0-8018-6679-0 (alk. paper)
    1. Cities and towns. 2. City planning. 3. Urban
renewal. I. Title. II. Series.
    HT153 K64 2001
    307.3'416—dc21
00-011532

ISBN 0-8018-7730-X (pbk.)

A catalog record for this book is available from the
British Library.

TO *Jane, Amanda,* AND *Theodore*

Make no little plans; they have no magic to stir men's blood and probably themselves will not be realized. Make big plans; aim high in hope and work, remembering that a noble, logical diagram once recorded will never die, but long after we are gone will be a living thing, asserting itself with ever-growing insistency.

—DANIEL BURNHAM

CONTENTS

ILLUSTRATIONS

ACKNOWLEDGMENTS

THAT SERENDIPITY IS GREATLY UNDERRATED AS A SHAPER
of scholarship is the lesson I am inclined to draw from having devoted
the better part of a professional career to a series of teaching assign-
ments and research projects leading—haltingly and circuitously—to
this book.

In 1975, while spending a semester at John Cabot International
College in Rome, a deceptively simple question was planted in my
mind, the same one with which Witold Rybczynski, with Paris in
mind, begins his book *City Life: Urban Expectations in a New World*
(1995): "Why aren't our cities like that?" Ever since, I have been
wrestling with this question and the related question of what kinds
of cities Americans can legitimately aspire to—even as the Ameri-
canization of European cities continues to narrow the urban quality
gap. Given my academic training, I was inclined at first to think that
these were essentially political questions. I continue to think that they
are political in a very profound sense, although they are not exclusively political, and there are aesthetic dimensions that must be considered as well. As insights go, that one might not be very original,
but it was a revelation to me, and I have many friends and associates
to thank for clueing me in.

During the late 1970s and early 1980s, a number of colleagues and
students at Hiram College—John Strassburger, Michael Starr, David
Anderson, Charles McKinley, Dave Fratus, Stephen Zabor, Thomas
Pascarella, Thomas Hellie, Mary G. Ragins, Paulette Gaia, and Julie
Seaman, to name a few—pursued with me some of the issues implicit
in Rybczynski's question, frequently testing them against the docu-
mented experience of community building in northeastern Ohio.
Strassburger and Ragins introduced me to the historic preservation
movement and the writings of John Brinckerhoff Jackson and John
Stilgoe. From Starr, I acquired a taste for the eclectic genius of Robert
Venturi. Under the auspices of Hiram's regional studies program, I

served an internship in the Cleveland City Planning Department that led me into the Cleveland Public Library, the Western Reserve Historical Society, the Case Western Reserve University Library, and the Shaker Heights Museum. Research in those collections forms the basis of chapters 3, 4, 5, and 6, earlier drafts of which were read with differing degrees of sympathy by Clevelanders Norman Krumholz, Hunter Morrison, John Grabowski, Eric Johannesen, Patricia Forjak, and Walter Leedy. Subsequent revisions of those chapters reflect my growing conviction that, just as the nineteenth-century city suffered from a dearth of planning, the twentieth-century city suffered from a surfeit of it. That such an argument should be considered heretical at City Hall might not be surprising; that there should be resistance to it at the Growth Association would, however, seem to speak volumes about urban politics in early-twenty-first-century America.

Outside the friendly confines of Ohio, I have incurred other debts—to Paul Farmer of the Pittsburgh City Planning Department; to Andre Darmagnac of Evry New Town, in France; to Coenraad van der Wal of the IJsellmeerpolders Development Authority in the Netherlands; and to a number of young planners in the Washington, D.C., area who took my course at Georgetown University in the early 1990s. In recent years I have profited from the richly stimulating environment of the University Honors Program at the University of Maryland, College Park, where my students have included citizens of, and articulate critics of, Greenbelt and Columbia, Maryland. The National Endowment for the Humanities, my employer since 1985, nurtured my professional development with two grants of released time for research on pre-Columbian North American urbanism, the subject of chapter 2. At the Endowment and elsewhere I have been blessed when it comes to supervisors—Richard Ekman, Guinevere L. Griest, Jerry L. Martin, James Herbert, and Maynard Mack Jr. have in common a singularly enlightened attitude about the way that individual research scholarship contributes to institutional mission. Margot Wells Backas and Enayet Rahim have helped me in any number of ways, for which I am deeply grateful. I have been inspired by other colleagues who have proved many times over that teaching and research can be complementary activities, and that they inform public service in a wholly salutary way.

This book began to take shape in 1998, when I was a John Adams Fellow at the Institute of United States Studies, University of London, and a fellow at the Eccles Centre for American Studies at the

British Library. Mention of the latter fellowship is a matter of full disclosure as well as an expression of gratitude; the British Library happens to be the subject of chapter 9. I owe much to my several editors: George F. Thompson, Frederick R. Steiner, Randall Jones, Julie McCarthy, and Nancy Trotic. I wish, finally, to acknowledge the many friends and long-suffering family members who shared the burden of big authorial plans. I trust my creditors will consider it a down payment on my debt if they are absolved of responsibility for what follows. Let me state emphatically that any opinions, findings, and conclusions or recommendations expressed in this book are those of the author and do not necessarily reflect the views of the NEH or the U.S. Government.

INTRODUCTION

ODDLY, TWO OF THE MOST INFLUENTIAL BOOKS EVER written on the subject of cities—their essential nature and the factors associated with their success or failure—were published in the same year: 1961. One, Lewis Mumford's *The City in History*, was the magnum opus of a famous man of letters who had been writing widely on cultural affairs—art, architecture, and literature, as well as urbanism—for more than three decades. *The City in History* is a comprehensive review of human communities from the Garden of Eden to Welwyn Garden City and beyond. One of its most memorable themes—the dangers posed by utopian thinkers such as Plato and by master planners "from Hippodamos to Haussmann"[1]—reinforced Mumford's reputation, earned the hard way through mortal combat with Robert Moses,[2] as the sworn enemy of regimentation.

But Mumford's hostility to particular master planners does not bespeak opposition to social engineering per se. On the contrary, few books extol the virtues of purposeful community planning more ardently than *The City in History*, celebrating as it does a series of regimes—for example, the Greek polis, the medieval commune, the little theocracies of colonial New England, and the greenbelt towns of the New Deal—that favored master planning and sanctioned various restraints on individual freedom. Consider, for instance, Mumford's account of the golden age of Amsterdam. The secret of the success of all the Dutch towns, Mumford argues, is to be found in the controls imposed by municipal authorities—Water Catchment Boards, specifically. The glory of Amsterdam, in short, derives not from market capitalism, but from enlightened state planning. Lest anyone miss the point, Mumford, later in *The City in History*, explains that the greatness of Ebenezer Howard's Garden City concept boils down to its being the antithesis of the city of classical liberalism:

Above all, by his insight into the corporate and unified structure of a city, Howard called attention to the fact that the growth of a city must be in the hands of a representative public authority; and that the best results could be achieved only if this authority had power to assemble and hold the land, plan the city, time the order of building, and provide the necessary services. No longer were the most essential agents of city development to be left to the individual investor, whether speculator or owner, dealing with individual building lots, individual houses, individual business sites; for no individual exercise of either foresight or public spirit could produce the equivalent of a co-ordinated and meaningful whole. Nor was the city's responsibility to provide for the well-being of all its inhabitants to be recognized only after the maximum amount of disorder had been created by unregulated private effort.[3]

The second great book of 1961, Jane Jacobs's *The Death and Life of Great American Cities,* was much less hostile to "unregulated private effort."[4] By directing attention to the virtues of diversity, lively streets, varied land use, aged buildings, and incremental, parcel-by-parcel adaptation, Jacobs in effect declared that American cities—including the least glamorous of that homely breed, and *in spite of* the best efforts of city planners—were, to borrow an expression from the architect Robert Venturi, almost all right.[5] While celebrating complexity and the organic urban tissue generated by a profusion of unfettered private interests, Jacobs issued a withering critique of the planning ethos, for which she coined an all-purpose epithet—Radiant Garden City Beautiful—that managed to indict equally the authoritarian cereal boxes of Le Corbusier, the anti-urban greenbelts of Howard, and the retrograde academic classicism of Richard Morris Hunt. Jacobs was something of an *enfant terrible* who enjoyed expressing perfectly reasonable propositions in terms that were slightly outrageous, with the predictable result that her arguments, while memorable, could easily be caricatured: crowds are good, zoning is bad, parks are dangerous, children should play in the street. She insisted on drawing explicit comparisons between city planning and the medical practice of bloodletting. Many readers were appalled that Jacobs was not content to limit her indictment to planning bullies such as Robert Moses, but actually went out of her way to target more cerebral, donnish types, such as Howard, the "heroic simpleton."[6] And Lewis Mumford.

Both *The City in History* and *The Death and Life of Great Ameri-*

can Cities were nominated for the National Book Award in the non-fiction category, and although the former was chosen, the critical acclaim bestowed on Jacobs's book seems to have constituted a kind of monsoon on Mumford's victory parade. In the *New Yorker,* Mumford complained that "Mrs. Jacobs" was lacking in "historical knowledge and scholarly scruple."[7] He addressed her as if she were a naïf ("As one who has spent more than fifty years in New York, speaking to a native of Scranton who has not . . ."),[8] charged that she was obsessed with the threat of criminal violence in American cities, and denounced her for denying that a city could be a work of art ("The citizens of Florence, Siena, Venice, and Turin will please take note!").[9] In sum, Mumford dismissed *The Death and Life* as "a mingling of sense and sensibility, of mature judgments and schoolgirl howlers."[10] Setting aside the patronizing, intemperate, and sexist tone of Mumford's attack, one observes with wonder how readily he dismissed Jacobs's celebration of freedom and diversity, her passionate argument against redlining and the "turf" mind-set, her deep appreciation of human scale and organic growth, and her hearty condemnation of arbitrary power and regimentation. This—despite Mumford's willingness to sanction power and regimentation when exercised by *enlightened* planners—was the very gospel that the man had been preaching all his adult life!

In truth, the two books have much in common. For one thing, both Mumford and Jacobs adopt what is essentially a pedestrian's perspective on the drama of urban life. Like the "groundlings" who stood in the pit below the thrust stage of an Elizabethan theater, both Mumford and Jacobs eschew the stalls in order to learn how things look—and sound and taste and feel and smell—from close up. They are interested in the lived experience.

Consider the ordinary city sidewalk. For Jacobs, sidewalks, "their bordering uses, and their users, are active participants in the drama of civilization versus barbarism in cities."[11] This proposition derives from her sense that what is fundamental about the city, as opposed to villages and towns, is that they are "full of strangers." She perceives in the interactions of strangers on the streets and sidewalks of the city an unchoreographed ballet, the vigor of which is the measure of a city's health:

Under the seeming disorder of the old city, wherever the old city is working successfully, is a marvelous order for maintaining the safety of the streets and the freedom of the city. It is a complex order. Its essence is intricacy of sidewalk use, bringing with it a constant succession of eyes. This order is all composed of movement and change, and although it is life, not art, we may fancifully call it the art form of the city and liken it to the dance—not to a simple-minded precision dance with everyone kicking up at the same time, twirling in unison and bowing off en masse, but to an intricate ballet in which the individual dancers and ensembles all have distinctive parts which miraculously reinforce each other and compose an orderly whole. The ballet of the city sidewalk never repeats itself from place to place, and in any one place is always replete with new improvisations.[12]

Mumford may have ridiculed Jacobs's celebration of city streets "in all their higgledy-piggledy unplanned casualness,"[13] but that does not mean that he was insensible to their charms. On the contrary, he was well aware of the earthy sensuousness of healthy urban tissue. Consider, for example, the imagery in his account of life in the Middle Ages:

In the main, then, the medieval town was not merely a stimulating social complex; it was likewise a more thriving biological environment than one might suspect from looking at its decayed remains. There were smoky rooms to endure; but there was also perfume in the garden behind the burghers' houses; for fragrant flowers and herbs were widely cultivated. There was the smell of the barnyard in the street, diminishing in the sixteenth century, except for the growing presence of horses and stables. But there would also be the odor of flowering orchards in the spring, or the scent of the new-mown grain, floating across the fields in early summer.[14]

In *The City in History,* Mumford arranges for us to hear the plainchant emanating from the monastery and the whistling of the humble milkmaid. He escorts us to the agora of ancient Athens and turns us loose among citizens who regarded themselves as nothing less than the polis incarnate. His account of the hedonistic excesses of ancient Rome is enough to send us careening to the vomitorium. He unleashes the carriages of early modern Paris, and we run for cover. When finally we arrive at the nineteenth century, about three-quarters of the way through his magisterial book, Mumford fills our nostrils with the stench of Coketown's noxious fumes. Reading *The City in History* is a visceral experience, one that recalls the palpable blubber of *Moby Dick*. Come to think of it, Melville was a favorite of Mumford's.

Jacobs's aesthetic sensibilities are much the same. Cities, Jacobs has observed, "are thoroughly physical places," and in seeking to understand them, we should be intent on "observing what occurs tangibly and physically, instead of sailing off on metaphysical fancies,"[15] such as those that Descartes sailed off on when he "complained that not all French cities were built according to the same well-thought-out plan."[16] The problem is that "from Plato to Ebenezer Howard, . . . philosophers and urban planners have been preoccupied with the perfect city and have replaced continuous creative design with a mode of thought that attempts to preprogram life."[17] Such thinking is on display at any number of exotic urban stage sets—the Venetian new town of Palma Nuova, for example, but also around the corner or down the street, for, as John Brinckerhoff Jackson has observed, the "reality which rises to obstruct our view or intensify a traffic jam" is likely to have originated in some "architect's or engineer's dream."[18] The problem with such dreams is that the abstract figure "delimits the social contents, instead of being derived from them and in some degree conforming to them. The institutions of the city no longer generate the plan: the function of the plan is rather to bring about conformity to the prince's will in the institutions."[19]

In this book, metaphysical fancies are referred to generically as Big Plans. Everyone knows that they are not easily effected. For one thing, the Big Plans that people generate compete with one another, which means that the execution of any particular one may require a measure of force or fraud. When imposed, they often have unintended consequences, or consequences that were intended but not advertised at the outset. Big Plans have a way of becoming ends in themselves. And not infrequently, they contain the seeds of their own destruction.

I will argue in these pages that while Big Plans are generally considered effete, impotent—in a word, utopian—they are, on the contrary, all too dangerously efficacious in arousing complicated human passions and expectations that they are unable to fulfill. It would seem important in the early years of the twenty-first century, given the ascendancy of a self-confident modernist revival that has planners

FIGURE I
*Palma Nuova, a new town founded by the Republic of Venice in 1593. This image
from the Braun and Hogenburg atlas has been reprinted often because it is the
archetypal expression of urban rationality and order. Characteristically, Le Corbusier
suggests that Palma Nuova was one of those "golden moments when the power of the
mind dominated the rabble."*

claiming to be the agents of "smart growth," and with every Rust Belt
metropolis hitching its wagon to some crinkled titanium star—Zenith
as the next Bilbao—to consider a far less glitzy alternative. Call it the
case for futilitarianism.

In these pages I will frequently be exploring "the boundary between necessary planning and the unplannable."[20] Let me hasten to
say that by laying stress on disappointment and the psychology of
deflation—dashed hopes, clipped wings, frustrated ambitions—I do
not mean to be calling attention to engineering or technical challenges, although those are important and interesting in their own
right. Nor am I much interested in the baneful influence of politics
as that term is usually understood. The subject that fascinates me
is the way that human nature first spawns and then thwarts the
planning instinct, generating a dynamic of seduction and resistance,

with rape and willing submission never far off stage.[21] Much of this book, therefore, is about the imperatives of human cussedness and whimsy—that streak of perversity that functions as an imponderable constant in a world infested with variables, sometimes sealing our doom and at other times providing the means of our salvation.

Or both at the same time. I have in mind a moving tale related by Alexander Solzhenitsyn in *The Gulag Archipelago*. To make a long story short, at a district party conference in Moscow province, the audience, including of course the party leaders and other eminentoes on the dais, would leap to their feet in wild applause at every mention of Stalin's name. The problem was that in order for these ovations to end, someone had to be the first to stop applauding. And so,

in that obscure, small hall, unknown to the Leader, the applause went on—six, seven, eight minutes! They were done for! Their goose was cooked! They couldn't stop now till they collapsed with heart attacks! . . . With make-believe enthusiasm on their faces, looking at each other with faint hope, the district leaders were just going to go on and on applauding till they fell where they stood, till they were carried out of the hall on stretchers! And even then those who were left would not falter. . . . Then, after eleven minutes, the director of the paper factory assumed a businesslike expression and sat down in his seat. And, oh, a miracle took place! Where had the universal, uninhibited, indescribable enthusiasm gone? To a man, everyone else stopped dead and sat down. They had been saved![22]

Solzhenitsyn reports, however, that the director of the paper factory was arrested later that night.

The other side of this tragicomic coin is that we are as likely to be saved by our vices as destroyed by our virtues. It was, after all, the collective sigh of the Thermidorean Reaction, a moment of ideological relaxation in which the Paris dance halls spontaneously reopened, that put the Reign of Terror genie back in his bottle. To say that we sometimes improvise our route to redemption is not to suggest that our vices are to be relished, exactly, only given their due. Some part of our nature seems to find solace in human imperfectability. Otherwise, it would be hard to explain why people who stand at the gates of the Emerald City persist in praying for their deliverance to Kansas.

It isn't always easy to tell the difference. Consider the movie *Pleasantville*, in which a pair of 1990s teenagers are transported into a black-and-white 1950s sitcom, complete with Ward and June Cleaver look-alikes cast as Mom and Dad. It doesn't take long for the worldly-wise '90s kids to ply the innocents of Pleasantville with sex, rock 'n' roll, race consciousness, and feminist politics—although what makes the film interesting is that waging their campaign to corrupt the nerds restores to the time-travelers a measure of their own lost innocence. By the end of the movie, our teenaged protagonists have raised their sights and their standards of behavior—transcended their own so-phistication, as it were. And in the process characters on both sides of the Pleasantville divide learn that the perfect can be the enemy of the good.

Another example might help. *Back to the Drawing Board!*, an un-derappreciated gem of a book by Wolf Von Eckardt, contains an illus-tration of a little house that Le Corbusier designed for a workers' vil-lage at Pessac, France, in 1926. It is pure modernist form—all clean lines and horizontality—covered by a trim flat roof, swathed in stucco, and painted in a primary color. Von Eckardt also provides a sketch of the house after its occupants have had a chance to work their will on it. The front yard has been enclosed by a tidy picket fence. Curtains have been hung in the front window. The roof has been pitched; the original flat roof had no doubt leaked. Von Eckardt tells us that the patio has been enclosed, a lean-to has been added for storing garden tools, and so on. These accretions were emphatically not part of the plan; they are elements of the vernacular. As J. B. Jackson has writ-ten, the vernacular "does not aspire to express universal principles of design; it is contingent; it responds to environmental influences—social as well as natural—and alters as those influences alter."[23] The point is that the designer of a house—whether in France, Kansas, or Pleasantville—needs to anticipate the intrusion of the vernacular, and not expect the imposition of his or her conceits to go uncontested. Von Eckardt makes the point more colorfully: "Where people can-not legally change their modern habitat, they fight it with vandal-ism."[24] And what is true of houses is all the more true of cities, and Potemkin villages.

I do not mean by citing the case of Le Corbusier's workers' cottage to suggest that the Thermidorean impulse is fundamentally anarchi-cal. Consider the inspiring tale of Hickory Cluster, one of the origi-nal townhouse nodes around which the 1960s new town of Reston, Virginia, was organized. The work of architect Charles Goodman, Hickory Cluster was oriented toward a modernist plaza that was perched on top of a parking garage. Goodman's design expressed the "belief that people in a community must be cooperative, considerate, and helpful to one another for a community to succeed," meaning that a "higher degree of cooperation is required of residents in this development than most Americans are comfortable with."[25] That Hickory Cluster succeeded in actually attracting or nurturing citizens devoted to the common weal is attested to by a recent controversy involving the core of Goodman's design. The plaza was from the

PESSAC BEFORE   PESSAC AFTER

FIGURE 2
Workers' housing by Le Corbusier: Pessac before and after the "vandalism" wrought by tenants

beginning underused; eventually, it fell into decay. When the parking garage was finally condemned in 1998, fifty-four of the ninety residents of Hickory Cluster—most of whom did not have direct access to the parking garage or plaza—nevertheless assumed responsibility for removing the offending structures and replacing them with a conventional courtyard. The *Washington Post* reports that the fifty-four homeowners "raised $500,000 to make the $1.2 million project possible; the rest will come from a bank loan and homeowners association reserves."[26] In other words, the homeowners took collective action—at a cost of $11,200 apiece—to demolish a monument to the *ideal* of community action. The vernacular strikes back!

But where, it might be asked, does the vernacular come from, if not from universal principles of design? To a certain extent, as with the little house at Pessac, it comes from a simple-minded concern for convenience: if you don't have a shed, what are you going to do with your garden tools? But the vernacular also originates in the sense that things should be done in a certain way, or have a certain look to them, because they have been done or looked this way from time out of mind. Was it Walter Bagehot who referred to this as the "cake of custom?" The reader may recall learning in an undergraduate art history class about the vestigial elements of ancient Greek architecture. Above the architrave and beneath the cornice is the frieze, consisting of alternating metopes and triglyphs (see fig. 3). The former are rectangular spaces, here blank, but often decorated. The latter contain narrow vertical features spanning the three horizontal features and tying them together. In Archaic times, when Greek temples were made of wood, this was literally the case. The triglyphs consisted of rods, or dowels, that were strictly functional—they held the entablature in place. The ends of the dowels, called guttae, stuck out at the bottom. When the Greeks began to build their temples out of more durable materials there was, of course, absolutely no need for these gewgaws, but a Doric temple would have looked naked without its triglyphs and guttae. The inoperative window shutters of their day, they completed an idea—a very powerful and complex idea, the ghosts of which persist to this day.

There is something else important about the relationship between metaphysical fancies and mundane physical reality: they tend toward conflation. A few years ago, the *New York Review of Books* published a remarkable article describing the relationship between the USSR and the Exhibition of the Achievement of the People's Economy, a kind of theme park on the outskirts of Moscow, better known by the acronym VDNX. The author, Jamey Gambrell, explained that the Exhibition "was a kind of laboratory model of the perfect socialist country, and was quite literally meant to be 'the motherland in miniature.'" Eventually the Exhibition ascended to the status of "mandala of the Soviet state," one "invested with near supernatural properties," so that whatever existed "at the Exhibition was supposed to exist in

FIGURE 3
The power of aesthetics: The Temple of Neptune at Paestum, showing features of the Doric order that came to be considered essential despite their uselessness.

the country, and vice-versa." Ultimately, the VDNX developed an aesthetic that not only expressed the ideology of the Soviet state, but had the capacity to breathe life into that withered body. "There was a certain intensity," Gambrell writes, associated with the visual images of the VDNX that "reinforced the dialectics of Stalinist materialism, according to which it was enough to say or portray something for it to be true." "It was," Gambrell concludes, "as if the images themselves gave birth to the reality."[27] Abstract images and models, in other words, have "agency," even if the aspirations they express are ultimately unattainable. One might well be reminded of the poignancy of Italo Calvino's imaginary city, "Fedora":

> In the center of Fedora, that gray stone metropolis, stands a metal building with a crystal globe in every room. Looking into each globe, you see a blue city, the model of a different Fedora. These are the forms the city could have taken if, for one reason or another, it had not become what we see today. In every age someone, looking at Fedora as it was, imagined a way of making it the ideal city, but while he constructed his miniature model, Fedora was already no longer the same as before, and what had been until yesterday a possible future became only a toy in a glass globe.
>
> The building with the globes is now Fedora's museum: every inhabitant visits it, chooses the city that corresponds to his desires, contemplates it, imagining his reflection in the medusa pond that would have collected the waters of the canal (if it had not been dried up), the view from the high canopied box along the avenue reserved for elephants (now banished from the city), the fun of sliding down the spiral, twisting minaret (which never found a pedestal from which to rise).[28]

Abstract ideals are not just elusive, they can be self-destructive. Mumford demonstrated how pride in the polis devolved into a kind of civic narcissism that prevented the ancient Greeks from devising practical solutions—some form of federation, for example—to address their larger political and diplomatic problems. Just so, the interstate highway system, a monument to modern freedom and rationality, is responsible for no small amount of the architectural kudzu that threatens to strangle American suburbia. Even the triumphs of science sometimes come with ironies attached. Consider that the terrifying polio epidemics of the twentieth century were caused in part by improvements in sanitation: microbes that had once been ubiquitous, and for some reason harmless when exposure occurred in early childhood, developed the capacity to cripple and kill when, thanks to improved sanitation, they became scarce, with exposure being deferred until adolescence or adulthood.[29] It is a classic case of noble causes freighted with unintended consequences, and it helps to account for a world—our world—in which no good deed goes unpunished.

A large part of this book is concerned with visual images—architectural drawings, three-dimensional models, watercolors, bird's-eye views, maps, plats, and digitized computer images—and the way that they give expression to the fantasies of their creators and fire the imaginations of those who receive, or "consume," them. These images have a powerful allure because they convey aspirations that are distinctly utopian. I will argue that such images tend to overstate the role of rationality in human affairs, even as they implicitly concede, insofar as they rely on appeals that are ultimately aesthetic, the power of forces that are profoundly subrational, even instinctual. In fact, the primary intention of this book is to direct attention away from the glorious images and their solitary creators who, from Vitruvius to Frederick Law Olmsted, have dominated the official history of urban planning. The point is not to disparage the geniuses, but to balance the ledger with common folk, who can as easily be discovered improvising clever solutions to complex social problems (e.g., patronizing inherently counterrevolutionary dance halls or building much-beloved shantytowns on the outskirts of Brasília) as capitulating—even to the point of participating in their own demise—to the metaphysical fancies of long-dead visionaries. Nor is it the point of this book that people should cease to dream. The point is that those wishing to implement their dreams should proceed with caution, and on their own nickel.

I should say something, finally, about the plan and architecture of this book. Geographically, it encompasses much of Western Europe and North America. Chronologically, its reach extends roughly from the fourth millennium B.C. to the Millennium Dome. At times I shall be dealing with huge swatches of urban form—I. M. Pei's Erieview, for example—and at other times I will concentrate on minute samples of urban tissue, even individual streets or buildings. The subjects treated by this book, while almost invariably profane, range from the most formal and monumental to the most improvisational and transitory. Since I wish to bring to the fore those qualities of the city that cannot be accounted for by formal plans, an element of nonlinearity is introduced to simulate the role of spontaneity, even randomness, in the urban experience.

In keeping with the architectural imagery employed thus far, perhaps it should be said that the aim of this book is not so much to construct a new edifice as to stabilize an existing structure by means of some modest scholarly tuck-pointing. I believe that a spirited eclecticism honors both Mumford and Jacobs, and I hope that what follows will demonstrate that *The City in History* and *The Death and Life of Great American Cities* continue—especially in juxtaposition—to reward careful study.

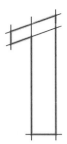

A FUNNY
THING
HAPPENED
ON THE WAY
TO TRAJAN'S
FORUM

IN 1972, JAMES E. PACKER OF THE
classics department at Northwestern University, fresh off an exhaustive study of Ostia, the
port of Rome,[1] set out to research the Forum
of Trajan, a formal grouping of public buildings designed for the emperor by Apollodorus
of Damascus and executed during the first
several decades of the second century A.D.
Trajan's Forum included twin libraries—one
for Greek materials, the other for Latin—plus
an impressive basilica and temple, a victory
column, and a space for public gatherings.
Attached to the Forum was a multilevel shopping complex, Trajan's Market. "Immediately
after its construction," Georgina Masson observed in her classic guide to Rome, Trajan's
Forum "was already considered to be one of
the wonders of the classical world, even after
the building of the new Imperial capital Constantinople."[2] Packer tells us that Ammianus
Marcellinus, a historian of the late fourth century, "summed up the late classical view when
he described it as 'a gigantic complex . . . beggaring description and never again to be imitated by mortal men.'"[3]

Given the historical and architectural importance of the Forum of Trajan, one might
suppose that when Packer embarked on his
recovery mission, he would have had a substantial scholarly base on which to build. But
based on his experience at Ostia ("it was

extraordinary how much hadn't been done"),[4] Packer knew better. In fact, like so many of the monuments of ancient Rome, Trajan's Forum had never been properly studied. The few trustworthy efforts to document the site, such as the Forma Urbis, were badly damaged or lost. There were some contemporary accounts. There was some numismatic evidence. Packer was granted permission to clean, measure, and survey the site, which has a footprint the size of twelve football fields, and to carefully document remaining fragments. In 1997, after twenty-five years of research, he published *The Forum of Trajan in Rome: A Study of the Monuments,* a multivolume work produced with the assistance of the architect Kevin Lee Sarring and containing detailed plans by Sarring and Packer and stunning full-color drawings by Gilbert Gorski. Reviewers have been lavish in their praise of a "sumptuous"[5] limited edition retailing for six hundred dollars.

These handsome volumes reveal "a construction unique under the heavens,"[6] uniquely grand as monumental architecture, and exemplary as public space:

> *Trajan's column was the hallmark of the imperial forum, the northernmost, most opulent and the last of those open spaces in Rome that provided citizens with a kilometer of partly covered walkways and a parade of public art. The forum was Trajan's most magnificent gift to his city and was probably the largest paved area (at least until then) ever given over to pedestrians. It was designed to be the climax of a sequence of forums, to which there would be no sequel. No monarch or tyrant of recent times—not even Hitler in his grandiose plan for Berlin—has provided as much relaxed magnificence for his subjects. Nor had any republic, however rich, ever spent such a fortune from the public purse for its prestige and the pleasure of its citizens.[7]*

As Garry Wills has observed, this was "one of the great urban experiences of all time," and now "we can walk, mentally, through Trajan's Forum as it has been painstakingly reimagined by James E. Packer and stunningly drawn by Gilbert Gorski. . . . The results are dramatic."[8]

Dramatic as they are, the images from *The Forum of Trajan in Rome* are now being augmented by advanced digital technology. As a story in *The Chronicle of Higher Education* explains, Packer found some high-tech collaborators at the Getty Center for the History of Art and the Humanities and the UCLA School of Architecture who have undertaken to digitize his images and "to construct a virtual-reality

Forum of Trajan," one that "will allow close up views."[9] The images in his book had contained a few "rough spots," and so, as Packer explains,

for a display on the Forum of Trajan at the opening of the new Getty Museum later this month, the Museum decided to make a three-dimensional computer model of the restored site. Since this model allowed clear visualization of all parts of the forum, my collaborator, architect Kevin Sarring, and I were able to revise and improve our restorations of its buildings in the various important areas discussed and shown on the Getty computer model. These changes have not only resulted in a more tightly organized coherent reconstruction of Trajan's Forum, but they have also created an arresting three-dimensional artifact. As has not been possible for the last 1,500 years, viewers can experience first-hand the splendours of Trajan's elegant buildings and can understand in a lively and immediate fashion why this "gigantic complex" so impressed Ammianus and taxed the descriptive powers of his contemporaries. The technology of the early twenty-first century has now revealed the true character of one of ancient Rome's greatest architectural achievements.[10]

A FUNNY
THING
HAPPENED
ON THE WAY
TO TRAJAN'S
FORUM

To say that the computer images are impressive would considerably understate the case. This was made dramatically clear to those in attendance at a December 3, 1997, public lecture at the National Gallery of Art. Packer's introductory comments were delivered against the backdrop of one of the images, which appeared to be merely a decorative still until it suddenly began to "move," at which point the audience literally gasped. Sharon Waxman, writing in the *Washington Post*, reports that museum-goers do the same thing at the Getty's exhibit: "They gasp. Then they gawk."[11]

The exhibit exploits "technology dreamed up for flight simulators and Hollywood special effects" in order to produce something akin to "computerized time travel."[12] According to Packer,

It is a major breakthrough. The problem in trying to explain to students or anyone else the real character of Roman buildings is that we don't have them, or what you have is a series of shattered ruins. The whole response people have to architecture is through space, light, movement and the shaping of forms as you move through a sequence of spaces.

What computer imaging allows you to do is to see the building's original sequence, shape and form in virtually a three-dimensional way. You can lie on your back on the pavement and look up at the building, or look at it through the top. Computer modeling allows you to look at the way the buildings are constructed, with all the marble, all the decorations on them.[13]

In his lecture at the National Gallery, Packer demonstrated this by panning the facade, occasionally zooming in for a close-up look at a frieze or some other architectural detail. Then he escorted his audience to the second floor of the basilica for a bird's-eye view of the complex. We "moved" across the piazza and through a colonnade. Someone called out, "What are we walking on?" In response, Packer lowered our virtual-reality eyes, and we seemed to look down on marble steps. Then he raised our eyes, and we began our ascent. Every detail seemed to be accounted for; there were no "rough spots," and the three-dimensionality of the model was entirely convincing.[14] Once we were upstairs, situated against the balustrade and looking out over the piazza, it was up to us whether we wanted to spin around to study Roman barrel-vaulting techniques, think about what kind of statuary would have filled up a particular niche, or zoom in on the Column of Trajan, which loomed just over our shoulder. The exhibit at the Getty Museum appears to offer a very similar experience. According to Waxman, the "tour" there

takes place on a large screen in a room filled with actual remains from the forum, including the torso of a Dacian, one of the peoples conquered by Trajan. There are also winged lions from a frieze. The visitor has the sensation of moving through the forum much as moviegoers feel as they fly through future cityscapes in movies like "Star Wars." Here, the visitor visually "enters" through the front portico, moves across a vast courtyard and through colonnaded hallways and a two-story basilica. The colors and textures are vivid, scanned into the computer from actual marble samples from the forum's ruins and other similar standing monuments like the Pantheon.[15]

If the visual images produced by Packer, and in turn by the Getty, give an impression of having been fashioned out of whole cloth by an original genius, Packer explains that in fact the Forum reflected residual influences "from the large-scale temples of Egypt and Mesopotamia, from the markets or shrines of the Hellenistic East, from the early imperial legionary camps of the northern frontier, or from the urban architecture of provincial northern Italy of the first century after Christ." According to Packer, "All these earlier prototypes influenced the design of Trajan's prestigious Forum, which was itself later widely imitated in the provinces." Packer maintains that there were also local prototypes, and that among these were the Theater and Portico of Pompey, the Portico of Octavia, the Temple of Peace, and the Forum of Augustus. In fact, he insists that the composition should not be considered in isolation from its urban context, because it was conceived as "the triumphant climax in the series of imperial fora" executed as extensions of the original Forum Romanum—the forum of the republic. Trajan and Apollodorus developed a rhetoric that "would complete and unify the total design of all the fora, which, taken together, had evolved into an uncoordinated assemblage of temples, public squares, and colonnades." The entire Forum of Trajan seems to have been

19

A FUNNY
THING
HAPPENED
ON THE WAY
TO TRAJAN'S
FORUM

conceived in the manner of a contemporary literary essay. That is, although an original monument in its own right, it was assembled from familiar parts that echoed those of its other famous neighbors. Repeating their achievements, it surpassed them on their own terms. As we have seen, the plan and its large-scale measurement came directly from the Temple of Peace, but lesser elements also constituted major visual references. The marble pavements in the Hemicycles varied the pavement in the lateral colonnades of the Forum of Augustus, and, with their long lines of Dacian captives bearing elaborate cornices, the attics of the East and West Colonnades and the Basilica unmistakably quoted the attics of the same colonnades and recalled the façade of the Basilica Aemilia [in the Forum Romanum] and perhaps even statues on attics above the garden colonnades in back of the Theater of Pompey.[16]

Furthermore, the Forum of Trajan turns out to be an exercise in propaganda—a celebration of Trajan himself, extolling his virtues as general and emperor and anticipating his deification, and also a celebration of the Roman political regime, for the grandeur of Apollodorus's design "merely continued on a larger and more splendid scale the traditions both of the recent imperial past and of the ancient Republic. Consequently, the magnificent monuments of Trajan's

Forum—and the great events they commemorated—were to be understood not as a revolutionary break with the revered past but only as the newly achieved perfection of preexisting artistic—and, by implication, political—forms."[17]

While Packer the scholar carefully documents the ways in which architectural prototypes and the emperor's political agenda informed the Forum of Trajan, his images themselves are considerably less revealing on that score, for in conveying an impression of architectonic unity they conceal precisely that which the text expounds. To really understand the layered qualities of the Forum of Trajan, we would need images on which Egyptian or Mesopotamian influences are identifiable as such, and distinguishable from that which is reflective of local prototypes and from the blatant self-promotion. In addition, we would want overlays that highlight what is "original," as opposed to what has been derived from secondary sources, or by means of extrapolation from other sites, or sheer conjecture. Standard historic preservation practice is based on this principle and thus requires that restorative work be readily apparent as such; undoubtedly, this becomes problematic when the primary sources are, like those of the Forum of Trajan, profoundly fragmentary.

The point is that Packer's images, unlike his narrative, oversimplify, it being the nature of the visual arts to dazzle or beguile rather than to split scholarly hairs. This applies with even greater force to the jaw-dropping images of the Getty's virtual model, which may account for its having spawned a legion of "vociferous detractors."[18] Sharon Waxman explains:

> In a scathing review, the Los Angeles Times's art critic charged the exhibit's curators with debasing ancient art. "Goodbye high art; hello, high technology," Christopher Knight seethed. The computerized display, he said, is "a fiction wholly dependent on modern expectations shaped by tracking shots in movies and TV shows. . . . This is less an art exhibition than a high-toned version of the kind of corporate trade show you'd expect to see at a convention center. . . . The product being touted here isn't ancient art, but merely the corporate activities of the Getty Trust."[19]

To put this point somewhat more politely, the images in Packer's book, and those that have been digitally remastered by the Getty, invite viewers to look away from the *historical* forum—the forum of classical antiquity, with all of its antecedents and contextual meaning; the multilayered medieval forum; and today's rubble yard—and to gaze upon the Platonic form of the imperial forum. But human beings—ancient ones and modern ones alike—are creatures endowed with limited faculties for comprehending Platonic forms, and images constructed to convey such abstractions will inevitably dazzle the mind's eye "as the sun dazzles the body's eye."[20] As Kenneth Burke has explained, "There is a difference between an abstract term naming the 'idea' . . . and a concrete image designed to stand for this idea, and to 'place it before our very eyes.' For one thing, if the image employs the full resources of imagination, it will not represent merely one idea, but will contain a whole bundle of principles[,] even ones that would be mutually contradictory if reduced to their purely ideational equivalents."[21]

A FUNNY
THING
HAPPENED
ON THE WAY
TO TRAJAN'S
FORUM

A truly faithful snapshot of Trajan's Forum in A.D. 112, even one containing a fully convincing account of the motives of the emperor and his architect, would not, moreover, constitute the whole story of this important feature of the Roman cityscape. I would submit—without, I hope, succumbing to the worst excesses of postmodernism—that while the effort to establish the Forum of Trajan as a "definitive" text and to discover "authorial intent" is worthwhile, it can never fully succeed in telling us everything we want to know, and that this applies to any cultural artifact—its origins, its production, its reception, how it might have changed over time, how it might have been appropriated to other ends, and so on. I do not mean to suggest that the problem is essentially technological. For even when the most high-powered tools of the digital age have been employed to depict the organic growth of urban tissue, the results have been only modestly convincing. The real problem is that the visual images through which Packer conveys his scholarship, and the Getty's digitization of those images, are profoundly ahistorical.

As a vital part of the civic center of Imperial Rome, the Forum of Trajan must have been put to heavy and varied use for many centuries. It would have been shaped by context and contingency—as political symbolism changed, as the pagan religion was gradually eclipsed by Christianity, as the neighborhood changed, as the empire divided, and as the monument to a nearly forgotten emperor was appropriated or plundered by his successors. Any *real* city is at any given point in time a multiplicity of negotiated landscapes. Thus, one wonders about the state of Trajan's Forum during the reign of Theodoric (454–526), when, Masson reports, it was still "in good condition," or at the beginning of the seventh century, when "the Romans still gathered in Trajan's forum—possibly in one of the libraries—to listen to Virgil being read aloud."[22] Likewise, the computer model can tell us very little about the "medieval" forum, or about the forlorn ruins that now lie in the long, dark shadow of the Victor Em-

FIGURE 4
Gilbert Gorski drawing of reconstructed Basilica Ulpia, Forum of Trajan, Rome.

manuel Monument.[23] Through his prose, Packer tells us a great deal about the Forum of Trajan in its several incarnations, but his gorgeous images convey none of this layering of lived experience.

It might be suggested that the inability of Packer's drawings and the digital reconstructions of the Getty to represent patterns of use over time is a minor defect, and that it is unreasonable to expect more of them. But Packer's whole point is that the Forum must be understood as urban tissue, not as art for art's sake. That point is crucial, especially for a monument in Rome—a city that "architecturally, as in its way of life, is a palimpsest." Rome, quite simply, is the opposite of "a museum city, preserved in a vacuum as an *objet d'art*."[24] "All through the centuries," Masson explains, the Romans "have ruthlessly destroyed the old to build up something new, with the same indifference with which Roman housewives have hung out their washing upon imperial ruins or the terraces of the princely Renaissance villas and palaces which rose above them, and Roman children play football or hop-scotch among the baroque splendours of fountains and piazzas that stand upon the site of classical circuses." Masson maintains that the Romans—"appallingly and terrifyingly"—are in the habit of "treating the grandeur of their inheritance with complete insouciance." Her point is vividly illustrated by modern manhole covers and garbage trucks bearing the inscription "S.P.Q.R."[25] Another perceptive writer has referred to the "delicious banality of conducting daily life" in a city that lives "its sedimented past as the most mundane condition of existence."[26]

FIGURE 5
View across the Forum of Trajan toward Trajan's Market and modern apartments behind, 1999.

The remarkable thing is that Rome's qualities as a palimpsest are so often on conspicuous, stratigraphic display. Domitian's Circus Agonalis lives on in the contours of the Piazza Navona. In the old Jewish ghetto, at the end of a row of Renaissance houses, there appear "the stumps of classical columns, relics of the famous Portico of Octavia, rising out of the pavement at the far end."[27] One learns to remove the overlays and to read the history that lies underneath; for example, an ancient temple sprouting anomalous baroque bell towers is a sure sign that consecration has saved a relic of the pagan empire. And there is sure to be more below.

The hardy Roman pilgrim can search out subterranean vestiges of *urbs.* At the Basilica of San Clemente, for example, one enters a baroque church only to discover three strata of Christian churches underneath, and under those, a center of Mithraic worship and the first-century house of a Roman citizen named Clement or Clemens. At its lowest levels, where the sound of running water from an ancient aqueduct feeding into the Cloaca Maxima is clearly audible, San Clemente is in fact "a rather eerie experience,"[28] one that underscores the intricacy of deeply rooted urban tissue, reminding us perhaps of the encomium to the vernacular delivered by the protagonist in *Brideshead Revisited:* "I have always loved building, holding it to be not only the highest achievement of man but one in which at the

FIGURE 6

The city as palimpsest: The church of S. Nicola in Carcere in Rome. A church with a mannerist façade has been constructed atop three temples dating from the third century B.C. Behind this may be seen the mass of medieval apartments built into the ancient Theater of Marcellus.

moment of consummation, things were most clearly taken out of his hands and perfected, without his intention, by other means. . . . More even than the work of the great architects, I loved buildings that grew silently with the centuries, catching and keeping the best of each generation, while time curbed the artist's pride and the Philistine's vulgarity, and repaired the clumsiness of the dull workman."[29] It is precisely this patina of the vernacular—a patina that adorns all cities that have not bulldozed the detritus of the past—that gets removed in architectural reconstructions such as those produced by Packer and his associates.[30]

Consider the Roman neighborhood where I passed the winter of 1975, in the raucous company of a couple dozen undergraduates. We were accommodated in a small hotel not more than half a mile from Trajan's Forum, in the heart of what appeared to be a residential neighborhood but that revealed itself over time to be a highly complex mixed-use district. The hotel itself was managed by an adjacent monastery, and there was some sharing of facilities. Immediately next door was an apartment building with a street-level shop selling wines and oils. Around the corner, to the west, was a basement machine shop and, down the street, a mom-and-pop grocery store, a butcher shop, a cabinetmaker, and a travel agency catering primarily to local residents. About a block away in the same direction were two restaurants. Nearby was a "bar" managed by a gentleman who enjoyed making fun—good-natured fun, for the most part—of my fractured Italian. At the end of the street, next to a small shop that sold antiquities, a man repaired motor scooters.

In the block just north of our hotel were some rather upscale row houses, one of which was being used as an embassy. About a block to the south were more apartment buildings, and also an ancient church and a monument dating from imperial times. Of the cultural and commercial establishments in our neighborhood, only two catered to tourists in a serious way: the greengrocer always stocked plenty of film and kept the *International Herald Tribune* on prominent display; and the antique store displayed English- and Japanese-language signs.

A FUNNY
THING
HAPPENED
ON THE WAY
TO TRAJAN'S
FORUM

The population density of this neighborhood must have been quite high, for nearly all the buildings were three or four stories tall, and flush with the narrow streets. The apartment buildings—all of them dressed in some variation of the distinctive Roman ochre—typically had central courtyards with reserved parking for residents. It was impossible to tell when these buildings had been constructed, since in terms of style they adhered to a strict if somewhat bland classicism. My guess is that some were quite ancient, but that most had been built in the nineteenth century; nearly all had been seriously renovated at one time or another.

There were many children in the neighborhood. After school—to the consternation of no one, it seemed—the boys and girls, most of them in school uniforms, played soccer in the street. There were also a large number of older people. Some were habitués of the bar, although they never seemed to order anything to drink. In my mind's eye I remember this neighborhood as a vertical and vital place, where the foot traffic was heavy enough, and the parked cars numerous enough, to slow down the Cinquecentos, if not the bicycles and Vespas. I also have a vivid sense of a cool, dark place, where one might find some relief from the summer heat. And despite—or perhaps, as Jane Jacobs would argue, because of—the high level of activity, even rowdiness, I recall a sense of security. During our semester in residence, we heard of no crimes in our neighborhood. It may be worth noting that two of my students were robbed at gunpoint after dark on a wide street abutting the Circus Maximus—a green yet desolate monolith with an unsavory reputation. Jacobs would have predicted as much, and the students, having read her, should have known better than to go there. Jacobs, were she to have accompanied us on our Roman holiday, also would have observed that our neighborhood, like her beloved Hudson Street in Greenwich Village, met the four criteria for generating urban diversity: the district, divided into short blocks, was densely populated, contained a mixture of new and old buildings, and generated activities of various kinds on different schedules.[31] There really is no way of creating a dazzling image of our

FIGURE 7
*Aerial view of
the Getty Center,
Los Angeles.*

neighborhood, for the simple reason that—recalling Kenneth Burke's commentary on the relationship between concrete images and their "ideational equivalents"—this type of cityscape is deeply rooted in principles that are mutually contradictory; that is the secret of its charm. Or, I should say, that *was* the secret of its charm, for the neighborhood, like almost all of the historic center of Rome, has been sadly gentrified, and rendered far less lively, in the course of the past quarter-century.

Back to Trajan's Forum. I would submit that, as abstractions cut loose from earlier prototypes and from the process of vernacular adaptation, the sumptuous drawings in Packer's book and the three-dimensional images of the Getty model may tell us less about the Forum itself—as it was conceived and executed by Apollodorus and Trajan; as it endured, finally succumbing to the ravages of time; and in its afterlife as stone quarry and ruin—than about the values and aspirations of its several reconstructors and their patrons. Packer suggests much the same thing about his nineteenth-century predecessors, who thought they had recovered Christian basilicas or ornate Beaux-Arts palaces from Trajan's rubble yard.[32] I would submit that Packer has brought preconceptions of his own to the place. Consider his use of such terms as "geometrical," "austere," "plain," and "undecorated," and his argument that the "true character" of the Forum of Trajan is that of an essentially Augustan civic center. According to Packer, the "cleanly elegant architectural ornamentation" of the Forum of Trajan expresses the "chaste, classicizing forms that characterized Augustus' Forum."[33] Can it be a coincidence that these are the very terms employed to describe the most ambitious designs of high modernism?

The funny thing that happened to Professor Packer on his way to the Forum of Trajan is that he ended up at Le Corbusier's Radiant City—or, to put a fine point on it, at the Getty Center in Los Angeles, a $4 billion composition that has been described as a "campus, clad largely in cleft-cut, Italian travertine," "organized around a central arrival plaza." There is "a bright openness to the complex," an essentially horizontal motif suggesting "a connection between the organization of the Center and the layout of the city's grid." The Getty Center is a white city designed to capture the sun, "reflecting sharply during morning hours and emitting a honeyed warmth in the afternoon." It may be significant that architect Richard Meier's choice of building material was based in part on the fact that stone "is often associated with public architecture."[34] Although I do not want for a minute to disparage Packer's stupendous achievement at the Forum of Trajan, it does seem as if the campus of the Getty Center, too, could be fairly described as a gigantic complex beggaring description, never again to be imitated by mortal men.

THE "HIDDEN CITIES" OF ANCIENT NORTH AMERICA

STANDING IN FRONT OF THE RUINS of an ancient human settlement not far from present-day East St. Louis, Illinois, the explorer Henry Brackenridge exclaimed in 1814, "What a stupendous pile of earth!" He professed to be "struck with a degree of astonishment . . . not unlike that which is experienced in contemplating the Egyptian pyramids."[1]

Brackenridge is not the only one to have noticed the parallels between the public architecture of the ancient peoples of the Mississippi basin and that of ancient Egypt, parallels that also must have impressed the founders of Cairo, Illinois, and Memphis, Tennessee. In the nineteenth century, it was generally accepted that the monumental earthworks of the American interior had been constructed by wayfaring Israelites, Welshmen, Vikings, Martians—or a lost race of "moundbuilders." Later, when it was recognized that the mounds had in fact been built by ancestors of the distinctly unglamorous Indians from whom the American frontier was being energetically wrested, the earthworks lost all their mystery and appeal. Recently, scholars have not only rediscovered the mounds but have argued that they are the remnants of "hidden cities" wantonly destroyed and systematically covered up by the dominant European-American culture.[2] But demonstrating that the architectural achievements of ancient North American peoples have been disparaged or obliterated by racists is not the same thing as proving that the ancient mound centers were in fact cities. Let us consider the evidence.

The place to begin is at Cahokia, the site that inspired Bracken-ridge's rapture.[3] Cahokia seems to have been the chief center of a late prehistoric culture that we know by the name Mississippian. This civilization, which prospered during the period A.D.900–1300, stretched from Georgia to Oklahoma to Wisconsin and was supported by the cultivation of maize and extensive trade networks. The Mississippians left behind many artifacts, none more impressive than the massive earthen mound complexes that appear to have been the locus of civic and religious life.[4] Monks Mound at Cahokia, a pedestal on which was constructed the residence of the chief, is the largest Indian mound in the United States and the third largest pre-Columbian structure anywhere in the Western Hemisphere. It helps, in assessing the achievement of this culture, to consider that in A.D. 1000 Cahokia, home to perhaps fifteen thousand souls,[5] may have been larger than contemporary London; there would be no more populous settlement within the limits of the present-day United States until late in the eighteenth century. Cahokia has been described as "a great capital of politics, religion, commerce and art"—it is called the City of the Sun at the site's interpretive center—home to merchants and bureaucrats who played key roles in a complex economy of "unparalleled wealth and power."[6]

There were in all 120 mounds at Cahokia. Mississippian settlements typically had a plaza, or open civic space, usually situated in the thrall of the main mound.[7] It is said that the Native American plaza was a ceremonial area, and it might also have been the place where men played "chunkee," a game of skill involving spears and a rolling stone disc. The explorer William Bartram reported that the ancient ruins had other uses: "The sunken area, called by white traders the chunk yard, very likely served the same conveniency, that it has been appropriated to by the more modern and even present nations of Indians, that is, the place where they burnt and otherwise tortured the unhappy captives, that were condemned to die, as the area is surrounded by a bank, and sometimes two of them, one behind and above the other, as seats, to accommodate the spectators, at such tragical scenes, as well as the exhibition of games, shews and dances."[8]

At Cahokia, the main temple complex, with associated plaza and related structures, was separated from the rest of the settlement by an

elaborate palisade that would have served a defensive purpose as well
as to segregate the politico-religious elite from the hoi polloi.[9] Typically, elite domiciles, some of them "gigantic circular buildings or
rotundas," were constructed on the tops of the platform mounds.[10]
Archaeological excavations near Monks Mound have also revealed
evidence of four wooden structures, built and rebuilt at different times,
that Timothy R. Pauketat cautiously refers to as "Post-Circle Monuments," but that some, who prefer the term "woodhenge," interpret

FIGURE 8
*Cahokia Mounds State Historic Site, Illinois, painting by Lloyd K. Townsend. The
view is looking north over central Cahokia circa A.D. 1150, with the Twin Mounds,
probably a mortuary complex, in the foreground, then the Grand Plaza, with Monks
Mound at the opposite end.*

as solar calendars designed for recording the equinoxes and solstices.[11]
No description of Cahokia would be complete, alas, without some
reference to evidence of human sacrifice on a large scale. Stuart J.
Fiedel's description of Mound 72 is as good as any:

*The skeletons of more than 50 young women, between the ages of 18
and 23, had been neatly placed in a pit in Mound 72. There was no
evidence of violence, but it is nevertheless likely that the women had
been strangled. Nearby lay the bodies of four men, whose heads and
hands had been cut off. The individual whose death may have occa-
sioned this mass sacrifice was an adult male, whose body had been laid
out on a platform composed of 20,000 shell beads. Next to him were
placed the bundled or partially disarticulated remains of several individuals. Evidently as part of the same funeral rite, the bodies of six*

high-status individuals—three men and three women—had been buried nearby.[12]

Some insight into Mound 72 may be gleaned from the practices of a vestigial Mississippian group, the Natchez, for whom there is a historical record. The Natchez lived primarily on family farmsteads and were drawn to their monuments for ceremonial occasions, which included monthly feasts but also, much more memorably, mass funerals. Natchez society was minutely ranked, and while it was dominated by males, noble status was transmitted by the women. Thus, a sort of "circulation of the elites"[13] ensued, as some sons of the nobility, called Suns, were required to marry commoners, or "stinkards," as they were referred to—discreetly, no doubt. The main building at the Grand Village of the Natchez was a truncated pyramid, a plinth for a wooden shrine where a perpetual fire was maintained in the inner sanctum; access, for those permitted it, would have been by a ramp that extended out beyond the base of the pyramid, a signature feature of Mississippian architecture. At the Grand Village, in 1725, a delegation of Frenchmen from the nearby garrison of Fort Rosalie witnessed the ritual burial of the war chief Stung Serpent. It seems that upon the death of a "Great Sun," or his war chief, wives and retainers were routinely strangled to provide service in the next life. Afterward, his house was burned, "and the mound raised to a new height upon which the house of his successor was erected."[14] Because even a lesser Sun was entitled, upon his death, to the same consideration, albeit on a lesser scale, Le Page du Pratz was well justified in pointing out "how ruinous such an inhuman custom would be among a nation who had so many princes as the Natches."[15]

Mississippian societies seem to have been highly regimented,[16] and so we should not be surprised by evidence of orderly land-use patterns. Thus, John A. Walthall reports that Moundville, a Mississippian site in Alabama, "was a planned community. . . . There were areas for domestic occupation, for public compounds, and for industrial activities such as pottery making, shell-bead manufacturing, and the weaving of cane mats and baskets. Certain areas were also used as game courts. Large public buildings were built near the northern end of the plaza. Domestic dwellings were located in the curved strip between the stockade and the plaza and in the area near the river."[17] Evidence of environmental design at Moundville includes artificial ponds, from which archaeologists have retrieved numerous fish hooks.

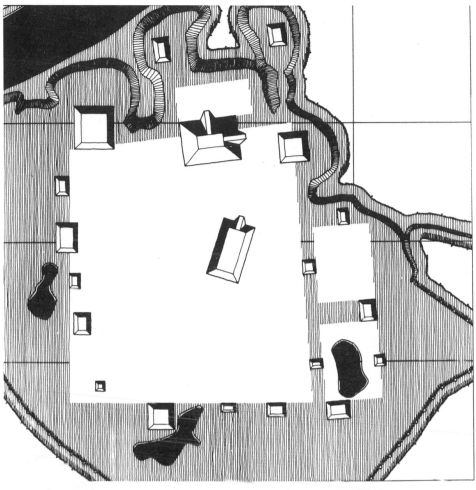

FIGURE 9
Reconstruction
of Moundville, a
Mississippian
site in Alabama,
by William N.
Morgan.

FIGURE 10
One of the
mounds at
Moundville,
1995.

Mound centers in Florida, including the Mount Royal site that William Bartram visited, were highly geometric in their planning, with sunken "avenues" or causeways radiating out from central plazas and integrating artificial mounds, islands, or various natural features of the terrain into the composition.[18] The resemblance of these forms to certain aspects of baroque design underscores William N. Morgan's observation that "movement through space, both vertically and horizontally, seems to have been an essential element of many prehistoric American sites."[19]

The Mississippian civilization exhausted itself long before the arrival of European explorers and colonists. At Cahokia, construction ceased altogether at some point in the fourteenth century; the site was long abandoned by the time of European contact. Climatic change and ecological stress are ordinarily cited as leading causes of the collapse of the Mississippian order. Endemic warfare is another possibility. Fiedel notes that a more mundane explanation involves the introduction, starting around 1200, of beans, a dietary innovation that might have allowed for a reduced population density, thus depriving the ceremonial and administrative centers of critical mass.[20] But the Mississippians were only the last of a long line of indigenous peoples who were arguably urban.

In the American Southwest, the maize-based Anasazi culture experienced a florescence in the San Juan River basin of northwestern New Mexico during the period A.D. 850–1130. At this time a Chaco Canyon elite established its preeminence because of its control over either water or agricultural surpluses and trade, or both. As Lynne Sebastian has written, "Archaeological remains from this period include sophisticated public architecture, an extensive and well-engineered road network, and widespread evidence for water-control technology. Likewise, there is evidence of participation in a very active trade network that involved both regionally produced goods and items transported from the Pacific and Gulf coasts and from Mesoamerica."[21]

For our purposes, the "Chaco phenomenon" boils down to the construction during this period of eight planned towns, or pueblos— great houses, really—on the north side of the canyon, and four more on adjacent mesas. These towns were constructed out of masonry covered by mud plaster, with the necessary wood beams—as many as two hundred thousand—being imported from forests up to seventy-five miles away. Some have argued not only that the architectural geometry of Chaco "apparently incorporated sophisticated astronomical alignments, with the major walls oriented to celestial phenomena," but that the entire complex of towns in Chaco Canyon displays a strict geometrical formality.[22] Each town, as Fiedel explains, "contained several hundred contiguous rooms, arranged in tiers around a central plaza, and rising to four stories at the rear. The largest of them was Pueblo Bonito, which covered 1.2 hectares (three acres) and contained 650 to 800 rooms. It was a planned community, laid out in the form of a giant D."[23]

THE
"HIDDEN
CITIES" OF
ANCIENT
NORTH
AMERICA

On the southern side of the canyon were at least two hundred identifiable villages, and there exists evidence of colonization at considerable distances—up to a hundred miles—from the canyon itself. The Chaco colonies, or "outliers," can, according to Fiedel, "be recognized by their planned, D-shaped layout, neat masonry, and kivas, which duplicate those of the pueblos within the canyon."[24] Charles L. Redman argues that a pattern of repetitiveness—"large sites, in fact, appear to be simply multiples of small sites"—ordinarily bespeaks an absence of complex social hierarchies, but he also concedes not only that the "great kivas and massive architecture used in both central and peripheral sites are suggestive of a central institution," but that there is evidence of "even larger, perhaps interregional, great kivas."[25]

In terms of urban form, the most remarkable feature of Chaco is a road system—the vast extent of it was disclosed only by aerial photography—that is positively Roman in its relentlessness. Broad thoroughfares, generally thirty feet wide, respond to obstacles in their path by devolving into stairways and footholds rather than deviating from strict linearity. Sebastian notes that most of "these perfectly straight, well-engineered features connect outlier sites to one another and ultimately the entire road network converges on Chaco Canyon."[26] Considering the absence of wheeled vehicles, Fiedel contends that the significance of the road network was primarily symbolic—that is, "as a concrete manifestation of the unity of the Chacoan sociopolitical system."[27]

Citing the scholarship of John M. Fritz,[28] Redman notes how the "magnificent architecture in Chaco Canyon appears to have been built according to a master plan, employing symmetrical positioning and repeating detailed themes." This would have had two major effects: "First, only those with access to this special knowledge could design the construction of important buildings; and second, while living or performing rituals in these buildings the inhabitants would be forced to follow certain pathways and see certain vistas, all of which contributed to a prearranged effect. Fritz hypothesizes that the impact of these orientations is to provide a parallel on the ground to the cosmological divisions in the universe, and thereby reinforce the class distinction between the two major divisions in the population."[29]

For reasons that remain obscure, the Chaco phenomenon began to unravel early in the twelfth century. Those impressed by the importance of Chaco as a redistributive system stress the disruption of relations with Mesoamerican trade partners attendant upon the establishment of Casas Grandes as a key Mexican outpost starting in the twelfth century.[30] Sebastian, who strongly resists this redistribution thesis, points out that a number of massive construction projects were commenced after 1090, "a time of serious decrease in agricultural production." Why? She is inclined to think that droughts undermined the credibility of the Chaco elite "as mediators with the supernatural," and so "the large construction efforts of the late 1000s could be viewed as a desperation measure" on their part.[31]

Given Redman's point about class distinctions, we should perhaps not be surprised to learn that there is evidence of extraordinary competition at Chaco—competition that probably was essentially political but that also found architectural expression. This competition "among the patron groups in Chaco Canyon was a major fact of political life during the eleventh century. Archaeologically, architecture may be the clearest evidence of such competition, but competitive sponsorship of major ritual events, perhaps drawing people from a wide area of the basin, is also a possibility. Competitive acquisition, display, and even conspicuous consumption of 'expensive' and exotic items—macaws, copper bells, turquoise, shell—could have occurred as well."[32] One is reminded of Lewis Mumford's account of the competitive forces unleashed among Tuscan families during the later Middle Ages.[33] Certainly, among the possible causes of Chaco's demise, war—internecine or otherwise—cannot be ruled out.[34] The archaeologist Stephen LeBlanc of the University of Southern California has been quoted to the effect that the surviving pueblo peoples of the Southwest "are basically the victors" of several centuries of intense warfare among Anasazi groups.[35]

Another prehistoric Native American group with a town planning tradition is the Hohokam. Fiedel has written that village life "based on intensive irrigation agriculture was apparently brought into the Gila River valley around 300 B.C. by immigrants from Mexico who established a settlement at Snaketown."[36] Hohokam culture matured after around A.D. 200 and bloomed during periods called the Sedentary (900–1175 or thereabouts) and the Classic (1175–1420). The fortunes of the Hohokam were intimately bound up with a vast canal system that carried water over long distances—more than fifteen miles, in several cases—through the Sonoran Desert of southern Arizona. Irrigation made possible a semiannual harvest, obviously a very productive cycle of agriculture. The Hohokam grew maize, beans, various grains, squash, and cotton; practiced cremation of the dead; manufactured a distinctive red-on-buff pottery; and maintained active trade relations with producers of obsidian, shell, and other exotic goods.

Hohokam towns were densely and permanently populated. Pre-Classic public architecture typically included ballcourts, platform mounds, and residential groupings laid out in concentric rings around a central plaza, a formal arrangement with clear "Mesoamerican antecedents."[37] The "consistency of form wherever the ballcourts are found suggests a shared conception of how to construct them and of the proper form and meaning of the activities that were conducted in them."[38] The type of ball game played on Hohokam courts presumably would have expressed fundamental cosmological notions that may have originated in Mesoamerica, but that would have in any event reinforced, and been reinforced by, other ritualistic activities.[39] At a certain point during the late Sedentary period, the ballcourts, as conveyors of cultural meaning, seem to have been superseded by platform mounds. David Gregory contends that in contrast to ballcourts, "the mounds were restricted in terms of both spatial and visual access, and it is probable that highly specialized (ritual?) activities were associated with them. Whatever these activities may have been, available evidence shows that neither the mounds nor the structures associated with them served as conventional residential space during the Sedentary period."[40]

What is curious is that the mounds underwent a transformation of their own later, during the Classic period. Sometime in the first half of the thirteenth century, existing mounds were modified and reinforced so as to render them much more "massive in character." In addition, "while palisades or walls around earlier forms separated nearby structures from the mounds themselves, Classic period compound walls enclose associated structures."[41] As David Wilcox observes, the "people who began living on top of the mounds were not

THE
"HIDDEN
CITIES" OF
ANCIENT
NORTH
AMERICA

ordinary residents."[42] Thus, "for the first time, there is clear architectural evidence for social differentiation involving status and power relationships among residential groups within Hohokam villages."[43] This may well have been the consequence of a breakdown of the regional political order.

Traditionally, research on the Hohokam has been stimulated by modern development in the Phoenix basin and has focused on core-periphery issues. However, recent research has disparaged the core-periphery model and cast into doubt the conventional view of the Hohokam as "peaceful maize farmers who cooperated to build canals."[44] Elaborating on the present controversy, *Science* reports that some researchers have theorized "that a powerful centralized authority lived in the village nearest the canal head gate on the river and peacefully controlled water and economic life along the canal. But in Hohokam settlements east of Phoenix, [archaeologist Glen] Rice found no trace of centralized wealth and authority. Instead, in the architecture atop large earthen mounds at the center of Hohokam communities, he found public council rooms that were in paired and opposing arrangements. This plus traces of distinct ceremonial regalia, indicated the presence of two or more opposing elites, he says. And some communities contained two or more of these mounds, each with their own sets of elites." Some archaeologists now claim that "conflicts over water actually defined" Hohokam society.[45] Neal Salisbury notes that there exists some ethnographic evidence, drawn from the folkloric traditions of Pima and Papago Indians—the putative descendants of the Hohokam—to support the proposition that Hohokam civilization met with a violent end.[46] Indeed, it might not be going too far to say that war is making something of a theoretical comeback in archaeology,[47] and some researchers are beginning to look again at evidence of apparent cannibalism in the Southwest.[48]

Following the trail of public architecture back in time and east of the Mississippi, there are two Woodland peoples to be considered. The Adena were a round-headed group of hunters and foragers who, starting at around 500 B.C., built conical burial mounds and earthen enclosures, used ceramics, lived in makeshift villages, and did some rudimentary farming. The Hopewell were a long-headed people whose archaeological presence becomes discernible several centuries later. Both were ranked societies, widely dispersed throughout the eastern United States and Canada. By 100 B.C. or thereabouts, the Adena and Hopewell had merged or otherwise become a single culture.[49]

The Hopewell flourished from about 200 B.C. until around A.D. 500, and it is worth noting that they maintained a far-flung trade network, through which they imported silver from Ontario, copper from Wisconsin, obsidian from Wyoming, shark teeth from the Chesapeake Bay, mica from the Great Smoky Mountains, and shell from the Gulf Coast. The Hopewell were fishers, hunters, and gatherers; in Ohio, they are known to have cultivated a few crops on the floodplain of the Scioto River. Hickory nuts formed an important part of the Hopewell diet; maize did not.[50] The Hopewell turned the idea of burial mounds into both an art form and an exact science—namely, geometry. Consider the following excerpt from an account of Hopewell architecture in Ohio: "Within thirty-two kilometers of Oldtown are four similar earthworks, each composed of a 329-meter square, a 524-meter-diameter circle, or major portion thereof, and a 235-meter-diameter circle. The uniformity of dimensions and the accuracy of square corners suggest that the builders used a standard measurement length and understood a method of laying out exact squares, octagons, and other geometric shapes, a difficult task, at best, without accurate instruments. The arrangement of each of the four sites varies according to the natural terrain, particularly water-courses."[51]

It is the Hopewell who bear responsibility for most of the truly grand circles, squares, and octagons—sometimes connected by graded processional ways or embankments—that so astonished European settlers throughout the Ohio Valley (see fig. 11). Hopewell mortuary centers were characteristically bounded by earthen enclosures, with mounds inside at the breaks of the *enceinte*. These enclosures were primarily ceremonial and carried on the funerary cult of the Adena. Both groups constructed effigy mounds, many of which survive in the upper Midwest, particularly Wisconsin—although the single most spectacular effigy mound is the great Serpent Mound of southern Ohio. Neither group built platform mounds, or truncated pyramids.

Perhaps because the Adena and Hopewell lavished so much attention on their mortuary centers, we know relatively little about the communities in which they lived, which were probably rather modest, quasi-permanent villages. Certainly, they had some craftsmen in their midst; Hopewell artisans were not only masters of realistic detail, but, within the limits of accepted motifs, imaginative and playful artists. In part because Hopewell culture prospered along the Gulf Coast, particularly in western Florida, long after it had become moribund in Ohio, it may be justified to think of this group as the evolutionary link between Archaic Indians and the more advanced Mississippians. That the Mississippians sometimes incorporated Hopewell mounds into their complexes, adding their distinctive ramps, is often interpreted as evidence of cultural continuity and as such tends to undermine arguments for Mesoamerican influence by way of cultural diffusion or migration.

One thing we don't know about the Adena and Hopewell cultures is whether their origins were extrinsic or intrinsic to eastern North

FIGURE 11
*Squier and
Davis's rendering
of the Hopewell
complex at
Newark, Ohio.*

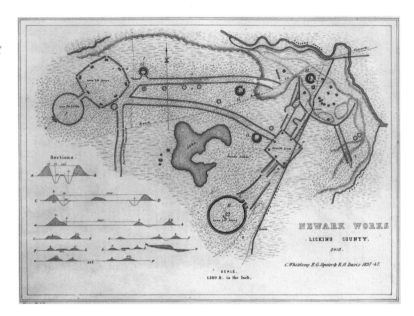

America. Certainly, the case for indigenous origins would be strengthened by the identification of plausible precursor cultures of the late Archaic period. Therein, at least in part, lies the importance of Poverty Point, which dates to 1200 B.C., give or take five hundred years. Poverty Point and other Louisiana sites may offer opportunities for studying cultures that were both pre-maize and not entirely sedentary, and yet arguably urban.[52]

The archaeological significance of Poverty Point, which is tucked away on the banks of the Bayou Maçon in the forlorn northeastern corner of Louisiana, went unrecognized until the 1950s, when aerial photography confirmed the suspicions of locals who had long puzzled over the terrain. Subsequent surveying and digging revealed evidence of an ancient settlement in the form of a terraced semicircle—sort of a flattened Greek theater—on six human-made ridges surrounding a

spacious plaza, presumably the site of politico-religious ceremonies.[53]
The Poverty Point people engaged in trade, importing goods from
sources more than six hundred miles away. There was no maize; the
main crops, supplementing a hunting and gathering economy, were
bottle gourds and squash.

The most prominent of several earthen structures built by the inhabitants of Poverty Point is a mound that measures roughly 640 by
710 feet at its base and stands about 70 feet high. Some have suggested that it is an effigy mound in the form of a great falcon in flight,
but that is highly speculative. The dirt used to form this mound and
others at the site would have been hauled by hand, in baskets, fifty
pounds at a time; National Park Service archaeologists estimate that
this exercise in manual engineering required at least five million hours
of human labor. Such figures encourage comparisons between Indian
mounds and other colossal structures, such as Gothic cathedrals, and
in so doing suggest that they were constructed by advanced and
highly organized civilizations. By other calculations these feats appear far less prodigious. According to Brian M. Fagan, for example,
five thousand moderately industrious people could have constructed
Cahokia's Monks Mound in fewer than two hundred days.[54]

It appears that Poverty Point was not a permanent settlement, but
was used by a substantial number of people—up to two thousand,
perhaps—for a part of each year over a period of many hundreds of
years. As Clarence H. Webb has written, there is "no direct evidence
of houses," but there are unquestionable signs of intensive domestic
use. For example, the eastern part of the site, nearest the Bayou Maçon,
has yielded a very large number of culinary objects, including baked
clay balls, stone vessel fragments, and potsherds; according to Webb,
this "indicates a heavy concentration of cooking—hence of family
habitation." While the denizens of Poverty Point knew how to make
pottery, they didn't begin to exploit its potential for fashioning pots
and other vessels, preferring to bake their food in earthen ovens by a
method that involved firing the aforementioned clay balls. Webb refers to this as "a hallmark of Poverty Point culture," while noting that
the technology "began in preceramic Archaic contexts along the South
Atlantic and Gulf coasts from the Carolinas to Louisiana."[55]

The pattern in which artifacts distributed themselves around the
Poverty Point site suggests a high degree of specialization, that is, division of labor. The southwest sector yielded most of the microflint
blades and blade tools, which "indicates specialized activity areas, pre-

41

THE
"HIDDEN
CITIES" OF
ANCIENT
NORTH
AMERICA

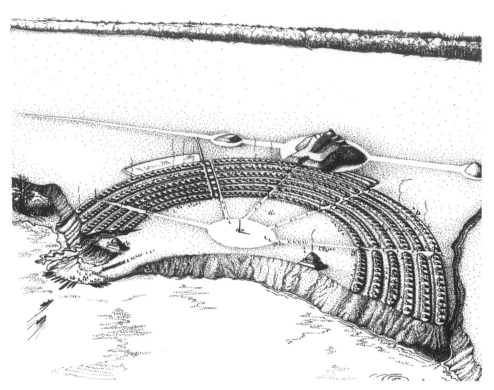

sumably frequented by male artisans involved in the shaping of bone, antler, and wood objects." Somewhat surprisingly, ornamental and exotic objects, presumed to have had a ceremonial function, were widely distributed throughout the site. The western sector proved to be the source of a "relatively large number of beads and other lapidary items, polished problematicals, and stone pipe fragments, conceivably the result of this sector's proximity to the great ceremonial mound."[56]

Because it is so distant—in geographical and chronological, as well as aesthetic, terms—from both its Paleo-Indian ancestors and the later Adena and Hopewell cultures, Poverty Point has been considered, as Fagan has put it, "isolated and enigmatic."[57] Recent research in Louisiana, however, has revealed the existence of even more ancient and mysterious cultures;[58] one of these, Watson Brake, dates roughly to 3400 B.C.—fully two *millennia* before Poverty Point.

Watson Brake is a complex of eleven mounds—a ring, really—that was "occupied by hunter-gatherers who seasonally exploited aquatic resources and collected plant species that later became the first domesticates in eastern North America."[59] Although the site is modest in size, researchers have unearthed impressive quantities of fish and shell-fish remains; over 175,000 pieces of bone were recovered from one mound alone. Of the seeds found, none "exhibit morphological features associated with evolution under cultivation," which is to say that they were gathered, not grown. One important point of contrast with Poverty Point is that there are no signs of external trade at Watson Brake. For our purposes, however, the most interesting revelation at Watson Brake has to do with the architecture:

THE
"HIDDEN
CITIES" OF
ANCIENT
NORTH
AMERICA

Planned large-scale earthworks such as Watson Brake were previously considered to be beyond the leadership and organizational skills of seasonally mobile hunter-gatherers. Poverty Point was considered the exception, and its extensive trade was cited as evidence for sophisticated socioeconomic organization. Our data imply that less complex mound building societies flourished in the southeast more than 1900 years before Poverty Point. Furthermore, not only did these Middle Archaic societies establish monumental architecture in the southeast, but they also may have initiated ecological relationships that led to the eventual domestication of weedy annuals in eastern North America.[60]

Watson Brake is an extraordinarily important site, not only because it helps to contextualize Poverty Point, which until recently had seemed to arise out of nowhere, but also because it pushes the origins of settled life back at least a thousand years beyond the shell rings of St. Simon's Island and Sapelo Island, which have heretofore been recognized as the most ancient public architecture in North America.[61]

At this writing, evidence of prehistoric public architecture effectively ends at Watson Brake, although domestic architecture can be traced to the Koster site in Illinois, circa 5500 B.C. Then, too, Paleo-Indian campsites such as Lindenmeier in northern Colorado, circa 8800 B.C., may be of interest to students of urbanism because they were rendezvous points for widely scattered Folsom bands who may have been impelled by motives that were social and economic.[62]

So what are we to make of all this? Certainly, it is fair to say that human culture in the Americas is now recognized as being of far greater antiquity, diversity, and complexity than most of us ever imagined.[63] Whether such human settlements as those described above deserve to be called *cities* is another matter. It was V. Gordon Childe who, in the 1930s, devised the standard test for distinguishing advanced societies that had arguably undergone an "urban revolution" (yes, Childe was a Marxist) from less advanced societies that had not.[64] Childe's formulation involves ten criteria, which have been fairly summarized as "(1) densely populated settlements, (2) specialization of labor, (3) surplus capital controlled by an elite, (4) monumental public works, (5) social stratification, (6) recording and exact systems, (7) writing, (8) great art styles, (9) long-distance trade, and (10) state organization."[65] In 1972, in a seminal article in the journal *Archaeology*, Patricia J. O'Brien put Cahokia—of all pre-Columbian population centers, by far the most promising candidate—to Childe's ten-part test.

O'Brien concluded that Cahokia easily met conditions 1, 2, 3, 4, 5, 9, and 10, but that 7—the literacy requirement—clearly was not met, and, as she put it, "the data are incomplete on numbers 6 and 8," number 6 being recording and exact systems and number 8 being great art styles. Thus, while she was unwilling to declare Cahokia a "city," she argued that "the process of urbanization was operating in Middle Mississippian culture"—then immediately qualified that by acknowledging that at Cahokia "we are seeing the early end of these processes rather than their more elaborated flowering."[66] Given the tentativeness of O'Brien's verdict, it is not realistic to think that Childe's hurdles could be cleared by any of the other settlements of ancient North America—not Spiro or Snaketown or Pueblo Bonito or Chillicothe or Poverty Point. Certainly not Watson Brake.

Of course, one can challenge the validity of Childe's test. The clay pipes fashioned by Hopewell craftsmen and the shell gorgets of Moundville happen to be very much to the taste of this writer. So are the Hopewell and Mississippian mound complexes, particularly as they have been rendered by modern artists and archaeologists. But do these pipes and gorgets and mounds constitute "great" art? That is harder to say. Most of us probably have fewer fixed ideas about what constitutes great art than people did in the 1930s. We might regard the literacy requirement, too, as unenlightened in its denigration of cultures that specialized in the more ephemeral of the arts, such as the performing arts, and oral or nonverbal means of communication.

I would submit that a diminished confidence in our ability to judge these facets of other cultures, coupled with the paucity of data bearing on pre-Columbian peoples, has lowered the bar for ancient settlements being put to the Childe test. For example, Roger Kennedy's argument in *Hidden Cities: The Discovery and Loss of Ancient North American Civilization* (1994) recognizes no particular distinction between mound centers and cities. An earlier generation of scholars, much influenced by Childe, would have rejected out of hand the suggestion that because indigenous peoples—the Hopewell, for instance—were skilled geometers, masons, or horticulturists, their societies must have been clever and complex enough to have invented cities. For his part, Lewis Mumford, ever mindful of the difference between a city and a mere "thickening of population," would have insisted that we "beg the whole question of the nature of the city if we look only for permanent structures huddled together behind a wall."[67] In other words, a city is more a cultural than a physical phenomenon.

But, of course, the image—of a thick population settled in permanent domiciles near a complex of platform mounds—is a very powerful one, as Kennedy well knew when he chose the painting by Lloyd K. Townsend introduced earlier as figure 8 to adorn the jacket of his book. Take another look at that arresting image. Left of center, on the plaza, a group of humans, dwarfed by the monumental architecture, appear to be engaged in a chunkee game or some other type of innocent activity. Perched on top of the mounds are tidy wooden temples with thatched and steeply pitched hip roofs; at first blush, they look a little like an orderly gaggle of solar collectors or satellite dishes. Monks Mound looms majestically over a wide expanse of carefully manicured greenery, the occasional pylon contributing to a scene reminiscent of the Old Course at St. Andrews. Or perhaps the artist had in mind a kind of grassy Chartres. The entire composition is highly speculative, a sanitized account designed to deflect the charge—in the unlikely event that anyone should ever be so politically incorrect as to level it—that savages, noble or otherwise, dwelled here. Townsend's painterly rhetoric, in short, constitutes an overture for Kennedy's contention that a glorious cultural legacy, nearly lost to racism and greed, is ours for the reclaiming, an assertion reinforced by David McCullough's dust-jacket blurb: "The world of the first Americans was richer, greater, more wondrous by far, than most of us have ever imagined or than most histories have ever even implied." This is quite a benign image. McCullough, Kennedy, and Townsend are giving the pre-Columbian peoples the benefit of every doubt, while the evidence, as we have seen, is highly inconclusive.

Townsend is by no means the first artist to have produced grandiloquent images of pre-Columbian earthworks. That tradition was established in the nineteenth century by Squier and Davis (look again

THE
"HIDDEN
CITIES" OF
ANCIENT
NORTH
AMERICA

at fig. 11). As David J. Meltzer has noted in the introduction to the recently reissued *Ancient Monuments of the Mississippi Valley*—the very first book published by the Smithsonian Institution—Squier and Davis claimed that the Hopewell earthworks "were perfect circles and squares," thus explaining Squier and Davis's predilection for "rounded numbers and squared corners."[68] How this manifested itself in their drawings is explained by Meltzer in the passage below (the parenthetical references are in the original):

See, for example, the roads running through—and breaching the walls—at the Hopewell site (Plate X), and the Ancient Work, Liberty Township (Plate XX). Since Squier and Davis believed that the enclosure wall must have "extended uninterruptedly through," they drew it as such (Ancient Monuments, p. 27). The walls and other features of earthwork were normally shown as being of uniform thickness, although that mostly reflects the limitations of lithography. They themselves appreciated that wall thickness varied. Only occasionally did they admit of ambiguity, at least in regard to the form and features of earthworks. The Stone Work, near Bourneville, for example, was assumed to have an encircling wall, even though it was not regularly laid, was missing in some areas, and appeared at first glance to be the natural outcrop of the hilltop (Ancient Monuments, pp. 11–12). Generally, they were confident in their ability to tell the difference between natural features and artificial ones (Ancient Monuments, p. 34).[69]

The work of William N. Morgan is very much in the same tradition, although Morgan is refreshingly explicit about the principles he followed in producing his images of ancient Indian earthworks. Morgan says that the "precision" of his drawings is based on a number of factors, one of which is "the linear clarity with which prehistoric artists executed their engravings and designs."[70] In other words, his depiction of Moundville (look back at fig. 9) is based in part on the linear clarity of such objects as the engraved stone disc reproduced here as figure 13 and represented by a line drawing in Morgan's book. Whatever its virtues—Morgan's drawings are stunning—his approach would seem to ignore the differing receptivity of the media (namely, stone or shell versus dirt) to precise craftsmanship, and in that degree to exaggerate the level of precision to which ancient Indian structures were designed and built.

To his credit, Morgan also takes care to warn his readers not to infer too much from the level of detail included in his drawings. In addition to some liberties taken with tree lines and watercourses, the caveat applies to the "precisely square corners on orthogonal mounds." Morgan is in fact trying to explain how he gets from the existing evidence to his speculative reconstructions—from, say, figure 10 to figure 9. This reader is not reassured when Morgan writes by way of justification that square corners "have clear precedents in the presentation of Mesoamerican site plans," or when he notes blithely that "this convention has not been applied to sites in the Eastern United States." On this point, he argues that visitors "to Uxmal, Palenque, Xachicalco, Copán, or other Mesoamerican sites probably would be unable to understand many of the still amorphous features of these sites without architectural reconstructions of their probable original shapes rather than their existing contours."[71] To be sure. But that statement, employing the word "probable" as a verbal airbrush, begs the question of how the "probable original shapes" of Indian mounds are to be discovered in the first place, and it contributes to an escalation of the rhetoric about "hidden cities" by ignoring the profound differences between the qualities inhering in earth and stone as building materials (a useful exercise is to look again at figure 10 and compare it in the mind's eye to one of the temples at Teotihuacán). The Mesoamerican spin that he uses to justify his methodology seems ill-advised, too, for the relationship between Mesoamerica and the ancient peoples of the American Midwest and Southwest is vigorously contested ground. That would seem to be reason enough for avoiding a method likely to highlight similarities and to generate what many will inevitably perceive as "family" resemblances. In fairness, let it be said that within the limits of a rather questionable method, Morgan is a restrained and sobersided scholar; falcons in flight, for example, are conspicuously absent from his drawings of the earthworks at Poverty Point.

FIGURE 13
Engraved stone disc with eye-in-palm motif, Moundville.

One fears that the application of computer imaging software to the study of prehistoric North American urban form will only contribute to the prevailing urban grade inflation. At the University of Cincinnati, for instance, scholars at the Center for the Electronic Reconstruction of Historical and Archaeological Sites (CERHAS) "are digitally rebuilding the ancient landscape" of Ohio, "including restorations of many of the earthwork complexes."[72] Like Townsend's painting and Morgan's rigorously geometric images, the CERHAS images are idealizations of Indian mounds; the circles and rectangles are perfectly formed, all the corners are squared, and all the platforms and plazas are covered with closely cropped Bermuda grass. Such fastidiousness is perhaps inevitable when one is dealing with pixels instead of mud, but to me it seems obvious that the proliferation of computer-generated images will only accelerate the claims made on behalf of the human settlements of prehistoric North America.

It might be suggested that ultimately the question of whether pre-Columbian urban form was as regular and monumental as suggested by such images as those produced by Squier and Davis, Townsend, Gibson, Morgan, and the CERHAS scholars is not a very interesting or important one. It might be suggested, too, that Childe's ten-part test ought to be abandoned because it reflects the lingering and pernicious influence of old and false dichotomies, such as civilized/barbarous and advanced/primitive. I might be inclined to grant these points, and to accept the basic premise of the "hidden cities" thesis, if its partisans were less adept at portraying Cahokia as the rustic equivalent of the Forum of Trajan.

Why is it so important that North America have an urban prehistory that is rich, great, wondrous? In her admirable book about Teotihuacán, Esther Pasztory notes that modern students of the ancient New World "have a deep desire for a 'good'—that is, 'humanistic'—Pre-Columbian civilization that we can love with a clear conscience." And so, rather than dwelling on the ancient Americans' failure to invent the wheel, we marvel at their having "done the impossible with simple stone and bone tools."[73] It could be that continuing research in the urban prehistory of North America will reveal that erring in *either* direction—dwelling on shortcomings or marveling at achievements—effectively alienates us from peoples who, like the ancient Greeks, were probably a lot more, and less, like us than we might care to believe.

CLEVELAND
AS CITY
BEAUTIFUL

SETTING ASIDE THE QUESTION OF
whether North America can be understood as
having an urban prehistory, the colonial period introduced a number of European city
planning traditions into the "New World." As
John W. Reps has demonstrated, the pro-
totypic colonial town owed more than a little to Hippodamus and Vitruvius, as well as
to medieval forms, including the "bastide"
that had fortified sundry European frontiers.
Reps's point applies to Dutch, Spanish, and
French settlements as well as to the English
towns, and among the latter it applies to the
more adventurous, including those of James
Oglethorpe at Savannah and William Penn
at Philadelphia. Modern European ideas also
were influential. Francis Nicholson's ingenious
plan of Annapolis recalls (however dimly) the
Wren and Evelyn proposals for the replatting
of London after the fire of 1666.[1] One can't
help but be struck by how intent these gen-
tlemen were on transplanting an old world
even as they were making a new one. Certainly, that can be said of the Puritans.

Plymouth, Massachusetts, and all subsequent Puritan plantations were fashioned on
the principle of Christian love, a utopian
aspiration tempered by the recognition that
such an ideal can be only imperfectly realized—at least in this life. Every freeman in a
Puritan community shared, albeit unequally,

in the public lands and in government. The covenant implied voluntary restraint—disputes were to be settled within the community, not by appeal to higher authorities—and it implied exclusion. Private property was by no means abolished, but members of the community worked the fields together; apparently, livestock was tended the same way. In England, the legal term for such a community was "tithing," male members of which were said to be in "frankpledge," meaning that each was responsible for the good conduct of, and for damage done by, all the members.[2] Part town, part kibbutz, the Puritan settlement was both a utopia and a vestige of medieval communal organization. John R. Stilgoe has taught us that such communities owed much to the medieval *landschaft*, which "was not a town, exactly, or a manor or a village, but a collection of dwellings and other structures crowded together within a circle of pasture, meadow, and planting fields and surrounded by unimproved forest or marsh. Like the Anglo-Saxon *tithing* and Old French *vill*, the word meant more than an organization of space; it connoted too the inhabitants of the place and their obligations to one another and to the land." The *landschaft* was an alternative to wilderness; as landscape, it represented "a mix of natural and man-made form," and in that way differed from "cityscape," which is wholly artificial.[3]

Even so ethereal a vision of the city as John Winthrop's evocation, in his famous 1630 sermon aboard the *Arbella,* of a "Citty upon a Hill" has architectonic implications. But the Puritans were not essentially concerned with patterns of land use or urban design; they were not preoccupied, for example, with the question of what the ideal village commons might look like.[4] For them, town planning was less civic art than a means of engendering civic virtue.[5] For the Puritan community constituted, as J. B. Jackson has put it, a kind of "superfamily." A community organized around a "Place for Sabbath Assembly" reproduced the familiar arrangements of medieval England, where "family and village had been almost interchangeable terms" and where a social hierarchy that stressed deference to the proprietor class echoed the Puritan church, with "its hierarchy of elders, deacons, and ministers." The meetinghouse was more than just a church; it was "school and forum for the discussion of civic affairs," it was a barracks and armory, and it was "the spot for community gatherings and celebrations." Most of all, the meetinghouse was a place that validated basic conceptions about the way the world was ordered—that is, hierarchically.[6] Stilgoe, summarizing a 1635 document called *The Ordering*

of Towns, the work of an anonymous New Englander, concludes that
the "ideal spatial arrangement . . . ought to mirror the divinely sanctioned social hierarchy."[7]

It has been argued that the last New England experiment in town
planning was conducted, with high hopes, in Connecticut's "Western Reserve." Of all the former colonies with vague western boundaries—its 1662 charter set its western limit at the "south seas"—only
Connecticut managed to wrest from the Continental Congress valid
title to a major chunk of trans-Appalachian land, a 120-mile-long
tract on Lake Erie's southern shore. In 1795, the Connecticut General
Assembly quitclaimed most of the Reserve to a group of investors
organized as the Connecticut Land Company, a syndicate that sur-
veyed the territory, divided it into unique six-mile-square townships,
and then distributed the land among its shareholders by means of a
lottery. The surveying expedition, led in 1796 by Moses Cleaveland—a Yale graduate, general in the state militia, and practicing
attorney in Canterbury—laid out the intended capital of New Connecticut a few hundred yards from the Lake Erie shore, at the mouth
of the Cuyahoga River; it was the only time Cleaveland ever visited
the place.[8]

Some of the settlements of the Western Reserve aimed simply to
reproduce familiar Connecticut institutions. But others were, and are,
quite distinctive. In Trumbull County, Mesopotamia—the whole

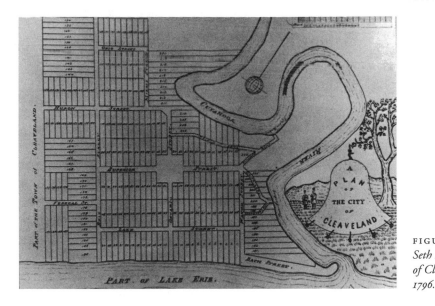

FIGURE 14
*Seth Pease map
of Cleveland,
1796.*

town is on the National Register of Historic Places—was laid out around a large central commons by John Stark Edwards, grandson of the great Puritan minister Jonathan Edwards. What sets such foundations apart is that, unlike in the rest of the American West, where families settled by themselves on more or less isolated homesteads, at Mesopotamia they built their houses around a village green; they shared quarters, in effect, and commuted to work in nearby fields. Stilgoe demonstrates that "outliving" was strongly discouraged by preachers who assumed, with John Cotton, that "society in all sorts of human affairs is better than solitariness."[9] Thus, we should not be surprised by evidence in several towns of the early Western Reserve of "warning out," a practice with colonial New England origins that had the effect of denying residential status. A man who was warned out was denied the right to vote and to be maintained by his neighbors in the event of his becoming indigent. There were also cases of expulsion from the church, again reflecting the corporate ethos that pervaded these communities.[10]

The lesson would seem to be that the Connecticut Yankees who migrated to the Western Reserve, far from abandoning Puritan traditions and adopting the boisterous, democratic individualism that we identify with the American frontier, were—Frederick Jackson Turner notwithstanding—intent on preserving, resurrecting, or contriving forms that reflected their view of community and hierarchy as two sides of the same coin. If some of these frontier towns wore their social conservatism lightly, because they took it for granted, others were more self-consciously rhetorical. At Tallmadge, thirty-five miles south of Cleveland, David Bacon laid out a little theocracy on an asterisk plan, eight boulevards radiating from an elegant Congregational church built in the Federal style in the 1820s.[11] Even in "shelled over"[12] Connecticut, where Congregationalism was the established church until 1818, the Federal style might have been considered passé by this time. But never mind. David Bacon was a man with Big Plans for Tallmadge, and those plans included a branch campus of his alma mater, Yale.

Its founders had Big Plans for Cleveland, too. Unlike Mesopotamia and other Reserve villages that have retained a sleepy, preindustrial aspect, there is but little aside from Public Square, the commons laid out by Moses Cleaveland's surveyors, to betray the capital's origins as a fragment of, or a nostalgic yearning after, Puritan utopianism. Lacking a class of resident patricians and with liberal institutions, such as fee simple land ownership, everywhere in the ascendancy, the town was free to be shaped by unalloyed capitalism. And it was. Early on, Cleveland competed with neighboring Painesville, Lorain, Sandusky, and even Ohio City, just across the Cuyahoga on the west bank, for preeminence on the lakeshore. In those days, every Gopher Prairie aspired to be Zenith, and every city had its Martin Chuzzlewits.[13]

What saved Cleveland in the early days was a canal—the brainchild of a prominent banker and politician named Alfred Kelley—linking the Western Reserve with the Ohio River via the Cuyahoga and providing access to distant markets; later, Kelley was instrumental in bringing the railroad to Cleveland.[14] Nowadays in the Western Reserve, wherever one finds a railroad town, with its lumberyard and Victorian commercial block, historic preservationists know to look a few miles away for a Greek Revival church and town hall grouped around a forlorn commons—the vestiges of New Connecticut preserved in the amber of economic ruin. Aesthetically, the contrast between winners and losers in the battle for the railroad reminds us of what we knew all along: development is a mixed blessing. Still, landowners in Mecca or Hiram Rapids, spectacular boomtowns that went bust, must find little solace in that.

In the course of the nineteenth century, the physical development of the city of Cleveland was driven by economic forces with little in the way of municipal controls. During the 1850s, the discovery of huge ore deposits and the development of shipping and oil refining converted Cleveland into one of the capital ports of America's first industrial heartland. Although Cleveland never captured the public's imagination in quite the way Chicago did, the city was, in the middle and late nineteenth century, a breeding ground for stories worthy of Horatio Alger. In the case of John D. Rockefeller, founder of the Standard Oil empire headquartered in Cleveland, that was literally true. Rockefeller and other men of technological or financial genius—in Cleveland they bore such names as Mather, Chisholm, Wade, Stone, Brush, and Hanna, and many were directly descended from Connecticut Yankees—built what Lewis Mumford called the paleotechnic city, perhaps their most enduring legacy.

The many changes wrought by the industrial and urban revolution also gave rise to what Richard Hofstadter famously characterized as the Age of Reform.[15] New cities, new wealth, and new problems engendered attempts to fashion a new politics that implicitly or explicitly charged America's plutocrats with having neglected their civic obligations. It wasn't hard to make the charge stick. In Cleveland, to take one homely example, reformers raking the 1896 tax duplicates discovered, amidst mounds of muck, John D. Rockefeller's claim to personal property worth only three thousand dollars; Rockefeller claimed neither horse, carriage, nor piano—not even a watch.[16] In cities across the United States, the move to formulate a new politics gave rise to attempts to fashion new models of the American city based on a distinctive conception of civic virtue. In Cleveland the embodiment of this story is Tom L. Johnson. And the complexity of Johnson's story, deriving from the extent of his own involvement in the rise of the new wealth, sheds light on the complicated nature of the Progressive movement.

Johnson, a man of humble origins, had gone to work at fifteen. By the time he was seventeen he was superintendent of a street railway in Louisville, Kentucky. He invented the coin farebox and used his profits to buy a failing street railway in Indianapolis, quickly setting it right. In 1879 he purchased the Pearl Street Line, one of eight street railways then operating in Cleveland under franchise—the method by which cities provided such services in those days, and a system subject to abuse. Johnson's street railway empire in Cleveland expanded, and he built a steel mill, later part of the United States Steel Corporation, to manufacture a grooved streetcar rail of his own devising. To succeed in business, he had to contend not only with a rapidly changing technology (the world's first electric streetcar was introduced, in Cleveland, in 1884) but with a "traction war" that he waged for more than two decades with Marcus Alonzo Hanna, a Cleveland businessman and Republican kingmaker. It was the franchise system (not, as is often suggested, an obsession with beating Hanna at his own game) that led Johnson into politics. He was a Democrat.[17]

Mark Hanna had also begun life inauspiciously. As a young man, he had shrewdly married the daughter of Daniel P. Rhodes, a coal and iron baron who took him into the business destined to be known as M. A. Hanna and Company, then Hanna Mining. The company's interest in street railways necessarily involved him in local politics; the Garfield campaign of 1880 aroused his participation in national affairs. Spurred by the conviction that businessmen ought to be directly involved in politics instead of just "spreading the green," he made the GOP peculiarly dependent on the state of Ohio, and so became known as the "boss of bosses." Despite his much-sullied reputation, Hanna's politics are not so easily stereotyped; he was not, for example, unsympathetic to the union movement.[18]

With Johnson's election as mayor in 1901, the city braced for a showdown between Progressivism and plutocracy. But Hanna died in 1904, and Johnson never did succeed in establishing a fully municipalized transit system; that was not to happen until after World War II. In retrospect, the melodramatic traction war and Johnson's "three-cent fare" rhetoric[19] seem to have fostered the view that Johnson's administration, and perhaps Progressivism generally, was smoke from the distant fire of class warfare. But sometimes it seemed as if the new politics had less to do with class conflict than with the idea of a unitary public interest, discoverable through right reason, weighing in against the unfettered pursuit of private gain.[20] Patricians especially were inclined to this view.

Johnson had no objection to business; as we have seen, he was a Big Business man himself. He objected to privilege—specifically, the privilege of using city government (through the franchise system, in this case) as a means of self-enrichment. Accordingly, Johnson's program went well beyond low streetcar fares. In the period before home rule, municipalities could command few resources and so provided little in the way of public services; Cleveland, for example, did almost nothing beyond furnishing a water supply. Johnson and his disciples wanted to change that. In fact, they worked toward the redemption of municipal government in the United States—which was "the worst in Christendom," according to Andrew D. White.[21] Fighting the entrenched utilities, the city acquired a Municipal Light Plant (the same Muny Light upon which the career of Mayor Dennis J. Kucinich was to be impaled seven decades later; Kucinich has always referred to Johnson as his "idol"). The Cleveland Progressives operated a municipal garbage plant; they took over street cleaning; they took credit for the city's first municipal bathhouse (in the Jewish quarter); they built a tuberculosis hospital in the then-distant suburb of Warrensville. Newton D. Baker, who was later to serve as mayor and then as Woodrow Wilson's Secretary of War, took the lead in applying new principles to the penal system ("Kind acts have taken the place of the club at the Work House," city clerk Peter Witt boasted in a letter to William Allen White).[22] A juvenile court was established. The reformers opened a "Single Tax Sunday School" in the public library, where they preached the gospel according to Henry George. By the end of Johnson's administration (he was defeated in his bid for reelection in 1909), Cleveland was being called the City on a Hill, recalling Winthrop's *Arbella* sermon. According to Lincoln Steffens, Cleveland under Johnson was "the best-governed city in the United States."[23] Prior to Johnson's administration, as one history of the city explains, "most people regarded city planning as an engineering necessity related to opening a street, constructing a bridge, or providing a park. The building of a community that would serve the health, wealth, and happiness of the citizenship was not generally understood."[24]

In terms of the physical city, the Progressives' inspiration was the famous plaster of paris "White City" that Frederick Law Olmsted and America's leading architects—including Daniel Burnham, Richard Morris Hunt, Charles McKim, Robert Peabody, and George B. Post—built at the World's Columbian Exposition at Chicago.[25] The operative principle of the 1893 fair, and later of the City Beautiful movement, was Burnham's dictum about the necessity of making big plans, since little plans "have no magic to stir men's blood."[26] Whether Burnham himself was interested in reconstituting the American city as a genuine community is not entirely clear, but Cleveland's Progressives had just that in mind. For example, Frederic C. Howe, one of Johnson's closest and most articulate aides, wrote that he harbored "an architectonic vision of what a city might be." Howe continues: "I saw it as a picture. It was not economy, efficiency, and business methods that interested me so much as a city planned, built, and conducted as a community enterprise. . . . It was a unit, a thing with a mind, with a conscious purpose, seeing far in advance of the present and taking precautions for the future. I had this picture of Cleveland long before the advent of city-planning proposals."[27] Howe, of course, was not alone in thinking of the city in architectural terms. As J. B. Jackson has observed, "Most of us still like to visualize the city in terms of architecture—in terms of massive blocks of solid, well-designed buildings that we can admire on foot." The monumental plazas and *palazzi* of the City Beautiful movement should be interpreted, according to Jackson, "as belated expressions of the belief that architecture, particularly classical architecture, is the essence of the city."[28]

The City Beautiful movement, so closely identified in Cleveland with Tom L. Johnson, actually antedated his administration, and its history reveals that it expressed more general aspirations than Johnson's partisanship would suggest.[29] In 1895 and then again in 1898, the Cleveland Architectural Club sponsored competitions aimed at generating a plan for the formal grouping of Cleveland's public buildings. The moment was propitious inasmuch as the federal, county, and municipal governments all had at least tentative plans for new construction. Later, after the Ohio legislature passed the enabling legislation, a Group Plan Commission was formed to coordinate the development of Cleveland's civic center. Three members were appointed on the recommendation of Mayor Johnson: Burnham of Chicago and John M. Carrere and Arnold W. Brunner of New York. Brunner had already been designated architect of the Federal Building planned for the northeastern corner of Public Square. The commission regarded its charge—"grouping the principal buildings of a city of the size of Cleveland and providing them with proper setting in the way of approaches and other accessories"—as unprecedented.[30] The political significance of the Group Plan was made explicit by Howe: the creation of the commission was "the most significant forward step in the matter of municipal art taken in America. It is comparable to the designs of Napoleon III, who remade Paris, with the aid of Baron Haussmann. . . . Here is a city among the most radical in its democratic tendencies of any city in the country courageously authorizing the expenditure of from ten to fifteen million dollars in the development of an idea. It suggests a new conception of the municipality."[31]

The Group Plan proposed the removal of numerous structures on a forty-four-acre site. Public buildings were to be arranged around a "Mall" laid out on a north-south axis and extending from the northeast corner of Public Square to the lakefront. The south end of that axis was to be adorned by twin buildings—the Federal Building and the Cleveland Public Library, both fronting on Superior Avenue. The Mall itself was conceived as a five-hundred foot wide monumental Court of Honor, the city's official gateway, a kind of *sacra via* joining a lakefront railroad station to the historic heart of the New Connecticut town—Public Square.

The composition was formed roughly on a cruciform pattern, the Court of Honor corresponding to the nave, flanked by Ontario and Bond (East Sixth) Streets. Ontario, just west of and parallel to the Court of Honor, would begin at Public Square and terminate at the Cuyahoga County Courthouse, to be built on a bluff overlooking the lake. Bond would lead to a new City Hall (the city had never before owned its own quarters), set in counterpoise to the courthouse. An east-west axis was conceived as a formally landscaped Esplanade featuring fountains worthy of Bernini. (In fact, the Group Plan super-

FIGURE 15

The Group Plan, Cleveland, designed by Daniel H. Burnham and other members of the Group Plan Commission. Bird's-eye view, looking south, from high above the lakefront railroad station. At the end of the main axis of the Mall (top, center) is Public Square.

visors included in their report evocative photographs of some of the European sites from which they had drawn inspiration, including the Palais Royal, the Place de la Concorde, and the Unter den Linden.) Since "in such a composition as this, uniformity of architecture is of first importance" (a lesson "taught by the Court of Honor of the World's Fair"),[32] the plan imposed a single architectural style—Italian Renaissance—and employed the usual devices (monumentality, symmetry, uniform cornice lines, etc.) aimed at enhancing the impression of unity that had been, from all accounts, one of the most compelling features of the White City: "Unlike any city which ever existed in substance, this one has been built all at once, by one impulse, at one period, at one stage of knowledge and arts. . . . No gradual growth of idea is to be traced, no budding of new thought upon a formulated scheme. The whole thing seems to have sprung into being fully conceived and perfectly planned without progressive development or widening of scope."[33]

The anchor of Cleveland's Group Plan was the proposed railroad station. The land on which the union depot was to have been built had been painstakingly reclaimed by the city, and for years the city had quarreled with the railroads over ownership. (On the day after the Group Plan was unveiled, the *Plain Dealer* reported that Mayor Johnson "declared . . . that adequate concessions should be made by the railroad companies in return for this valuable land." According to the newspaper, spokesmen for the railroads were not immediately available for comment.)[34] It is in fact hard to imagine a better symbol of Progressive government—insisting as it did on the subordination of previously ungovernable private interests to the common good—than a union depot conceived as the focal point of a work of civic art. It is also hard to imagine a better object lesson in the perils of master planning than the story of how the union depot eluded the Group Plan and the lakefront, winding up instead at the southwestern corner of Public Square.[35]

Despite the loss of the lakefront union depot, the Cleveland Group Plan is, after nearly a century of sporadic effort, one of the most fully realized of all City Beautiful plans outside of Washington, D.C., and John Nolen's Madison, Wisconsin. Still, the Group Plan, a grandiose government complex conceived as the heart of a provincial industrial city, leaves room for disappointment.

Because of its colossal dimensions, the integrity of the scheme, so convincing to the bird's eye, is scarcely discernible on the ground. Streetside, one can appreciate axial views of the courthouse and city hall, but from that perspective other parts of the plan—the larger elements of the design—are imperceptible. From the pedestrian paths of the Mall, one has a nice view of the fountains and the backs of the *palazzi;* their main facades are on the street, probably where they belong. Major thoroughfares cutting through the plan laterally, east to west, are another distraction. The result is that the City Beautiful composition, whatever its abstract merits, is not very successful as civic art. Perhaps this is what Lewis Mumford meant in referring to the "meretricious pictures of the City Beautiful."[36]

More importantly, the Group Plan fails as urban space because it is neither park nor street, but something in between, and because it is monolithic in both form and function. Let us consider each point in turn.

Parks are places of recreation. At noon on a warm summer day, with the fountains flowing, a Dixieland band performing, and street vendors (once outlawed by the city) offering luncheon fare, the Mall has often served as a lively and successful recreation area. But at other times, unless one were to bring a soccer ball, a Frisbee, or roller skates, there really is nothing to do on the Mall. Unlike with the great Chicago parks, there is no easy access to the lake—not even to lake *views*. And for those who, like the thousands of people who gravitate to London's Regent's Park on a Sunday afternoon, would be content to just lie on the grass, there is precious little of that, either. Most of the time, as former City Council president George Forbes once observed, the Mall has amounted to little more than "a few pools where only reefer

FIGURE 16
No "Stranger's Path" here. Artist's rendering of lakefront railroad station proposed by Group Plan Commission for downtown Cleveland, from early-twentieth-century postcard.

heads hang out."[37] This is one of the reasons that the vast expanse of the Mall has long tempted private developers—and a city with famously shallow pockets.

If the Mall does not measure up to the standards of a good park, it must be said that it also has none of the virtues of a good street. When Clevelanders looked at Daniel Burnham's drawings for the Group Plan, they must have imagined huge throngs promenading down the Court of Honor, as they did at the great Chicago fair, the World's Columbian Exposition of 1893. But there were exhibition halls at the fair, not to mention a Ferris wheel and Little Egypt, the exotic dancer. There were places to promenade *to*, and *from*, at the Chicago fair. And there were places to eat. Once the Group Plan separated the civic heart of the city from the center of commercial activity—the street, generally, and Euclid Avenue in particular—it was inevitable that people looking for visual stimulation, "retail therapy," food, or people-watching opportunities would stay away in droves. It must be said, too, that the Court of Honor as conceived by Burnham and his colleagues would have provided none of the services and attractions that people disembarking at a railroad station actually need and look for. They need the services associated with what J. B. Jackson has called the "Stranger's Path," that indispensable strip of coffee stands, diners, bars, newsstands, barber shops, pharmacies, and cheap hotels, the kinds of amenities to which the City Beautiful was constitutionally allergic.[38] The casual informality of such improvisations as street vendors and Dixieland bands suggests all too clearly the formal pomposity of the Group Plan, and why Cleveland's union depot probably deserved to be situated somewhere else.[39]

The City Beautiful was hostile not only to the honky-tonk of the "Stranger's Path," but to the commercial street itself. But healthy urban tissue, as Jane Jacobs has demonstrated, is composed of small blocks and plentiful streets, not superblocks and megastructures. In fact, she contends that streets naturally tend to proliferate: "In city districts that become successful or magnetic, streets are virtually never made to disappear. Quite the contrary. Where it is possible, they multiply. Thus in the Rittenhouse Square district of Philadelphia and in Georgetown in the District of Columbia, what were once back alleys down the centers of blocks have become streets with buildings fronting on them, and people using them like streets."[40]

The real problem with urban monoliths has more to do with function than with form; healthy urban tissue is generated when different uses are *mixed,* rather than segregated. The Group Plan, by contrast, is a single-use district, a government ghetto (not entirely unlike the Forum of Trajan in that respect). There is no room for commerce, industry, or residential use—only bureaucrats. Jacobs notes that Elbert Peets observed with dismay the same phenomenon when it materialized in Washington, D.C.:

Briefly, what is happening is this: the government capital is turning away from the city; the government buildings are being concentrated together and separated from the buildings of the city. This was not L'Enfant's idea. On the contrary, he made every effort to amalgamate the two, to make them serve each other. He distributed buildings, markets, seats of national societies, academies, and State memorials at points of architectural advantage throughout the city, as if with the definite purpose of putting the impress of the national capital on every part. This was sound sentiment and sound architectural judgment. . . .

There is no evidence, in this procedure, of feeling for the city as an organism, a matrix that is worthy of its monuments and friendly with them. . . . The loss is social, as well as esthetic.[41]

Jackson has issued the same lament about the modern civic center, with its "array of classical edifices, lost in the midst of waste space, the meaningless pomp of flagpoles and war memorials and dribbling fountains." The contrast with the "almost domestic intimacy" of the arche-

FIGURE 17
*"A few pools where only reefer heads hang out":
View of Hanna Fountains, the Group Plan, Cleveland, mid-1980s.*

typal courthouse square of small-town America, according to Jackson, provides "a pretty good measure of what is wrong with much American city planning; civic consciousness has been divorced from everyday life, put in a special zone all by itself."[42]

While people do come to the Mall to attend special events at Public Hall and the Convention Center—and some vitality is generated by Jacobs Field and the Rock 'n Roll Hall of Fame as well—there is only one major cultural institution, the Cleveland Public Library, on the Mall proper. One of the reasons for this is that Cleveland has a separate cultural quarter, called University Circle, some five miles away. Jacobs explains that the idea of a "decontaminated cultural district" was pioneered in Boston:

In 1859, a Committee of Institutes called for a "Cultural Conservation", setting aside a tract to be devoted "solely to institutions of an educational, scientific, and artistic character", a move that coincided with the beginning of Boston's long, slow decline as a live cultural leader among American cities. Whether the deliberate segregation and decon-tamination of numerous cultural institutions from the ordinary city and ordinary life was part of the cause of Boston's cultural decline, or whether it was simply a symptom and seal of a decadence already inevitable from other causes, I do not know. One thing is sure: Boston's downtown has suffered miserably from lack of good mixtures in its pri-mary uses, particularly good mixing in of night uses and of live (not museum-piece and once-upon-a-time) cultural uses.[43]

And so a frenetic Clevelander, or tourist, could conceivably spend a week attending events at the Cleveland Museum of Art, Severance Hall, the Museum of Natural History, the Garden Center, the Cleveland Playhouse, the Western Reserve Historical Society, Playhouse Square, and Case Western Reserve University (soon to have its own Frank Gehry shrine) without ever setting foot downtown, let alone on the Mall proper. At the same time, University Circle is not successful as urban space, which is why Cleveland's elite is currently mounting a revitalization campaign—a very shrewd one that aims to add density and diversity to the place: "People want University Circle to be a livelier place. Participants in the planning process repeatedly stated a desire to see more retail activity and more housing available for Circle living. They hope to see exciting new technology businesses grow out of the research that is occurring in the Circle. In general, people want more outdoor activity on the streets, in the parks, and between the institutional centers."[44] Here's hoping it succeeds, but one can't help but regret that the cultural institutions were not woven into the fabric of the city in the first place.

FIGURE 18
Artist's rendering of planned roundabout at University Circle in Cleveland, near Severance Hall.

Jacobs contends that urban monoliths—she mentions "railroad tracks, waterfronts, campuses, expressways, large parking areas, and large parks," in addition to civic centers and cultural centers uncontaminated by commerce—not only are bad in themselves, but generate problems at their edges, problems that she refers to as "border vacuums." Because single-use districts "are apt to form dead ends for most users of city streets," such areas get less intense use, which means that they generally run down. In fact, Jacobs mentions large-scale civic centers in particular as having scant use along their borders, "because the massive single elements that form them possess such a low intensity of land use relative to the great perimeters they possess."[45] It may not be a coincidence that when urban renewal descended upon downtown Cleveland in the 1960s (see chap. 5), its epicenter was the "blighted" parcel of land immediately adjacent to the eastern side of the Group Plan.

To sum up: Not all American cities were conceived by private profiteers in a spirit of pure greed and gain. To the extent that a vestigial (or resurrected) Puritan utopianism informed town planning in the Connecticut Western Reserve, Cleveland can be said to have aspired to a higher ideal. A hundred years after the founding of the city, Cleveland Progressives rekindled the vision of a city on a hill and commissioned several of the country's leading architects to express that vision formally in a grouping of monumental public buildings downtown. The Group Plan was to be the city's civic heart. Unlike Big Plans that collect dust on the shelves of City Hall, the Group Plan—save for the lakeside railroad station—was actually built. Whether the aspirations of its architects and Progressive sponsors were realized is another question. While it is hard to imagine a more alluring vision of the City Beautiful than the architectural renderings of Daniel Burnham and his colleagues, the Group Plan is what the political theorist Michael Walzer calls "single-minded," as opposed to "open-minded," urban space. And in its execution it suggests something of the practical limits of formal urban design.

EARLY IN THE TWENTIETH CENTURY, affluent suburbs were being developed to the east of Cleveland's University Circle—one of these, East Cleveland, growing up on what had been John D. Rockefeller's Forest Hill estate. Another venture, on a 1,400-acre parcel too remote for streetcar service, "said to be the largest residence development under single control in the world,"[1] was destined to become a development called Shaker Village, and then the City of Shaker Heights.

The property had been the site of a utopian community established in 1822 by the North Union Society of the Millennium Church of United Believers—the Shakers. As these things go (and especially considering their vows of celibacy), the colony was quite successful, but by 1889 it was ready to give up the ghost. The parcel of land, which included two large lakes built by the Shakers, changed hands several times before a syndicate organized by two brothers—Oris Paxton and Mantis James Van Sweringen—acquired it in 1905. In their politics, at least, the Van Sweringens were thoroughly conventional men; like most people of the time, they believed in the primacy of property rights. And yet they disparaged most suburbs as rootless dormitories, and they believed that a mass migration to suburbia that proceeded one homestead at a time—appropriate to a Lockean political culture—was inadequate to the task of protecting and promoting middle-class values ("Most communities just happen; the best are always planned").[2] The result was that their speculative venture aimed higher than most—typically, at the cost of some personal freedom.

Knowing that their real estate promotion ("delightful country estates removed from town and yet within easy distance of it")[3] depended utterly on their providing convenient transportation to downtown Cleveland, the Van Sweringens, in 1916, had to purchase the Nickel Plate Railroad in order to obtain several miles of right-of-way vital to their proposed "rapid transit" connection to downtown. Earlier, they had acquired some property on the southwest corner of Public Square (diagonally opposite the Federal Building, the Group Plan's toehold on the square), where they proposed to build their interurban terminal. Now that they owned the Nickel Plate, and with the union terminal on the lakefront still unbuilt, they upgraded their plans. On January 5, 1919, Cleveland voters passed a referendum approving a union depot for the Van Sweringens' Public Square site.[4]

It was on this site that the Van Sweringens built Terminal Tower. For many years it was, at 708 feet, the tallest structure in the United States outside Manhattan. Dedicated in 1930, the skyscraper rose up directly over the Van Sweringens' railroad station—but on separate piles, to minimize the danger posed by vibrations from the trains—and presided over a group of related and connected structures, including a department store, a hotel, a shopping concourse, and office buildings accommodating some of the city's leading business firms (Sohio, Hanna Mining, Sherwin-Williams, and Republic Steel, among others). A city-within-a-city remarkable primarily as a feat of engineering,[5] the complex effected a reorientation of the city away from the Mall and the lakefront and back toward Public Square, the original civic center, and Euclid Avenue, the commercial diagonal leading from it. Terminal Tower became the architectural symbol of Cleveland, much to the consternation of those inspired by the civic vision immanent in the Group Plan. The light rail connection—the Shaker Rapid—proved a huge practical success, and so did the garden suburb. In 1919, Shaker Village had a population of seventeen hundred; ten years later the community, soon to incorporate as the City of Shaker Heights, boasted sixteen thousand.[6]

Shaker Village was laid out in several stages by the F. A. Pease Engineering Company. Those chiefly responsible appear to have been William A. Pease, described by one source as a "garden city advocate,"[7] and Harry Gallimore, an "avid reader of English stories"[8] who is often said to have chosen street names out of an English postal book.[9] The plan itself was generally romantic, although nothing compared with Frederick Law Olmsted's 1873 plan for Tacoma, which was described by a contemporary as "the most fantastic plat of a town that was ever seen. There wasn't a straight line, a right angle, or a corner lot. The blocks were shaped like melons, pears, and sweet potatoes. One block, shaped like a banana, was 3,000 feet in length and had 250 lots. It was a pretty fair park plan but condemned itself for a town."[10] The Pease/Van Sweringen plan incorporated thoroughfares that were more or less straight, including the two boulevards with Shaker Rapid tracks running down their median strips.

The perceived "Englishness" of Shaker Village could be read as a reference to the informal English garden, as opposed to the formal landscaping traditions of the French. It also could refer to the residential squares that graced certain quarters of London, particularly Bloomsbury. The more direct English influence, however, is to be found in Hampstead Garden Suburb and in Letchworth, the first Garden City; both were the work of architects Raymond Unwin and Barry Parker.

The English Garden City movement was the brainchild of a humble London clerk named Ebenezer Howard, whose dream boiled down to a society distinguished by "beauty of nature, social opportunity, low rents, high wages, plenty to do, low prices, no sweating, pure air and water, bright homes and gardens, freedom, co-operation."[11] Harking back to pre-Raphaelite notions about the organic qualities of life, wherein technology was subordinate to politics and aesthetics, Garden City advocates in America—Lewis Mumford, most notably, most eloquently, most unremittingly, both on his own and through the Regional Planning Association of America—generated a powerful vision of a city that maintained close contact with the countryside, sustained both high and folk culture, and reconciled diversity and individual liberty with harmony and public authority—all the while preserving human scale and the dignity of labor.[12]

While leaving behind Howard's radical ideas about how to finance his Garden Cities (for more on this subject, see chap. 7), the Van Sweringens appropriated the rhetoric and symbolism of the movement and hand delivered their literature, appropriately inscribed, to likely prospects. There was never a strident sales pitch, for "Shaker Villagers are neighbors you would like as friends."[13] Publications of the Van

Sweringen Company advertised building lots, but they also sold an idea. The promotional booklet *Peaceful Shaker Village,* for example, is adorned on every page with stunning engravings exuding a kind of elegant rusticity, all accompanied by homely paeans to country life, such as:

Here along the southern wall
Keeps the bee his festival;
All is quite else—afar
Sounds of toil and turmoil are.[14]

In these publications, Shaker Village residences are romanticized to the point that the rooflines of English cottages appear, from the gable side, decidedly concave. In several cases, they look as if they might be thatched—fairy-tale facades pasted over balloon frames. On one page is a striking image of a log cabin: evocative enough, but of William Morris, or the Hameau at Versailles, where Marie-Antoinette earnestly played at churning butter—anything but local history. Log cabins had been no more in fashion with the Shaker communists than with the earlier Connecticut Yankees; certainly, the Van Sweringen Company was not proposing that prospective investors actually contemplate building in that style. One illustration in particular is a tour de force: Terminal Tower, then under construction, dramatically pierces a bank of billowy clouds representing Shaker Heights, replete with stockbroker Tudor mansions and faux châteaux hovering over Public Square (see frontispiece).

The Van Sweringens seem never to have doubted that when middle-class people think of "making it" in the upland moors, they see their personal success occurring in a social context: "On every family's horizon is a rainbow, and for many the pot of gold at the rainbow's end is Shaker Village."[15] Accordingly, they used some of their most valuable land to lure the kinds of institutions intimately associated with the bourgeois idea of success. Herein lay the origins of a number of Shaker Heights churches, as well as the Shaker Country Club. Above all, the brothers understood that education is the middle-class religion. Every neighborhood was organized around its own public elementary school. In addition, University School and two private girls' schools, Laurel and Hathaway Brown, accepted invitations to build campuses on land donated by the company; and St. Ignatius College—now John Carroll University—was transplanted from Cleveland's west side to University Heights. The brothers failed, however, in their effort to arrange a suburban marriage between Case Institute of Technology and Western Reserve University, rivals of long standing at University Circle.[16]

If the Van Sweringens—like the Puritans and Progressives—harbored an elevated vision of what community life entailed, they also never lost sight of the material basis of secular American urban life. Their Shaker Village was a community based upon a common inter-

FIGURE 19
A stylized gothic mansion, Shaker Village in Ohio.

est in schools and property values. In general, they thought of Shaker Village as a bastion of residential bliss: "It is large enough to be self-contained and self-sufficient. No matter what changes time may bring around it, no matter what waves of commercialism may beat upon its border, Shaker Village is secure . . . protected for all time."[17] The Van Sweringens were interested in aesthetics, but they were just as interested in the social character of housing: "Can you not realize what the influence of such homes must be upon the lives of children

FIGURE 20
Somewhere over the rainbow: "Their ways are ways of pleasant-ness, / And all their paths are peace." Elegant rusticity à la the Van Sweringens.

in them? Do not character and refinement depend much upon the manner in which they are housed? Yet, without neighborhood support, is not home influence ever in jeopardy?"[18]

They took care to insulate residential from commercial uses (the first zoning ordinance was adopted in 1927) and to separate more-affluent from less-affluent neighborhoods. By means of an imaginative street plan that exploited certain "natural" borders—the Country Club, the original Shaker lakes and two more that the Van Sweringen Company built, and the two branches of the Shaker Rapid—they were able to create a hierarchy of distinctive neighborhoods. The real estate agent's perspective, from north to south: right side of the right tracks; wrong side of the right tracks; right side of the wrong tracks; wrong side of the wrong tracks. Although most of Shaker Heights was zoned for detached, single-family residences, one parcel (wrong side of the wrong tracks) was reserved for two-family structures that the company insisted should not be identifiable from the street as duplexes; indeed, they are not. The duplex in disguise is another lesson learned from Unwin and Parker.

But mainly, the Van Sweringens relied on strict architectural controls. Having no taste for the "freakishness" of Victorian architecture ("the ugly residence injures surrounding property values"),[19] they devised a set of standards that has been described as "enforced historicism."[20] "Enforced" may be too strong a word, as there were virtually no objections—a strong prima facie case for their having succeeded in attracting a community of like-minded souls. But it cannot be denied that their code left little to the discretion of either architect or homeowner. The combination of style (English, French, or "Colonial") and structural material (brick, stone, shingle, or wood frame) dictated all the accessories. For instance, if one owned a brick Colonial, the appropriate color scheme depended on whether the house was made of sandmould colonial brick, common brick burned in beehive kilns, or overburned arch brick. If the last, trim and sashes, doors, and fly screens were to be painted white (not ivory), shutters dark green (as opposed to blue-green, bottle green, or olive green); the appropriate mortar was natural; and the roof was to be dark moss-green shingle (not mottled, rough-textured slate or dark weathered gray shingles). All permutations were equally prescriptive.

If one was building in an area zoned for single-family residences, one was bound to use the premises exclusively for that purpose. No additions were to be put on, or alterations made, without the company's permission. Structures generally had to be two stories high, and wider than deep. The main entrance had to face the street; driveways had to be located on a particular side of the house; no outbuildings (except for the exclusive use of the family or servants) were allowed on the premises. Trees and shrubbery, even statuary or fountains, were permitted on the front lawn, "but no vegetables, so-called, nor grains of the ordinary garden or field variety . . . and no weeds, underbrush or other unsightly growths." Chickens were verboten, as were other fowl and livestock, gas and oil derricks, billboards, advertising signs, and the manufacture or sale, either wholesale or retail, of any "spiritous, vinous or fermented liquors." Just to be on the safe side, the company reserved the right "to enter the property" of those not living up to the terms of the deed and to remove the offending "erection, thing or condition."[21]

The vision of community life that animated the Van Sweringens' garden suburb—again, inviting comparison with earlier utopias— implied exclusion. This was accomplished informally, for the most part, but matters were complicated in the mid-1920s when about three hundred African American families purchased farmland in what was destined to become the adjacent suburb of Beachwood. It cost the company three-quarters of a million dollars to remove this siege tower from the vicinity of their *enceinte,* and the incident seems to have intensified their already well-developed turf-guarding instincts.[22] From then on, every deed issued by the company contained a restrictive covenant aimed, apparently, at the exclusion of blacks, Jews, and Italians: "The premises here conveyed shall not be occupied, leased, rented, conveyed or otherwise alienated, nor shall the title or possession thereof pass to another without the written consent of the Grantor, except that the Grantor shall not withhold such consent if and after a written request has been made to the Grantor to permit such occupation, leasing, renting, conveyance, or alienation by a majority of the owners of the Sub Lots which adjoin or abut, and within a distance of five Sub Lots from the respective boundary lines of the said premises."[23] This restriction, however, applied only to the first generation of Shaker residents—to those dealing directly with the Van Sweringen Company. Passing it on to succeeding generations of owners required that sellers deed the property back to the company, so that the restriction might be inserted and conveyed. All of this was accomplished at the company's expense. One study estimates that about 75 percent of the owners agreed to the procedure when it was suggested to them by the company's agents.[24]

Exclusionary practices might offend modern sensibilities,[25] but a community by definition requires a sense of belonging, which depends in turn on boundaries—on being within, and therefore on keeping out. To say so is not to issue an apologia for bigotry, but merely to suggest that *genuine* diversity—as opposed to multicultural window dressing—can be thoroughly disagreeable. Those bent on denying that truth are also inclined to underestimate the extent to which exclusion is inherent in *any* community, not just a feature of bad ones. As we shall see, the Radburn concept favored by reformers such as Lewis Mumford (see chap. 7) depended on restrictive covenants to enforce architectural standards, and the FHA itself sanctioned their use as a "protection for residential development," which unfortunately "led to vicious racial and ethnic discrimination."[26] Even developments explicitly dedicated to promoting racial and socioeconomic diversity—Columbia, Maryland, for example—rely on more or less strict controls of various kinds. Columbia is no more tolerant of purple window shutters, or cardinals on mailboxes, than Shaker Heights.[27] The problem with such communities is, as one observer has put it, that they have "tried to fulfill the American dream with slightly un-American governments."[28]

One of the problems with Big Plans is that they compete against one another. In the case of Shaker Heights, a private-sector Big Plan competed directly with the Group Plan, and the Progressives' municipal vision was the loser. As we have seen, however, it would be wrong to conclude automatically from this that crass materialism drove out a more enlightened vision of community. American suburban development has often been described as "formless sprawl," but the Van Sweringens' development was neither formless nor anarchistic. On the contrary, it invited people into a community that did not shrink from the imposition of strict controls on individual members. Once enrolled in this community, Peaceful Shaker Villagers must have continued to yearn for freedom—"freedom from burdensome emotional ties with the environment, freedom from communal responsibilities, freedom from the tyranny of the traditional home and its possessions; the freedom from belonging to a tight-knit social order; and above all, the freedom to move on to somewhere else."[29] That kind of freedom was never the point of Shaker Heights, but it remains a powerful urge there nonetheless. That's what all those Jeep Grand Cherokees and Ford Explorers are doing in the driveways.

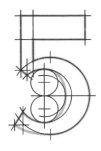

**URBAN
RENEWAL**

*"The Bugs Are
All Out"*

WHILE THE VAN SWERINGENS WERE developing Shaker Heights, and going broke in the process,[1] city planning was gradually becoming professionalized. No longer was planning confined to "widening streets, building boulevards and planning civic centers."[2] The new professionals looked for inspiration to Europe, where they discovered *regional* planning, as well as various alternatives to "unassisted private ventures" in housing.[3]

In Cleveland, City Councilman Ernest J. Bohn, who had "made himself a thorough student of slums,"[4] argued that decent housing for poor people might be provided "through government action, as in Vienna," or by "government subsidy, as in most German cities."[5] Bohn drafted the model for the public-housing statute adopted by the Ohio legislature in 1933; it was the first such act in the United States. In the same year, he became director of the Cleveland Metropolitan Housing Authority, another pioneering institution, where he oversaw construction of the nation's first public-housing "estate," Cedar Apartments. Through the National Association of Housing Officials, an organization he sired, Bohn led a public-housing propaganda blitz, at one point organizing a lecture tour for Sir Raymond Unwin, former president of the Royal Academy of Architects and veteran of the Garden City movement, and appearing with him on a public-affairs program broadcast nationally over the NBC radio network.

Besides looking for sites for future Garden Cities,[6] Cleveland reformers sought increased powers for the City Plan Commission, which had been created in 1914 to prepare a city plan, among other things, but had never done so. In 1942 voters approved a charter amendment giving the commission a new name ("Planning" instead of "Plan," emphasizing the ongoing, dynamic nature of their charge), a planning director with a professional staff, and greatly expanded powers, powers aimed at stopping the "slow insidious rot" allegedly plaguing the city.[7] It was also suggested that increased planning powers would help win World War II,[8] a line of argument not fully pursued. Bohn was named chairman of the City Planning Commission, and John T. Howard became planning director. It seemed certain that comprehensive planning had finally come of age in Cleveland. Now the city would finally have its General Plan (the term "master plan" being scrupulously avoided).[9] The 1949 General Plan has been aptly characterized as "a broad picture, expressed largely in maps and tables, of the chief things we can do, over the years, to make Cleveland in 1980 a far better and more livable city for its men, women, and children. The General Plan took up all the main categories of city planning: residential land use, by type of dwelling and by quality of area; business land use; industrial land use; recreational land use; major thoroughfares; rapid transit; lakefront development; and general public services. In each of these it studied our 1949 lacks and hindrances, and then it looked thirty years ahead and, with all possible good judgment, forecast our 1980 needs and the ways to meet them."[10]

While the General Plan was in many ways comprehensive, the Garden City utopianism that had marked John Howard's earlier work with the Regional Association of Cleveland is nowhere in sight. Why? Part of the answer must be that city planning had by this time ascended to the status of a profession, which was fitting considering its origins in the Progressive movement—but with the professionalization of planning, radical butterflies metamorphosed into bureaucratic caterpillars. Another way of putting it is that professional planners proved, on the whole, to be interested "not in utopian schemes and basic social change but in the more limited spheres of physical design and construction permitted by established groups and acceptable to the urban leadership. Planners generally accepted this role out of a desire to be practically useful and to find a niche for themselves in the existing scheme of things."[11] Increasingly, it seemed that being practically useful meant building highways and taking advantage of judicial expansion of the power of eminent domain and new federal subsidies available for public housing and "urban renewal." This concept was intimately associated with the design ideas of the International Style, as codified by the Charter of Athens. As Allan B. Jacobs has written:

The Charter of Athens could find realization on either new sites, like Chandigarh or Brasília, or in the older central cities. In the latter, there would have to be clearance of large unhealthy urban environments in order to rebuild at a scale necessary to have an impact. Here, the rejection of streets as places for people and for the making and expression of community was even stronger, in favor of efficiency, technology, and speed, and, to give credit, of health as well, as the prime determinants of street design. Building orientation to streets was seen as a fundamental wrong. The most memorable images of what those developments might look like are perspectives taken from a viewpoint high in the air with the uniform height of tall, tall buildings as the horizon line, or drawings of two people sitting at a table somehow overlooking a large, presumably public space with no one in it.[12]

Whatever else might be said of this type of planning, it proved to be good politics.

In Cleveland, Anthony J. Celebrezze, who was later to serve as President Kennedy's Secretary of Health, Education and Welfare, was mayor when Congress passed the 1954 Federal Housing Act. Four other men played important roles in bringing urban renewal to Cleveland: Bohn, chairman of the City Planning Commission and father of public housing not only in the city but, arguably, nationally; James M. Lister, planning director after 1949, when Howard resigned to accept a professorship at the Massachusetts Institute of Technology; Upshur Evans, a former Standard Oil executive recruited to head the Cleveland Development Foundation's effort to encourage private investment in the city; and Louis B. Seltzer, editor of the afternoon newspaper, the *Cleveland Press*.

At the heart of urban renewal was the concept of a public-private partnership, which allowed Evans to turn on the federal spigot by leveraging $2 million in "seed money." Cleveland's approach was considered exemplary. That Cleveland was setting the pace nationally was the point of remarks by Vice President Richard Nixon in which, in a special broadcast from Washington (preempting Arlene Francis's television show in Cleveland), he praised Cleveland "for having brought government and private enterprise together in a slum prevention program. . . . Nixon quoted his nine-year-old daughter in describing the slum problem. He said that on a recent ride with him through a slum area in Washington near the Capitol she asked, 'why is it boys and girls have to live in these crumped-upped old houses?' Cleveland, Nixon said, 'has recognized that the solution lies' in uniting private enterprise and capital with local, state and federal funds in municipal improvement programs."[13] In those days, there appear to have been no nattering nabobs of negativism at City Hall—or at the *Press:* "Cleveland can win its battle against blight within ten years. This forecast was made today by Planning Director James Lister and Ernest J. Bohn, chairman of the City Plan *[sic]* Commission. Both said slums can be eradicated and deteriorating residential areas spruced up within a decade if the city takes full advantage of federal subsidies and loans now available."[14]

Seltzer took the lead in orchestrating public support. It bears emphasizing that this was not a war on poverty, but a war on slums, the idea being that every form of human vice, including poverty, was environmentally induced. On December 31, 1954, for example, the *Press* averred that "indecent housing was the number one cause of juvenile delinquency."[15] When the slums had been dispatched, fire, rats, tuberculosis—and crime itself—would be under control. Bohn had provided the solution: "Public housing is a tested, proven weapon," asserted a May 14, 1956, *Press* editorial; "the bugs are all out."[16] That proposition was to be tested in Cleveland many times, but most dramatically at a project called Garden Valley.

Initiated by the Cleveland Development Foundation, Garden Valley was the first public-housing project financed under the 1954 Federal Housing Act; the project received $3,941,024 worth of federal grants plus $4,676,875 in loan funds. Oddly, Garden Valley seems not to have generated much opposition (aside from the African American city councilman who represented the ward in which it was to be built), in spite of the fact that it displaced at least seven thousand people, and despite a published report that of the first 358 families who had applied to live in Garden Valley, 132 were rejected because they could not afford the rents.[17] No one seems to have thought to ask where these 132 families were going to live, or for whom urban renewal legislation had been approved, if not for them. As for the lucky residents of Garden Valley, by July of 1959 the *Press* handed down a reluctant verdict: the project was an "eyesore."[18] That revelation did nothing to slow down the juggernaut of public housing.

Housing the poor was not the real purpose of urban renewal. It was not even the *stated* purpose. The official justification for urban renewal was cast in terms of removing "blight and obsolescence so as to restore the economic health and growth of downtown."[19] As for the process, the key was public acquisition of private properties, then turning the assembled parcel over to private developers. Accordingly, late in 1959 the Cleveland Development Foundation announced preliminary plans for a project called Erieview, the impetus for which had come from the city's Department of Urban Renewal and Housing, created in 1957 and now headed by Lister. I. M. Pei, the internationally known architect and Erieview's planner, argued that downtown development in a Radiant City style would "spread its rejuvenating influence—like ripples from a stone dropped in a pool—to neighboring blocks."[20]

FIGURE 21
Ernest J. Bohn (left) with Lady Bird Johnson at the opening of the Riverview housing estate, April 20, 1964. Next to Bohn is Anne M. Celebrezze, and on the far right is Rep. Charles Vanik.

Pei proposed development in two stages: Erieview I was principally commercial, Erieview II residential. Taken together, the plan was to decrease the amount of land devoted to streets (from 44.6 to 38.5 acres), industry (from 45.6 to 7.5 acres), public institutions (from 18.0 to 8.8 acres), and commerce (from 45.8 to 32.8 acres), while increasing the amount of land devoted to residential use (from 5.6 to 50.9 acres) and public parks (from 6.0 to 20.5 acres).[21] All this was possible because the plan involved building up, not out, and because of the suppression of what Le Corbusier referred to as "corridor-streets" (alleged to be wasteful of space) in favor of superblocks.

The site, northeast of Public Square and directly abutting the Group Plan, stretched along Cleveland's refractory lakefront from East Sixth to approximately East Seventeenth Street. Although admittedly a "choice piece of real estate" (to be acquired at bargain-basement prices through the good offices of the Urban Renewal Administration), the site was described in a Pei report as "a derelict neighborhood," lying "fallow and blighted," and "cluttered with small makeshift parking lots, a sure sign of urban decay." The existing land-use pattern ("a hodge-podge of unrelated uses") was an offense to every principle of modern planning. Pei's audacious plan ("undoubtedly the most ambitious project so far undertaken under the Federal urban Redevelopment Program")[22] had a price tag of $250 million, of which the city would contribute $10 million.

The bird's-eye view and elevations included in the Pei report were, of course, spectacular. Steel-and-glass towers sprang out of imposing horizontal slabs laid out in the form of a Greek fret. Numerous streets were to be replaced by formal landscaping ("more than half the total land area is given over to open lawns, tree-lined malls and parks").

Lending "majesty and repose" to the composition would be a forty-story office tower dramatically situated at the end of a reflecting pool, on what used to be East Twelfth Street. The Pei report, eschewing the future—not to mention the conditional—tense, elaborates: "In its spacious arrangement, Erieview is beautiful as well as useful. Long low silhouettes are interrupted by the clean vertical accents of taller buildings. Quiet, treelined residential streets open into malls and bustling plazas. Around nearly every corner lie sunny lawns and park-like gardens. On the south shore, a broad grassy terrace, built out over the shoreline railroad tracks, brings Clevelanders for the first time close to the natural beauties of their lake in the downtown area."[23]

As Pei's designers busied themselves at their drawing boards, the city of Cleveland did its part by conducting a careful, indeed fastidious, building-by-building survey of the site. Of the 237 structures, 169—71.3 percent, just enough to qualify for urban renewal funds—were found to be "substandard." On average, structures in the area were cited with five code violations. Moreover, the blight was "fairly evenly spread throughout the project area," meaning that practically everything would "have to be razed."[24] Urban Renewal Commissioner William L. Slayton, who had approved $10 million worth of grants and $33 million in loans, explained that "just as there are situations and times for sensitive, gentle approaches in urban renewal, there are situations and times for vigorous, more sweeping efforts."[25] Lister, relying on the familiar organic metaphor, referred to the need for "surgery . . . where the inroads of blight and deterioration had destroyed all hope of salvage."[26]

Later, an investigation by the Comptroller General of the United States revealed that the Urban Renewal Administration had funded Erieview "without making an adequate examination of the structural condition of the buildings." Evidently, only about 20 percent of the existing structures were "substandard because of building deficiencies which could not be corrected by normal maintenance." The other 80 percent were not "substandard requiring clearance." One twelve-year-old building assessed at $80,000 had been classified as substandard despite its having "but a few minor violations such as pointing of chimney and venting of toilets." Several other structurally sound buildings, one appraised at $620,000, another at $310,000, had been classified as substandard because of "incompatible uses" and because they were said to have a "blighting effect" on surrounding structures.

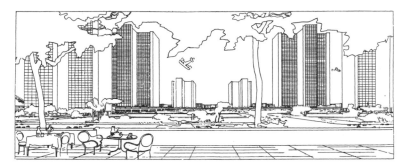

FIGURE 22

The Contemporary City, as conceived by Le Corbusier in the early 1920s. View from a terraced café overlooking "speedways" in the direction of the Great Central Station square and park. Those inspired by such images, such as the founders of Brasília, were to learn that Radiant Cities come with makeshift shantytowns built by construction workers in unconscious mockery of their masters' pretensions.

FIGURE 23

Erieview: Bird's-eye view from report published by I. M. Pei and Associates. Note Public Square and Terminal Tower on left, with adjacent Group Plan and tree-lined Mall. Is it a coincidence that a huge area of "blight" cropped up directly adjacent to the Group Plan?

One $300,000 building was, according to the Comptroller General, classified as "obsolete" because "it had no off-street loading facilities and because wood and glass paneled doors were not adequately fire resistive."[27] He concluded that "the findings indicate there may be a need for modification of the classification system now used by the City of Cleveland."[28]

At roughly this point, the federal bulldozer was stalled by similar revelations in other cities, by the diatribes of Lewis Mumford and Jane Jacobs, and by the scholarship of Martin Anderson.[29] According to Herbert J. Gans, writing in the mid-1960s, the accomplishments of the urban renewal program could be summarized as follows: "It has cleared slums to make room for luxury-housing and a few middle-income projects, and it has also provided inexpensive land for the expansion of colleges, hospitals, libraries, shopping areas, and other institutions located in slum areas. As of March 1961, 126,000 dwelling units had been demolished and about 28,000 new ones built."[30] In the east-side neighborhood of Hough, urban renewal was said to be "at a virtual standstill" despite the expenditure of some $16.4 million by the summer of 1966; a General Accounting Office study revealed that not one new residential unit had been started in the project.[31]

FIGURE 24
What, no terraced cafés? Erieview Tower, by I. M. Pei and Associates. The plaza in foreground was turned into the Galleria.

And so there commenced another kind of urban renewal project—this one far different from Erieview. The toll of rioting in Hough included 4 dead, 46 injured, and 187 arrested. Property damage, well into the millions, included a ransacked regional urban renewal office. The 1968 annual report of the Cleveland City Planning Commission makes no explicit reference to the Hough riots, but it does discreetly observe that "to clear wide acreages of slums, and create new and decent housing for people with small incomes, is [in 1968] more unattainable than a trip to the moon."[32]

Now Erieview, too, was at a standstill. For years—for decades, in fact—the site was a howling wind tunnel distinguished mainly by its makeshift parking lots, a sure sign of urban decay. There were, to be sure, powerful economic and demographic forces conspiring against the project. But one should not underestimate the defects of a Radiant City type of plan. For Erieview, no less than the Cleveland Group Plan, represents a kind of architecture that is monolithic and inherently secessionist: "This kind of architecture, usually corporate or public and occasionally residential, strives to free itself from a subordinate role to the street. The large building—office or hotel or bank—has often declared its independence of the uninterrupted flow of traffic and joined with other similar buildings to form a self-contained complex with its own surrounding buffer zone, its own orientation, its own patterns of movement: office complexes, shopping complexes, sports and convention complexes, and campuses."[33]

The residential part of Pei's scheme for Cleveland—Erieview II—was never realized to anything like the extent that I. M. Pei and Associates had in mind. In any event, no "crumped-upped houses" were ever at issue at the Erieview site, and no Garden Valley type of housing project was ever envisioned. Rather, the essence of Erieview was subsidized regentrification, in the form of "luxurious apartments" designed so as to "combine the utmost in elegance and in spaciousness with the unmatched view over the city, the waterfront, and the lake" (it being taken for granted that the opening of the St. Lawrence Seaway would render Cleveland the Rotterdam of the Midwest). Even with the subsidy, it didn't work. Moreover, Erieview had no discernible "ripple effect" on the surrounding area—and that was urban renewal's main justification. With the lake on the north and the Group Plan complex on the west, any ripple effect would have had to occur to the east and south; today, those areas continue to be Great Blights of Dullness—at best.

It might be argued that Erieview represented an improvement over the Group Plan by including a residential component, but Pei offers no argument, explicit or implicit, for why anyone would want to live there. From the text and illustrations in Pei's document, one learns nothing about the prospective tenants, except, of course, that they will be prosperous enough to pay the high rents that luxurious apartments always command, even in Cleveland. The Pei report refers to the need "to provide an orderly and attractive setting for the buildings and a pleasant environment for the people who occupy them."[34] But the identity of the residents—their values and their motivations for living there, as opposed to, say, in Shaker Heights—is never revealed. There is an offhand reference to a neighborhood school that would be squirreled away somewhere within the vast complex, but the document is otherwise silent on the bonds of community. Was this school to be part of the Cleveland public school system? What kind of inducement would that have been? Did Pei plan to lure private schools, or donate land for churches or country clubs, or design neighborhoods around public elementary schools (or racquetball courts or discotheques or designer coffee bars)? There is no evidence to suggest that he did. What were to be the terms of membership (and the principles of exclusion) in this community?

Cities are, by definition, high-density places. They are supposed to be thick with humanity, all talk of "clogged arteries" and "lonely crowds" notwithstanding. But Erieview is an architectural monolith. It is almost entirely given over to office space. It is not dense and complex urban tissue. It seems to have been conceived and executed in abstraction from any and all consideration of the distinction, in human terms, between an elementary school and an elevator shaft. Significantly, the liveliest part of Erieview today is the Galleria, a glass-covered retail establishment built in 1987 to replace the International Style plaza/reflecting pool pictured in figure 24. The Galleria was not part of the original Erieview concept; on the contrary, it was an inspired bit of adaptive reuse and, as such, a repudiation of Pei's plan.[35] As for the rest of Erieview, it lacks all the features associated with urban vitality: nightlife, outdoor cafés, store windows, street musicians, hot dog vendors—and other people. Nor would prospective residents be drawn to Erieview by the kinds of amenities that we ordinarily associate with the much-maligned suburbs: big lots, good schools, low crime rates.

Even so amiable a civic booster as the *Plain Dealer*'s George Condon was soured by Erieview. Recognizing that City Hall had become "the depository of some of the finest studies, reports and recommendations ever made," he suggested the city hold a rummage sale. The lucky purchaser of the Pei report, according to Condon, "would get a complete set of artists' conceptions of how Erieview I and Erieview II were supposed to look when they were finished, just for laughs if for nothing else."[36] But, of course, the laugh was on Condon. Pei's plan was not consigned to a shelf in a remote corner of City Hall. Over the decades it was gradually implemented, and it has not come close to realizing the claims made on its behalf by all the people who had a pecuniary interest in its construction—architects, planners, politicians, real estate tycoons, newspaper editors—not to mention ordinary men and women who, quite simply and innocently, were inspired by the International Style and harbored elevated aspirations for their hometown. And because Erieview has not "spread its rejuvenating influence" as it was supposed to do, it has given way to another Big Plan: "Civic Vision 2000 and Beyond."

In recent years a group of boosters known as Cleveland Tomorrow has commissioned another distinguished architectural firm, HOK, Inc., to reorganize the lakefront, adding new attractions and improving public access. Even now plans are being laid for a steamship museum, a dock for cruise ships and a ferry to Canada, a sports complex, and a new convention center/hotel complex that would be located adjacent to the spot that Daniel Burnham chose, a hundred years ago, for Cleveland's union railroad station. True to form, HOK and the Thompson Design Group have produced gorgeous watercolors and a glossy brochure that lay it all out in Technicolor. Empty stores and offices along Euclid Avenue are to be converted to housing. An ambitious transportation plan will significantly modify the Shoreway, which cuts the city off from the lakefront, and eventually link downtown with the cultural institutions at University Circle. A light rail system, opened in 1999, enhances access to the major attractions on the Cleveland midway.[37] Again, there are vague promises of downtown schools. Citizens are exhorted to support the use of eminent domain "to increase acquisition of land for green space, waterfront access, retail, housing developments and industrial parks."[38]

Much of what is wrong with "Civic Vision 2000 and Beyond" is discernible in its artwork. One drawing, "View of North Coast Harbor from Voinovich Park," shows a young couple pushing a stroller out onto the pier. Nearby, a woman walks with her bicycle, a man relaxes on a park bench, and several people lean on the railing and look out over a busy harbor. All the faces appear to be white. In the background are most of the architectural landmarks of downtown, including the Rock 'n Roll Hall of Fame. Another drawing offers a bird's-eye perspective on the East Ninth Street pier, which has been reconceived as a formally landscaped funfair. There is a carousel on the pier, a fleet of yachts moored in the harbor, another panorama of the city's skyscrapers, and scores of fun-seeking pedestrians; one supposes they might be looking in vain for Cap'n Frank's.[39] Another view features a fountain and flagpoles near the Great Lakes Science Center. Another rendering—this one more of an eagle's-eye view—shows the main axis of the Group Plan terminated by a massive Convention Center. A convention center hotel has been built on the west side of the Mall. Together, the two structures dwarf the adjacent Cleveland City Hall and the Cuyahoga County Courthouse. So much for Tom Johnson's and Daniel Burnham's civic vision.

Besides the Thompson Design Group, "Civic Vision 2000 and Beyond" features the artistic work of the Downtown Development Coordinators. Their images conjure up a sense of what Cleveland will be like after the lakefront project has waved its rejuvenating wand over downtown. One shows an electrified trolley line bringing customers to the Playhouse Galleria at Seventeenth Street (but won't that compete with the Galleria on East Ninth?). Another shows sidewalk cafés in front of the Cleveland Trust Building. Another, "East 13th Street and Euclid Avenue from Star Plaza," seems to have been inspired by Leicester Square on a Saturday night. How realistic is that?

The current revitalization project conceives of the lakefront as a weekend place, or, more precisely, given the severity of Cleveland's weather, a summer weekend place. Between Labor Day and Memorial Day, a full nine months, how many afternoons—never mind evenings—would anyone want to go promenading on the Cleveland lakefront, steamship museum or no? In "Civic Vision 2000 and Beyond," the lakefront has been transformed into a recreation center, a special district—a "tourist bubble"[40]—for play and leisure. The prototypes of this approach to downtown revitalization were developed by James Rouse, who converted Boston's Faneuil Hall Market Place and adjacent Quincy Market into "a new kind of urban shopping mall combining shops, restaurants, small cart-boutiques, and street performers."[41] Later projects, much celebrated, include New York's South Street Seaport and Baltimore's Harborplace. But it is a dubious concept. As Baltimoreans have found out, a shorefront theme park does little or nothing to inspire the revitalization of adjacent districts. It is just as likely that such projects suck money out of other parts of the city, or the region. As for "Civic Vision 2000 and Beyond," the extent to which everything depends on tax abatements and other concessions is not spelled out in the literature; the taxpayers will discover that in time. Or not. There are things to be said on behalf of the project: it does not call for building highways or skyscrapers, and it is sympathetic, at least in principle, to mixed uses, if naïve about what attracts people to a place.

Let no one imagine that Clevelanders are uniquely susceptible to seductive visions of lakefront splendor. In Chicago, the case for lake-

front redevelopment has been advanced by architecture critic Blair
Kamin, who wrote a Pulitzer Prize–winning series for the *Chicago Tribune* ("Nature didn't give Chicago its glorious shoreline. Good planning did")[42] and who conceives of lakefront parks as a nuclear weapon
in the war against blight. Kamin challenges Mayor Richard M. Daley
and his fellow Chicagoans to summon up the will to reclaim neglected
lakefront acreage that boasts—the legacy of Frederick Law Olmsted,
in the main—three thousand acres of parkland, twenty-nine beaches,
and eight harbors, amenities that "attract an estimated 65 million vis-
its a year." He argues that revamping public space along Lake Michigan could transform the city in any number of ways:

—*It could help bridge the racial chasm that has long split Chicago.*
—*It could begin to lift entire neighborhoods out of oblivion.*
—*It could heal us physically, especially as the population ages, and could*
   be an ever-renewable source of peace and fulfillment.
—*It could have a democratizing influence, allowing people from diverse*
   backgrounds to mix and come to appreciate one another.
—*It could celebrate not only dead presidents and generals, but also the*
   so-called ordinary men and women who endured extraordinary hard-
   ships to build this nation.[43]

"All this," Kamin promises, "is within our grasp."[44]

   Because Kamin makes no effort to show precisely how lakeshore
redevelopment can serve to "lift entire neighborhoods out of oblivion," or why the revival of these neighborhoods would not occur at
the expense of others—or why it should—it is hard to take the claim
seriously. More to the point, Kamin fails to identify the kinds of devices that could be employed to knit together redeveloped lakefront
parkland and run-down South Side neighborhoods. Huge swatches
of urban fabric do not get stitched together automatically. Unless edges
are cleverly turned into seams, human nature will treat them as bar-
riers. How does Kamin propose to prevent that from happening? And
if the point is to bridge racial chasms and lift entire neighborhoods
out of oblivion, then it needs to be shown why these goals can be better accomplished through lakefront redevelopment, or through construction projects generally, than by more direct means—by redis-
tributing income, for example.[45] If, on the other hand, Kamin's real
motive is simply to beautify the lakefront and make it a better recre-

ational center (there would be nothing wrong with that, although one could argue that it should be financed through users fees), then why the grandiose claims about addressing *spiritual* needs?

Experience with Big Plans and cataclysmic money[46] ought by now to have conditioned us to anticipate all the things that can go wrong. Lakefront redevelopment can raise real estate values and rents in poor neighborhoods to the point that low-income residents, many of them African Americans or other minorities, would be forced to flee (to where?). The rising tide of gentrification can turn entire neighborhoods from black to white, raising serious questions about how that would help to heal racial chasms in a riven city. Lakefront development can render a single-purpose district all the more monolithic by driving out every human use that is not recreational (Kamin writes off Meigs Field, for example) and even a few that are (he wants to evict the Bears from Soldiers Field). It can sometimes succeed in raising property values and stimulating growth in adjacent neighborhoods, but mightn't that occur at the expense of other Chicago neighborhoods? *Doesn't the blight have to go somewhere?* Finally, lakefront redevelopment is *very* expensive; Kamin argues that the $500 million budgeted for lakefront projects over the next twelve years is nowhere near enough.

But never mind. Big Government is back—not only in massive lakefront redevelopment schemes, but in the reinvention of public housing. Early in 2000 it was reported that Mayor Daley had signed an unprecedented agreement with the U.S. Department of Housing and Urban Development that will send $1.5 billion to Chicago "to demolish virtually all of the city's high-rise public housing developments, widely regarded as the nation's worst examples of failed public housing policy. Under the ambitious federal-city plan, 51 decaying high-rise buildings containing 16,000 apartment units will be razed and replaced with nearly 25,000 new or rehabilitated units, mostly low-density, mixed-income rental town houses on sites scattered across the city." According to HUD Secretary Andrew M. Cuomo, the Chicago Housing Authority has "agreed to safeguards to protect the rights of displaced tenants, including assurances of enough affordable housing in the Chicago market to temporarily absorb displaced families and guarantees that displaced residents can return to public or assisted housing when it becomes available."[47] By that time, no doubt, *all* the bugs will have been ironed out of public housing.

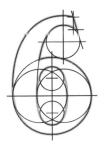

THE STRANGE CAREER OF ADVOCACY PLANNING

AFTER ALL IS SAID AND DONE, I. M. PEI'S Erieview plan might have been just another real estate hustle. But one wonders if its appeal—it had the near-unanimous support of upstanding Clevelanders, after all—lay not so much in its social-scientific pretensions ("Cleveland is growing," the Pei report declares authoritatively, and it "needs new office space and substantial amounts of new housing in the downtown area")[1] as in its technocratic utopianism, a genre as old as Francis Bacon's *The New Atlantis* and as new as Le Corbusier's Radiant City. Either way, the urban renewal fiasco—memorialized for posterity by the nationally televised 1973 implosion of the Pruitt-Igoe project in St. Louis—left the American city planning profession riven.

Traditionally, planners had had formal training in law, landscape architecture, or engineering. Often, their interest in planning had been inspired by the grand designs of the City Beautiful or the soaring visions of the Garden City movement, and so they were inclined to agree with Cleveland's John T. Howard that planning was concerned with "a good or bad pattern of land uses and population densities knitted into better or worse workability by systems of streets, utilities and public service facilities."[2] Planning, in short, was both civic art and the science of reordering the physical environment.

By the end of the 1960s, however, younger planners were recoiling from such a conception. Many had been trained in the social sciences, and they took it for granted that since urban politics "is above all the politics of land use, city planners were bound to be politicized."[3] They weren't scandalized by that. On the contrary, liberated from the technocrat-as-political-eunuch myth, they felt free, even obliged, to address the most fundamental issues of politics—the practical meaning of justice and equality, for example. Within the American Institute of Planners (AIP), a mainstream, even establishmentarian professional society whose ranks had been swollen by the influx of recent graduates of professional planning programs, these two groups squared off.

Since 1938, the AIP's constitution had defined their professional purpose as "the planning of the unified development of urban communities and their environs and of states, regions, and the nation, as expressed through determination of the comprehensive arrangement of land uses and land occupancy and the regulation thereof." In 1967 the annual conference of the AIP passed an amendment deleting the entire last phrase referring to land use, with the obvious implication "that it broadened the scope of professional concern by removing the apparent limitation on planning practice implied in the direct reference to land use."[4] A new concept of city planning variously called advocacy planning, equity planning, or policy planning was ushered in. Although it was to become fashionable in academic circles, advocacy planning had little impact on the day-to-day operations of municipal planning departments.

Except in Cleveland. There, in 1969, Norman Krumholz was appointed planning director, heralding a unique, ten-year experiment in advocacy planning. In part because of Krumholz's eloquence and prolificacy—his background was in journalism—Cleveland in the post-Hough-rioting era once again attracted national attention for its planning efforts. The major document of the Krumholz years, the *Policy Planning Report* of 1975,[5] utilized no conventional maps, no visionary architectural renderings, no land-use surveys with Technicolor overlays. The document relied on stark black-and-white photography to depict the lives of the ordinary people of Cleveland. Buses, old people, black children, mean streets, broken windows, and Victorian frame houses were prominently displayed. The things that Clevelanders were accustomed to boasting about—the Group Plan, the art museum, the Cleveland Orchestra, the office buildings of Erieview—were conspicuously absent; there was one grim shot of Terminal Tower. Among the city planning authorities cited by the *Policy Planning Report* were Thomas Jefferson, Andrew Jackson, Woodrow Wilson, Franklin D. Roosevelt, Lyndon B. Johnson, Mayor Carl Stokes, John Rawls, and Jesus Christ. Shifting the focus of planning away from the 1949 General Plan—still the official guide—the document stressed decentralization and announced that the overriding goal of the City Planning Commission was to promote "a wider range of choices for those Cleveland residents who have few, if any, choices."[6] Under Krumholz, city planners in Cleveland would be advocates for the city's have-nots.

Krumholz, who later became a professor at Cleveland State University—the university itself was conceived as part of an urban renewal project—describes the urban development process as "inherently exploitative of the poor and especially of the minority poor." Because exploitation is endemic to the system, Krumholz contended, city planners and other public officials must place "priority attention on the needs of the poor" so as to "provide them with countervailing power." Cleveland's advocacy planners, therefore, "deemphasized many of our concerns with zoning, land use, and urban design," altering "the planner's traditional posture as an apolitical technician serving a unitary public interest."[7] Layton K. Washburn, a landscape architect who worked with the City Planning Commission from 1938 into the early 1980s, says that while Krumholz "did respect the feelings of old guard physical planners, he was more interested in the reports prepared by the economists, geographers, and social scientists he brought in."[8]

The contrast between orthodox planning and advocacy planning may be seen in Krumholz's approach to transportation, the main preoccupation of the General Plan. Instead of concentrating on "rush hour congestion, auto access, or the need for more off-street parking," Krumholz focused on the problems of those city residents who did not own automobiles—by his reckoning, about a third of all Cleveland families. The Regional Transit Authority, which in 1975 consolidated the transit systems of the various municipalities in the metropolitan area, was seen by Krumholz as excessively suburb- and rail-oriented (at the time, 87 percent of RTA's ridership took the bus) and generally insensitive to the needs of Cleveland's "transit-dependent population." Krumholz lobbied hard for lower fares and for a Community Response Transit ("a door-to-door, dial-a-ride service") and in general "worked to discredit the rail expansion plan [of the

Regional Transit Authority] at the local, regional, and federal levels." This Krumholz claims as his "greatest success."[9]

Other highlights of his tenure as planning director included his (unsuccessful) opposition to the Tower City project, a downtown development plan organized around the Terminal complex and depending on tax abatements and extensive site improvements financed out of the federal pork barrel. Krumholz objected in principle to the use of tax abatements and suggested that the Tower City developers themselves finance the infrastructure improvements. For his pains, he and his associates in the City Planning Department were branded "a bunch of baboons" by the irrepressible chairman of the Cleveland City Council, George Forbes.[10] Krumholz also took up the cudgels for Tom Johnson's Municipal Light Plant by mounting a counteroffensive against the Cleveland Electric Illuminating Company, a campaign inextricably wedded to the city's ignominious 1979 default under Mayor Dennis Kucinich. He proposed (unsuccessfully) to build a "new town," called Warren's Ridge, on the site of Tom Johnson's old tuberculosis sanitorium and House of Corrections.[11] He also failed in his attempt to deregulate the city's woefully inadequate taxi business.

FIGURE 25
Terminal Tower: A Cleveland landmark on an overcast day. Advocacy planning recognized that the city was more than just architecture and public art.

Krumholz claims a number of successes. He was able to get a state law passed that "simplified the foreclosure procedure for tax delinquent and abandoned property"; he arranged for the transfer of the city's neglected shorefront parks to the state (an arrangement that was not wholly salutary; it was the state's first experience with urban parks, and the Park Commission, acting on instinct, immediately moved to get rid of all the baseball diamonds—to make room for nature trails, presumably); he worked to rationalize the procedures of the city's Waste Collection and Disposal Division; he "helped block" the construction of two freeways and "set in motion the events" that would decertify a troublesome (from the city's perspective) regional planning agency. But all things considered, it amounts to a fairly modest record, and even Krumholz is willing to acknowledge that Cleveland's advocacy planning experience had "little known application by practicing planning professionals in other cities." His "model, after all,

FIGURE 26
*Advocacy planning was about the mundane realities of everyday life. The sign on the
wall says, "We're proud of Cleveland." The woman pictured here might well be proud
of her hometown, but she likely has other matters on her mind.*

asked the city planners to be what few public administrators are: activist, risk-taking in style, and redistributive in objective. . . . Planning practice actually is cautious and conservative."[12]

Advocacy planning—Krumholz prefers "equity planning" or "policy planning"—is a paradox. On the one hand, it is avowedly parti-
san, in that it rejects the very idea of an objectively knowable and unitary public interest. On the other hand, it is political in the highest,
Aristotelian sense of being animated by a vision of a just and equi-
table society. In a curious way, then, it is an expression of that quest
for community that has served from Plymouth to Erieview as the
common thread in this narrative. But it lacked the power to inspire
perhaps because its basic principles were not conveyed well through
the kinds of visual images normally associated with Big Plans. Actually, that doesn't go far enough. As the photography in Krumholz's
Policy Planning Report makes clear, advocacy planning was constitutionally allergic to such visionary renderings and thus could never
hope to compete with those advocating grandiose construction projects of one kind or another. As the planner Michael Sorkin has observed, the modernist project of therapeutic cleansing "remains the
dominant model for the large-scale transformation of urban areas.

Most of us acknowledge that this is a disreputable and inappropriate model. But we find ourselves in the difficult situation of having no alternatives, or insufficient ones."[13]

Advocacy planning had its innings in Cleveland, but soon it was back to business as usual for a profession that is "virtually unable to resist the social pressures of capitalist economy and consumer sovereignty."[14] And so, in the 1980s and 1990s, Public Square submitted to a multimillion-dollar facelift; the Shaker Rapid was refurbished; there was renewed talk of building a Euclid Avenue subway, first proposed in 1917; the Playhouse Square Foundation raised funds to save the city's theater district; Tower City construction proceeded successfully, undeterred by the fact that there was a glut of office space in the city; yet another lakefront development plan was unveiled (see chap. 5); at City Hall, planners were again speaking of blight as if it were bacteriological. Some observed an irony: while Daniel Burnham's Cuyahoga Building (1893) was sacrificed to make way for British Petroleum's $200 million, forty-five-story headquarters on Public Square, James W. Rouse, developer of Columbia, Maryland, Baltimore's Harborplace, and other projects, was awarded an ovation in Cleveland by repeating Burnham's nostrum about the need to make Big Plans. In the early 1980s, Cleveland was beset by an outbreak of what Calvin Trillin has called "domeism,"[15] an effort to save the city's American League baseball franchise by building an indoor sports arena. What if that campaign had succeeded? About a decade later, when ideas about ballparks had radically changed, Cleveland built a state-of-the-art facility that draws rave reviews and capacity crowds every night.[16] A few years after that, the city built a new lakefront stadium as a lure for an NFL expansion franchise. In the meantime, Cleveland invited I. M. Pei back to design the Rock 'n Roll Hall of Fame and Museum. There seems to be no way of driving a stake through the heart of the "edifice complex" that equates public architecture with the city.

What remains to be demonstrated is that such projects—worthy of the Caesars, or even Robert Moses—will in any meaningful way enhance the quality of life of the majority of Clevelanders, or even fuel downtown redevelopment. As Richard Moe and Carter Wilkie have written, Cleveland's reputation as "the Comeback City" conceals as much as it reveals: "Few of the city's former residents are coming back. Many more are leaving. Thomas Bier, director of the Housing Policy Research Program at Cleveland State University, studied residential migration in the Cleveland metropolitan market from 1987 to 1991 and discovered that migration 'outward was five times greater than movement inward.'"[17] What Cleveland has created on its lakefront, with the help of massive public subsidies, is a recreation complex. What cities like Cleveland actually need is residents, attracted and retained by jobs, healthy neighborhoods, safe streets, and decent schools.[18]

On the basis of experience, we should expect massive downtown development projects to generate a very large dose of frustration—not because of the possibility that they will be aborted or compromised, but because they promise so much more than they can ever deliver. Curiously, those who stand to benefit *most* from the Disneyfication of downtown—prosperous, public-spirited suburbanites who can afford season tickets at the ballpark, and who might actually patronize the museums and aquariums or promenade in the parks—are likely to be disappointed, because a few evenings in the tourist bubble will not slake their thirst for community. Just as curiously, those who stand to benefit *least* from downtown development schemes—Norman Krumholz's natural constituency—seem least inclined to complain about them. Among the cultural contradictions of capitalism, this surely is among the more tragically delicious.

7

TWO CHEERS FOR SPRAWL

THE MODERN IMAGE OF THE VICTORIAN city—of smokestacks and sweatshops, of child labor and vice—owes something to Friedrich Engels's studies of Manchester, Patrick Geddes's analyses of Edinburgh, the Pittsburgh survey, and other pioneering ventures in social science. But it probably owes a lot more to a handful of creative artists, including Gustave Doré, Jacob Riis, and Charles Dickens, whose graphic accounts of "Coketown" raised the consciousness of the middle classes. There could hardly be a better case in point than Edward Bellamy's "utopian romance," *Looking Backward*,[1] which fired the imaginations of people the world around:

Published in Boston in 1888, Looking Backward had won immediate popularity in the United States and exercised a profound influence over such men as Thorstein Veblen and John Dewey. Written against the background of the industrial depression and growing labor unrest that engulfed both America and Europe in the third quarter of the nineteenth century, the book presented a graphic depiction of a society in which these problems had been overcome. The hero of the novel is a prosperous Bostonian who has the good fortune to sleep soundly from 1887 to 2000 and wake in a society organized on moral principles. Industry has been efficiently grouped into one govern-

*ment-owned cooperative Trust. Distribution has also been concentrated
into one great Department Store whose branches in every city and
village sell everything the nation has produced. Competition has been
replaced by centralized planning; poverty and unemployment are
unknown; all citizens between twenty-one and forty-five occupy ranks
in the "industrial army," and everyone receives an equal salary.*[2]

For an obscure and modest London clerk named Ebenezer Howard,
the experience of reading *Looking Backward* was transformative; the
book "made him an activist for the rest of his life."[3]

The self-educated Howard is remembered as the inventor of the
Garden City—a concept that had its roots in the eighteenth-century
practice known as "emparking," in which the landed gentry built
"estate villages" in the thrall of their country houses as part of an
effort to clear existing rural slums, and which later found expression
in enlightened company towns such as Saltaire, Bournville, and Port
Sunlight.[4] Building on such precedents, Howard wedded Bellamy's
utopian vision to the "single tax" program of Henry George, which
boiled down to confiscating income from rents and abolishing all
other taxes.[5] As such, the Garden City was part urban plan and part
financial scheme, the key being a nonprofit investment company organized to sell bonds "yielding a fixed rate (4 or 5 percent), purchase
6,000 acres of agricultural land, and lay out a city according to Howard's plans. They would build roads, power and water plants, and all
other necessities, and then seek to attract industry and residents. The
company would continue to own all the land; as the population rose,
the rents too would rise from the low rate per acre for agricultural
land to the more substantial rate of a city with 30,000 residents. All
rent would go to the company and would be used to repay the original investors. Any surplus that remained after the financial obligations had been discharged would provide additional services to the
community."[6]

The publication in 1898 of Howard's *To-morrow: A Peaceful Path
to Real Reform,* and its reappearance a few years later as *Garden Cities
of Tomorrow,*[7] gave birth to an international movement that sought
to take city planning out of the hands of both patricians and real
estate developers and turn it over to public servants trained to apply,
on a regional basis, neutral principles of good city design. Among its
progeny was a century-long, international search for some solution
to the problem of providing decent housing for the working classes,
it being assumed that the market was not up to the task.

At the core of the Garden City concept was the fusion of the best qualities of urban and rural life, for Howard

believed that the time had come to establish a new pattern of city development: one that would use modern technical facilities to break down the widening gap between the countryside, with its depleted economic and social facilities, and the city, with its equally depleted biological and natural advantages: he proposed to overcome both the prevalent apoplexy at the urban center, and the paralysis at the extremities, by promoting a new pattern of city growth. Unlike the advocates of continued urban expansion, he rejected the suburb as a tolerable compromise; indeed, he hardly considered it. Howard saw that the relief of congestion was not a matter of widening the dormitory areas of the city, but of decentralizing all its functions.[8]

Howard imagined that a full-grown Garden City might cover six thousand acres and contain a population of about thirty-two thousand; growth beyond that point would be through "hiving off." At the heart of each Garden City would be a railroad station and a Central Park, "an impressive and meaningful setting for the 'large public buildings': town hall, library, museum, concert and lecture hall, and the hospital. Here the highest values of the community are brought together—culture, philanthropy, health, and mutual cooperation."[9] In short, Howard "sought a stable marriage between city and country, not a weekend liaison,"[10] with the ultimate goal of "superseding capitalism and creating a civilization based on cooperation."[11] Another way of putting it is that he sought the re-creation of *landschaft*. But Howard insisted that the Garden City was less a romantic vision than a sensible alternative both to Coketown and to what Mumford called "conurbation," that is, formless urban sprawl. And it differed from the City Beautiful movement in being less about public buildings than about affordable housing.

Howard's aspirations were expressed in financial details and through meticulous yet restrained diagrams that are so familiar to students of the city that they need not be reproduced here. "The Three Magnets" depicted people as so many iron filings being inexorably drawn toward "town-country," the synthesis of urban and rural virtues. Who, after all, could resist "beauty of nature, social opportunity; fields and parks of easy access; low rents, high wages; low rates, plenty to do; low prices, no sweating; field for enterprise, flow of capital; pure air and water, good drainage; bright homes and gardens, no smoke, no slums; freedom, cooperation"?[12] His diagram of the Garden City ("N.B.: Diagram Only. Plan cannot be drawn until site selected") was an asterisk of broad boulevards overlaid on a set of concentric circles with a crystal palace in the bull's-eye, all these features floating in a greenbelt ("new forests," "allotments") adorned with sundry benevolent institutions ("agricultural college," "farm for epileptics"). These diagrams not only convey the sum and substance of the Garden City, but also make clear that the self-effacing Howard, unlike other utopian visionaries,[13] actually sought to avoid giving "the architectural and planning details the stamp of his own imagination."[14] In fact, Mumford insists that Howard's green-eyeshade utopianism "gained distinction precisely because he refused to be tied down to a particular physical image of the city or a particular method of planning or a particular type of building."[15]

Howard's "invention"—let's face it, it was the next best thing to the Big Rock Candy Mountain, where "they hung the jerk that invented work"—appealed to an odd coalition of radicals and paternalistic industrialists. Of the former, George Bernard Shaw may have been the most notable. Of the latter, one of the most interesting was a lawyer named Ralph Neville: "If Neville's interest in reform stemmed from a love of humanity, he was careful to hide it. He had the same horror of sentiment that he had of bankruptcy; he supported reform measures only when he believed they followed logically from the laws of biology and economics. When Neville concluded that the Garden City was 'based on sound economic principle,' it was the highest accolade he could bestow, and Howard was happy to receive it."[16] Largely as a result of this strain of pragmatism, Howard's utopian vision bore fruit—beginning in 1903 at Letchworth, on a remote site north of London and along the route to Cambridge, and then in 1920 at Welwyn Garden City, closer in but on the same rail line. These two communities were to have an enormous worldwide impact. Mumford explains that both ventures, "starting as private enterprises, with limited prospects of gain, not merely survived indifference and opposition, but have affected the pattern of housing and city-building in many areas, from Scotland to India. It was the success of these cities that led Sir Anthony Montague Barlow's parliamentary committee to recommend the industrial decentralization in garden cities as a remedy for the increasing congestion of London; and this led in turn to the New Towns Act of 1946, which projected a ring of New Towns around London and in various other parts of England."[17] In short, the Garden City concept engendered a town planning movement that was to inform the design of the English landscape, with global repercussions, throughout the remainder of the twentieth century. Even as unromantic a city as Cleveland found inspiration in the Garden City ideal (see fig. 27).

Although it was not Howard's doing, part of the legacy of the Garden City is a distinctive aesthetic. At Letchworth the architectural work was done by Barry Parker and Raymond Unwin, who, while sympathizing with Howard's goals, "had no use for his rationalistic, geometric methods of town planning." Accordingly, they "gave to the Garden City movement their own vision of the 'city greatly beautiful,' a vision derived from the medieval village as seen through the eyes of William Morris. . . . Parker and Unwin employed traditional designs to express the unity of a cooperatively organized community of equals. In the context of their time, their designs for Letchworth stood for cleanliness, simplicity, and the honest use of materials—qualities the arts-and-crafts movement associated with the fourteenth century and hoped to revive in the twentieth."[18]

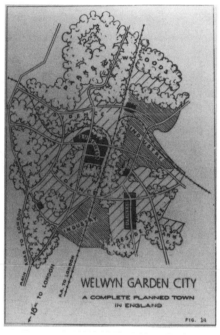

Letchworth housing recalls such traditions, evoking as it does the corporate qualities of the medieval cloister.[19] Robert Fishman has noted that Unwin's work with multi-unit dwellings in particular set an extremely high standard for workers' housing: "Unwin's designs show the Garden City movement at its best—pragmatic, democratic, responsive to the needs of the people it served. Unwin gave the same attention to these projects that other architects devoted to the rich man's villa. He made sure that every cottage got its share of sunlight, that every window and door were properly placed. That institutional bleakness which affects British (and not only British) architects when planning for the 'lower orders' was completely absent from Unwin's work. Instead, there was a real sense of individual well-being and community solidarity, precisely the 'organic unity' that Unwin had proclaimed." But this project had "one great deficiency. When the costs of the new houses were added up, only skilled workers could afford them." Fish-

FIGURE 27
*Model city:
Ebenezer
Howard comes
to Cleveland.
From John T.
Howard's*
What's Ahead
for Cleveland?

FIGURE 28

Letchworth, England, 1998: Unlike the City Beautiful, which was about government offices and other public buildings, the Garden City was largely about workers' housing. Howard's socialist utopia might not have been realized at Letchworth, but Parker and Unwin left their indelible, elegant mark.

FIGURE 29

The beguinage at Bruges, Belgium. Lewis Mumford taught us years ago that the Beguines were a lay order whose little cloisters well illustrate the principles of corporate building and medieval enclosure. Note chapel on right.

man absolves Parker and Unwin of any real blame, however: "If they were unable to build decent workers' housing without a subsidy, neither could anyone else."[20] This was to be a recurrent theme of twentieth-century planning.

Even Mumford had to concede that in addition to the prohibitive cost of Garden City housing, there were basic design flaws. For one thing, the site plans employed at Letchworth and Welwyn Garden City were "perhaps too open" to provide for appropriate urban density. In addition, Howard might have "underestimated the gravitational pull of a big metropolitan center,"[21] which is another way of saying that in the real world a city like London is a kind of invisible sun exerting an irresistible force on outlying communities. Thus, autonomy proved elusive for Letchworth and Welwyn Garden City, and the differences between Garden Cities and garden suburbs, distinctions that Howard considered fundamental, were largely lost.

This in turn is related to one further respect in which the Garden City movement was remarkable: to the extent that it succeeded, it did so "not as a social movement but as a planning movement."[22] In other words, the revolution was turned over to the professionals, which meant that the ideal of cooperative socialism was displaced by a concern for the various accoutrements of the Garden City: Howard's rhetorical flourishes; Parker and Unwin's "organic" architecture; romantic street and park plans reminiscent of Frederick Law Olmsted; and, above all, greenbelts and zoning.

As this sanitized version of Howard's vision was insinuating itself within the newly established town planning profession, England's actual Garden Cities were being put to any number of tests. As Richard T. LeGates and Frederic Stout explain, a century after the publication of *To-morrow: A Peaceful Path to Real Reform,*

Letchworth exists as a gracious city outside of London, the size Howard envisioned, surrounded by a greenbelt, with publicly owned land leased to the owners of gracious houses (many built by Unwin). Much of the increased land value created by the successful development has been invested back to the community just as Howard envisioned. But getting from Howard's vision to the completed city of Letchworth was tough work. The First Garden City Society fought neighboring landowners and hostile local officials who wanted nothing to do with what they considered outside socialist cranks. . . . When the project struggled financially, board members who wanted to keep all land in public

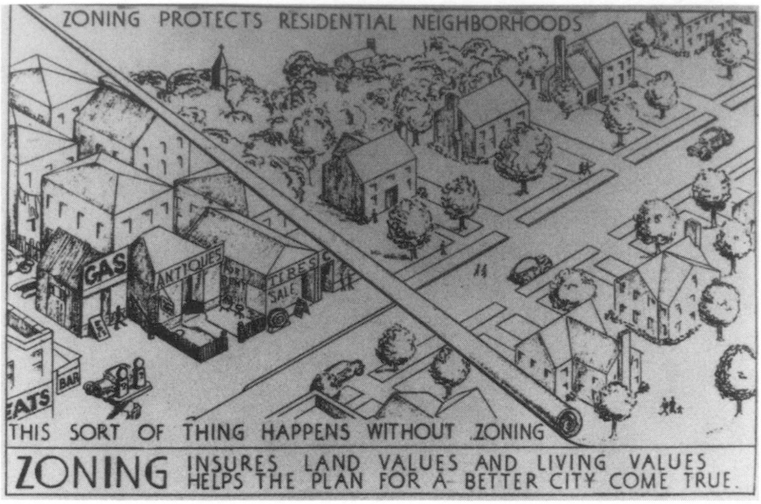

FIGURE 30

The banality of professionalism: When the Garden City vision was turned over to the experts, the predictable result was a profusion of zoning ordinances. From John T. Howard's What's Ahead for Cleveland?

FIGURE 31

Ebenezer Howard was a teetotaler, but others found that they worked up a powerful thirst building the socialist utopia. The Three Magnets pub, Letchworth, named in honor of a key Garden City concept, conveys the wackier side of the Thermidorean instinct.

ownership fought with members who wanted to sell some land for cash
to keep the city growing. Later, when the city was financially successful,
citizens fought directors to retain the "unearned increment" in
increased land value that Howard had predicted for community use
rather than stockholder profits.[23]

While still distinctive, Letchworth has to a certain extent been "main-
streamed" by instincts that may seem admirably Burkean or merely
bourgeois, depending on one's political proclivities. Either way, connoisseurs of dashed hopes and disappointment can savor the ironies:
where Howard decreed that there be a "Crystal Palace" celebrating a
"cooperatively organized community of equals," one now finds, in
Letchworth, the standard attractions of a pedestrian commercial precinct; in Welwyn Garden City, there is at the railroad station in the
heart of town a shopping mall—the Howard Centre!—and at a prime
location within, the Golden Arches of McDonald's. Howard himself
never lost the faith; late in life he took up Esperanto.[24]

The Garden City concept was retailed in the United States by
the Regional Planning Association of America, an organization that
counted Lewis Mumford, along with Clarence Stein and Henry
Wright, as prominent members. Founded in 1923, the RPAA was
involved in the development of Sunnyside Gardens, a pioneering
housing project in New York City; Lewis and Sophia Mumford, along
with Wright, were early residents. In the 1930s, the faithful rallied
round the Radburn project in New Jersey, a good example of how the
radical aspects of the Garden City ideal were jettisoned while its inci-
dental features were fetishized. Mumford, an indefatigable Radburn
promoter, offers the following account.

*The Radburn Plan, the first major departure in city planning since
Venice, was prompted by a suggestion from a layman, who conceived its
new layout as a "town for the Motor Age." But adaptation to the motor
car was only one of many distinguishing features: it utilized the separation of traffic by overpasses and underpasses, first demonstrated by
Olmsted in Central Park; the suburban superblock, with a more systematic use of the cul-de-sac for privacy and quiet; the continuous strip
park (also an invention of Olmsted's); the separation of neighborhood
access roads from main traffic arteries, as outlined by [Clarence] Perry's
neighborhood unit concept; and the school and swimming pool set in
the park, as the civic nucleus of a neighborhood.[25]*

Implicit in the "full Radburn ideal" were a number of objectives: "decentralized, self-contained settlements, organized to promote environmental considerations by conserving open space, harnessing the automobile, and promoting community life."[26] Architectural controls were enforced through restrictive covenants. Residential units fronted on interior parks, while automobiles were relegated to service alleys in the rear, and pedestrian traffic was routed along an extensive system of footpaths. The hierarchy of streets and other byways was often justified by an organic metaphor ("arterial" roads, etc.) that seems to have been in the air in the late twenties and early thirties. (Le Corbusier, who believed the number of streets in existing cities "should be diminished by two-thirds,"[27] developed a characteristically rigid taxonomy of streets that was to prove influential for decades.)

Although the prototype itself failed to survive the economic crisis of the 1930s, "various New Deal projects treated the Radburn design as dogma,"[28] as can be seen in a number of projects that were American variations on the Garden City theme, as well as President Roosevelt's answer to the "Hoovervilles" of the Great Depression. The "greenbelt towns" were built by the Resettlement Administration, headed by Rexford Guy Tugwell, with Clarence Stein serving as intellectual godfather.[29] The towns were based on the proposition that government can build better communities than the private sector, and on "the three basic ideas of the modern community: the Garden City, the Radburn Idea, and the Neighborhood Unit."[30] The principal ideas underlying Greenbelt, Maryland, for example, have been described as "the superblock of housing and open space where vehicular traffic is excluded; extensive use of walkways and underpasses to facilitate pedestrian movement; placing the service entrance of residences at the street side of the house, and the main entrance in the rear facing parkland; and establishing the elementary school as a focal point for the community. . . . Greenbelt is also significant for its development of cooperative forms of enterprise, including a housing cooperative, a coop grocery store and pharmacy, a community newspaper, and a cooperative nursery school, all of which continue to operate today."[31] The whole point to the panoply of Greenbelt co-ops was providing a substitute for the ideal of home ownership, which was dismissed as a cynical bourgeois scheme devised to defang the proletariat.

Like any Big Plan, Greenbelt had its nits. For one thing, as at Letchworth and Welwyn Garden City, the rents were too pricey for the truly poor; as William H. Wilson has put it, "the greenbelt towns were not inexpensive housing."[32] At the same time, the bureaucrats in charge of selecting the residents were required to enforce fairly strict income limitations, which meant that local allegiances were constantly being undermined by high turnover rates. How do you build a community when you're always having to kick people out? In addition, there were, despite an essentially attractive Olmstedian layout, some fundamental aesthetic problems: "In truth the styles of the thirties have not worn well. The flat-roofed houses were kin to the International Style, scarcely a fresh approach to housing design by 1935. The architectural *cognoscenti* of the day defended them over the neocolonial designs also used in the greenbelt towns. They forgot that the neocolonial, though derivative, is gracious and adaptable. The flat-roofed houses instead are period pieces, well-designed and functional, but too stark to be attractive."[33] Also, one could argue, following Christopher Alexander, that Greenbelt's physical organization was simply wrong-headed. The layout of Greenbelt (and later of Columbia, Maryland), which "suggests a hierarchy of stronger and stronger closed social groups," is utterly unrealistic, for there are "virtually no closed groups of people in modern society. The reality of today's social

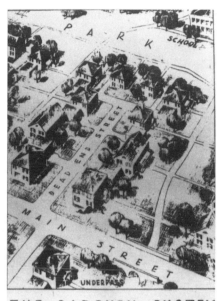

THE RADBURN SYSTEM

structure is thick with overlap—the systems of friends and acquaintances form a semi-lattice, not a tree."[34] Finally, the early greenbelt towns seem to have shared with Soviet collective farms of that period—early residents called themselves "pioneers"—a level of intensity that could not be long sustained. They were, in short, "over-organized civically and socially. The schedule of meetings was so crowded at first that stay-at-home weeks were declared."[35]

Other Radburn-inspired communities were conceived in the private sector, yet shared Greenbelt's—and the Garden City's—animus against home ownership. One of these, Chatham Village, continues to be an interesting case study in American residential planning. In 1929, a Pittsburgh department-store magnate named Henry Buhl left $13 million to a foundation devoted to great cultural projects, among

FIGURE 32
Radburn, New Jersey, from John T. Howard's What's Ahead for Cleveland? *Note the pedestrian underpass and the way that houses front on parkland.*

which was the provision of community housing for persons of limited income. In 1931, the foundation purchased the forty-five-acre Bigham Farm, an estate magnificently situated high atop Mt. Washington overlooking Pittsburgh's "Golden Triangle," where the Allegheny and Monongahela Rivers meet to form the Ohio. Chatham Village was built on that dramatic site.

According to Charles F. Lewis, director of the Buhl Foundation, what was distinctive about Chatham Village was its status as "the first planned garden homes urban community built in America to be retained in a single ownership and managed as an investment."[36] Residents did not purchase individual units, but rather memberships in the community, which were fixed at a fairly modest (but not nominal) rate. They paid a monthly fee that included their contribution to the "master mortgage," property taxes, school taxes, maintenance, property insurance, and security. In the beginning, the Buhl Foundation owned and managed the community; in 1960, these functions were assumed by a cooperative association, Chatham Village Homes Incorporated.

Writing for the foundation in the mid-1950s, Lewis documented the success of Chatham Village. By maintaining virtually 100 percent occupancy and an enviably low rate of tenant turnover (unlike in the greenbelt towns, there was no income cap), the foundation's investment had yielded a stable annual return of over 4 percent after depreciation. Lewis also noted that "the impact of Chatham Village upon community planning has been noteworthy. The site planners and architectural consultants—Clarence Stein and Henry Wright, of New York—turned the challenge of a hillside terrain into a composition of great beauty. To this site they—and the architects, Ingham and Boyd, of Pittsburgh—adapted buildings housing from two to eight families in such a way as to provide overall harmony with variety, individuality, and unusual privacy for family living." Any inventory of the amenities of Chatham Village would include the "Georgian" charm of the residential units; buried utilities; an on-site shopping center; the consignment of cars to cleverly concealed garage compounds; well-placed and well-equipped playgrounds and schools; and a community center, to which use the 1844 Bigham mansion was converted. Twenty-five acres of woodland served as a human retreat and bird sanctuary. "More and more, over the years," Lewis boasted,

Chatham Village has been hailed by national and international leaders as pioneering an important new phase in American urban housing.

*From all parts of the United States and from many foreign lands there
continue to come architects, planners, engineers, builders, financiers,
and public officials. They have been enthusiastic in their comments,
and many of them have gone away to build other fine communities on
the Chatham pattern in other cities. Sir Raymond Unwin, an early
and distinguished British authority, frequently expressed the ardent
hope that the example of Chatham Village would have just such a
stimulating effect. . . . Lewis Mumford, Catherine Bauer, and Louis
Brownlow are among leaders in housing who have visited Chatham
Village and have gone away to praise its contribution to American
housing.*[37]

It is true that Mumford was an ardent Chatham Village booster,
but in *The City in History* he laments its failure "to excite even local
imitation," which he deemed "inexplicable."[38] One reason was suggested by Jane Jacobs, who argued that "there is no public life here,
in any city sense." What there is, according to Jacobs, is "differing
degrees of extended private life." Given "the degree of chumminess
that neighborliness in Chatham Village entails," Jacobs maintained,
it was necessary that "the residents be similar to one another in their
standards, interests and backgrounds." Citing evidence that one representative court "contains as this is written four lawyers, two doc-
tors, two engineers, a dentist, a salesman, a banker, a railroad executive, a planning executive," she argued that Chatham Village is an
enclave of middle-class professionals who "set themselves apart from
the different people in the surrounding city."[39] To the extent that
Chatham Village has been a professional-class ghetto, its goal of providing housing for "moderate income clerical workers"[40] a quite
limited ambition at that—has proved elusive.

To this day, Chatham Village is a charming precinct for professional people tucked into a working-class section of Pittsburgh. In the
Radburn tradition, the architecture is communocentric; residences
front on courtyards, culs-de-sac, or common parkland, rather than
on the public street. What is lacking is any formal connection between
the basic social units of Chatham Village—families—and the surrounding urban tissue. Architecturally, in cities and suburbs alike, the
main point of contact between individual and community is the front
door, which invites social interaction while imparting to the citizen
a hedge against society's potential for intrusiveness. Point that front
door away from the city streets, and you make a secessionist statement—a first step in the direction of gated communities.

In the post–World War II period, the principle of the communo-centric residential enclave found favor in urban, as well as suburban, settings. In the cities it took the form of high-rise megastructures organized around elevator shafts or introspective superblocks facing on a common courtyard or shopping center. London's Brunswick Square is a particularly depressing example. Brunswick Square is an exercise in 1970s brutalism in which residents turn their backs (complete with fire escapes) to the street, presumably so they can better contemplate the cell block within. Sadly, it is situated in one of the liveliest precincts of Bloomsbury, across the street from the Russell Square tube stop and close by the University of London. All the architect needed to do was connect the residential complex to the surrounding urban tissue. And yet, somehow, he or she managed to alienate the private residences in Brunswick Square from both the lively streets outside *and* the "commons" area within. It could not have been easy.

If residential communities like Chatham Village and Brunswick Square have failed to develop the civic potential of the front door, it is because they suppose that individual self-expression needs no further inducement in a capitalist society; they postulate, rather, that the public interest requires the *suppression* of individualism. As we have seen, in Chatham Village, as in the greenbelt towns, this animus extended to the principle of home ownership itself—or, to put it more precisely, to "the American faith, almost a religious belief, in what is called 'home ownership.'"[41] For Clarence Stein, the lessons of the private market in real estate—learned the hard way at Sunnyside and Radburn—were unambiguous: "The Sunnyside people—and a good many of those at Radburn—found that when they could no longer pay interest on their mortgage, owning your own home was merely another form of tenancy. They had the minority holding in their dwelling; voting power was held by the lending institutions. They discovered that they had actually been the janitor, caring for the mortgagee's property. They found that all their savings which had gone into the maintenance of their home, the years of payment to reduce the mortgage, the interest they had regularly paid, were cancelled when the depression deprived them of job, income, and savings."[42]

However formidable such arguments might have been in the 1930s, they lost their force in the climate of postwar prosperity, when the dream of home ownership, at least for the middle classes, revived.[43] But Chatham Village residents, because of the "master mortgage" concept, did not participate in the postwar real estate boom; thus, they had no equity in their homes, much less the prospect of capital gains. Naturally, this bred resentment, and led—as at Letchworth— to pitched battles over the "unearned increment." Eventually, Chatham Village shareholders chose their pocketbooks over their ideology. A brochure spells out the current rules for prospective residents: "Chatham Village is a cooperative corporation owned by the Village residents. The corporation holds one title for all the property, including land and buildings. Each resident owns a certificate of member-

FIGURE 33
A Radburn principle turns ugly: Brunswick Square, London, where private residences turn their backsides to the street. This kind of architecture inadvertently marks out "turf" for people who are to be segregated from the rest of the city.

ship in the corporation, and the value of the certificate reflects the market value of the member's house. Like a conventional home, a certificate for a larger house or a house that has been improved, or is in an especially desirable location is worth more in the marketplace. It is actually these certificates that are bought and sold when a house changes hands."[44] It's not home ownership, exactly, but it allows for profit. In the sanitized rendition of the corporation it sounds unremarkable enough, but Clarence Stein would have regarded this concession to the real estate market as a betrayal of everything Chatham Village stood for—as the privatization of a public utility.

And so, once again, utopia succumbs to the lure of market forces and bourgeois sensibilities, which turn out to be astonishingly re-silient, and a source of constant frustration for master planners every-where. Over and over, democratic planners find that they must make the necessary accommodations, here finding ways to reconcile the profit motive with a culture of communism, there providing outlets for sentimentality in an officially rational city.

Town planning in Holland is an interesting case of the latter. The Dutch have a fundamental problem, which is that they live in a low-lying country that is constantly at risk of inundation by the sea. Thus, for a thousand years, they have fought back by reclaiming land, an enterprise that has taught them a thing or two about hydraulic engi-neering (and the efficiency of windmills).[45] In the nineteenth cen-tury, Dutch confidence in their land reclamation skills had reached the point that they began to think seriously about draining the Zuider Zee. This project was taken up in the early twentieth century by an engineer and politician named Cornelius Lely. Implementation of Lely's bold plan began in the 1920s, when a barrier dam was con-structed to cut the Zuider Zee off from the North Sea. The waters of the river IJssel gradually turned the sea into a freshwater lake, now called the IJsselmeer. That having been accomplished, the Dutch gov-ernment undertook the systematic reclamation of huge parcels of land, called polders.

After World War II, the Dutch got serious about draining the polders and building new towns as part of an ambitious plan to con-trol urban growth.[46] In the beginning, these towns, particularly Lely-stad (complete with agora), were, like their counterparts in Scandi-navia, thoroughly modernist ventures with a dash of Riverside and Radburn: "A salient feature of Almere-Haven," the new town de-picted in figure 34, "is the traffic separation system. Cyclists and pe-destrians can reach all parts of the town via their own path network. These paths pass either over or under the busy highways to which the only direct communication is via the bus stops and public transport vehicles circulate in their own lanes."[47] Almere-Haven incorporates the standard equipment of the Dutch town, including bicycles, buses, clock towers, and ersatz canals and canal houses with allusions to familiar motifs, including hoist beams and stepped gables, all done on the customary small scale.[48] The revival of the vernacular in the new towns of the polders reflected a rediscovery, during the 1970s and 1980s, of the charms of "the eighteenth-century picturesque, the love of disorder, the cultivation of the individual, distaste for the rational, passion for variety, pleasure in idiosyncracy, and suspicion of the generalized."[49]

More recently, however, Almere's planners have determined that despite a population of 120,000 (about halfway to the goal), the town is not "urban" enough, and so Rem Koolhaas, winner of the 2000 Pritzker Prize, has been brought in to do a makeover. Koolhaas, a modernist who loves crowds, is well known as the designer of Euralille, the Chunnel- and TGV-linked commercial complex vying to become the Flemish equivalent of Tyson's Corner. According to Koolhaas, Euralille is an expression of "a new wave of modernization which has to coexist with the historical décor, but which has nothing to do with it."[50] Peter Newman has written that Koolhaas's development "turns away from the old city to the flows of trains and financial and commercial information. . . . The commercial center, like all such developments, is clean, secure, and policed. Out of sight are the large housing estates typical of French city planning, with

FIGURE 34
Nostalgia as a design element in the Dutch new town. Here at Almere-Haven, government planners in the 1970s and 1980s recognized the legitimacy of the vernacular. What impact will Rem Koolhaas have on this scene?

FIGURE 35
Streetscape, the cheese market town of Edam. A large part of the charm of traditional Dutch architecture derives from its small scale, evident here.

high levels of unemployment and giving rise to periodic riots."[51]
There is even an Avenue le Corbusier at Euralille. One would think
that the modernist revival would have inspired questions about why
public authorities at such with-it places as Euralille and the Koolhaas-
enhanced Almere are trying to keep up with the vicissitudes of fashion, when that is what a market economy does best.

Which brings us to the New Urbanism, a market-oriented movement that has sometimes been associated with "smart growth," but
also with the motto "form follows finance."[52] The New Urbanism is
based on the idea that there is something profoundly wrong with
"the places where we live and work and go about our daily business,"
and on the conviction that Americans have lately come to realize
their unhappiness and to express it "in phrases like 'no sense of place'
and 'the loss of community.' We drive up and down the gruesome,
tragic suburban boulevards of commerce, and we're overwhelmed at
the fantastic, awesome, stupefying ugliness of absolutely everything
in sight—the fry pits, the big-box stores, the office units, the lube
joints, the carpet warehouses, the parking lagoons, the jive plastic
townhouse clusters, the uproar of signs, the highway itself clogged
with cars—as though the whole thing had been designed by some
diabolical force bent on making human beings miserable."[53]

According to one version of this critique of suburbia, the diabolical force behind sprawl is what Lewis Mumford liked to call the private motorcar. According to another version, it is government that is
cast in the role of Grendel; goaded on by General Motors and Big
Oil, government is cast as the financier of Sprawl—through large-
scale highway construction, the dismantling of mass transit, home
loan programs, tax rates that encouraged big mortgages and discouraged personal savings, low gasoline taxes, and local control of public
schools. However they may differ among themselves, the New Urban-
ists are united in posing a straightforward alternative, one that "is simple and timely: neighborhoods of housing, parks, and schools placed
within walking distance of shops, civic services, jobs, and transit—a
modern version of the traditional town."[54] In the 1990s, this con-
sciousness-raising enterprise spawned a national conversation on suburban growth. Benjamin Forgey has written that the New Urbanism
may be "the closest thing to a consequential urban reform movement
the United States has seen in at least three decades."[55]

The New Urbanist prototype is a community in the Florida pan-
handle called Seaside; it is the work of celebrated planners Andres

Duany and Elizabeth Plater-Zyberk and of a visionary developer, Robert Davis. Seaside would never be mistaken for a standard American subdivision:

Once travelers enter the eighty acres of Seaside, they discover a network of narrow streets surfaced with reddish concrete pavers—the contemporary, pale-looking equivalent of the red brick streets that rumble beneath motorists' tires in many old communities. Most of Seaside's streets are paved just eighteen feet wide, limiting the room for movement. Restricting passage further, vehicles park on the streets or the shoulders. Motorists have little choice but to slow down. Individuals on foot and on fat-tired bicycles give every impression of feeling on equal terms with cars, vans, and pickups.

The streets have been designed with affectionate detail. Enclosing their sides are white picket fences in dozens of different designs. Property owners individually select or invent the style of their own fence, which must differ from all others on their block. About sixteen feet behind the fences stand front porches. The distance was set so that people sitting on the porches can hold conversations with those going past without having to raise their voices.

By Seaside regulation, the porch typically extends along at least half of the house's façade, and it must be no less than eight feet deep—big enough so that people can use it comfortably. The houses are clad in clapboard, shingles, or board-and-batten siding—no vinyl, no aluminum. Their windows are mostly tall and narrow, in keeping with the old-fashioned character of picket fences and spacious wooden porches. Festive colors such as pink, yellow, and aqua predominate.[56]

If all of this seems somewhat authoritarian, it is important to understand that DPZ Associates did not introduce strict controls into a sector of the economy that had been an anarchist's paradise. On the contrary, they simply exchanged some regulations (building codes, mainly) for others (namely, zoning ordinances). When they started out, Duany and Plater-Zyberk were astonished to discover that traditional town design—that is, towns featuring a mixture of social classes residing in a fairly compact area adorned with small parks, sidewalks, front porches, back alleys, and other public spaces, as well as commercial and industrial activities—had been rendered *illegal* almost everywhere in the country. In short, whatever one might think of them, America's suburbs were *planned* to look and work the way they do. And so, as James Howard Kunstler explains, DPZ learned that there were times when they had to resort to sleight of hand: "When Mr. Duany's firm designed a development in Miami with narrow streets and old-fashioned service alleys, his client was denied a permit. They submitted a new set of blueprints on which the streets were relabeled 'parking lots' and the alleys were relabeled 'jogging paths'—and then the project won approval."[57]

It must be emphasized that Seaside is more than a distinctive aes-

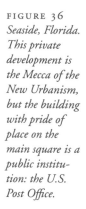

FIGURE 36
Seaside, Florida. This private development is the Mecca of the New Urbanism, but the building with pride of place on the main square is a public institution: the U.S. Post Office.

thetic. Implicit is the idea that the city is more than the sum of its parts, and the common good more than the residue left behind by the clash of private interests. Consider, for example, Seaside's handling of the beach as a public amenity, rather than as a resource to be appropriated by individual families; the result is that Seaside has resisted the syndrome in which property values plummet as one moves inland from the shoreline.[58] Appropriately, most structures on the beach side of the main road serve some public function, with the "beach pavilions" exploiting the Janus-faced quality of classical temples—that is, they gracefully preside over the beach, while bowing politely toward the town. Some lots in town are perhaps more desirable than others, but all homeowners (and renters) are within easy walking distance of the beach and the main commercial area. Whimsical Victorian towers provide Gulf views while contributing an element of the picturesque—or kitsch, depending on one's taste. Either way, it is surely significant that *The Truman Show,* which required a townscape that could double as a benevolent prison, was filmed in Seaside.

Other New Urbanist developments may have less rhetorical power than Seaside, but are interesting in their own ways. At Kentlands, a development in the Maryland suburbs of Washington, D.C., Duany and Plater-Zyberk have made particularly good use of the "granny flat," an outbuilding or over-the-garage unit that adds architectural complexity and density to the neighborhood while importantly altering the demographics of the community. Kunstler explains that granny flats and other "accessory apartments"—zoning violations in most jurisdictions—accommodate singles and lower-income residents who would otherwise be excluded: "Without provision for apartments, an unmarried sixth-grade schoolteacher could not afford to live near the children she taught. Nor could the housecleaner and the gardener—they had to commute for half an hour from some distant low-income ghetto."[59] In an unanticipated variation on the theme, granny flats in Kentlands have sometimes been initially inhabited by their owners, who rent out the adjacent big house until they are financially able to occupy it themselves. Recent development at Kentlands features "live-work units," where apartments are piggybacked on ground-floor stores.

Other features of the New Urbanism may be discerned most clearly at several developments in the United Kingdom. Anticipating a need "to build 4.4 million new homes by 2016, a 20 percent increase in the existing stock," the British have estimated that "that would consume 650 square miles of farm land if the 1980s pattern of suburban development continues."[60] The challenge is to find a less destructive model of growth. Crickhowell, a complex of medieval-looking structures in rural Wales, was designed with certain communal features but also is fully "wired" to encourage telecommuting; its developer, Acorn Tele-villages, has won the Royal Town Planning Institute's award for innovative and sustainable housing development. Poundbury, located just outside Dorchester in southwest England, is the work of the London-based architect Leon Krier, who also has been active at Seaside.[61] Architectural codes at Poundbury require work in the vernacular, "which in the case of Dorset means Purbeck marble and Portland stone and a rich local vocabulary of brick, chalk, roof slate and stucco called 'render.' There can be no decorative tricks like half-timbering or gaudy ornamentation. The houses may look antique from the out-side, but they have double-glazed windows, high-efficiency condens-ing boilers, extra insulation and computer-controlled energy-man-agement systems to reduce fuel consumption."[62]

Warren Hoge points out that all services at Poundbury—"tele-phone, electricity, gas and drainage—are buried in channels behind the housing; one large satellite dish hidden behind a high masonry wall serves the community."[63] It has been suggested that Poundbury

marries traditional design and materials with modern construction and planning techniques to produce an Olde English village that even-tually will be full of characterful stone houses, a pub, tower, inn, small stores, offices and some light industry. . . . Over the next 20 years, Poundbury is planned to have 2,000–3,000 homes spread over 400 acres and incorporate offices, workshops, a community center, market square and children's playground. The first houses are in stone and brick with slate or tile roofs. Unlike the cookie-cutter sameness of most modern subdivisions, each house is different, and they are clustered in groups of five or six. That type of construction costs 10 percent more than ordi-nary housing, builders say.[64]

In keeping with the ethos of the New Urbanism, houses "stand flush with the street so that when you step from your front door, you're already in town."[65] The point is to try to replicate the kind of intri-cate urban space that Jane Jacobs and Camillo Sitte so admired.[66]

It is instructive to consider the several ways in which Poundbury differs from Seaside and other New Urbanist ventures in the United States. For one thing, Poundbury is directly adjacent to the old city of Dorchester, and so it is essentially a town extension, meaning that the opportunity exists of grafting the new community onto living urban tissue. In the United States, we generally do not have that op-tion, and in any case residents are seeking autonomy, rather than fu-sion with existing communities. Moreover, Poundbury is being devel-oped on land owned by the Duchy of Cornwall, which is to say by His Royal Highness the Prince of Wales. In a sense, then, Poundbury is a vestige of noblesse oblige; in addition, 20 percent of the houses are to be rented to low-income people through the charitable Guin-ness Trust. In the United States, of course, there is no comparable tra-dition, and no discernible taste for integrating low-income families into middle-class communities.

Perhaps the most interesting thing about the New Urbanism—and this applies *mutatis mutandis* to either Seaside or Poundbury—is how utterly conventional it is, and how limited are its aspirations: the point is to enable people to get a newspaper or a loaf of bread, and possibly to commute to work or school, without jumping in their cars. Absent from the New Urbanism are the novel financing schemes of Letchworth and Chatham Village. Banished is the hostility to home ownership that marked the work of the Resettlement Administration. New Urbanist developments are convention-ally financed; they do not involve "cata-clysmic money," enforced transfer payments, or subsidies of any kind. In fact, the New Urbanism has often been criticized for being too market-oriented. More to the point, New Urbanist ventures have been, as Vincent Scully has put it, "largely luxury affairs."[67] That may not apply to Poundbury, but it is certainly evident in Seaside, where nearly all recent construction has been on a grand scale and where even modest houses are breath-takingly expensive. Small wonder that critics such as Forgey complain that the New Urbanism "offers scant help to the neediest levels of our society."[68]

What is it, then, that's so smart about "smart growth" (other than the way it clev-erly substitutes the word *smart* for the word *dense*)? That question might be best answered with reference to Port-land, Oregon, the city with the singular distinction of having turned a highway—the bastard child of Robert Moses, as a matter of fact—into a park, and the Mecca of the "sustainable cities" movement. Preservationists in Portland have led the campaign to create a metro-politan-wide government and a regional planning authority that has established an urban growth boundary (UGB), enforced a cap on downtown parking spaces, employed zoning as a tool to encourage socioeconomic diversity, and promoted the use of light rail as an alter-native to auto dependency. This last feature reflects the influence on the West Coast of the planner Peter Calthorpe, who stresses nodal development—"pedestrian pockets"—around light rail stations,[69] a scheme appropriate for retrofitting older suburbs. Philip Langdon elaborates:

FIGURE 37
A representative granny flat at another of the Duany and Plater-Zyberk develop-ments, Kentlands, in Gaithersburg, Maryland. Because these units are success-fully woven into the fabric of the town, there is no underscoring of architectural, or socioeconomic, inferiority.

The Portland area adopted an urban growth boundary in 1980. Modified since then, it now encompasses 362 square miles. Inside the boundary is a large supply of land available for building. Outside the boundary, governments discourage building by zoning agricultural areas for farm use only, by insisting on lot sizes that preclude much residential development, and by instituting policies such as refusing road improvements and sewer service. To help conserve land and generate affordable housing throughout the region, all Portland area municipalities have been required to enact plans allowing half their new housing to be apartments, townhouses, or other multifamily construction. The growth boundary and other regulations have significantly reduced suburban sprawl. The average size of a single-family lot has dropped from 13,200 to 8,700 square feet. By raising residential density the region has obtained the capacity to build as many as 310,000 houses and apartments inside its growth boundary—nearly double the number that could have been accommodated under previous planning and zoning.[70]

FIGURE 38
Worker's cottage, Seaside. In the spring of 2000, this 1-bedroom, 1.5-bath house, called "Our Place by the Sea," was listed for sale at $550,000.

But Portland is culturally distinctive and untypical of American cities. It is predominantly white and middle class, and it has a progressive political culture, which may do more to explain Portland's appeal than the "smart growth" measures themselves. Duany, for instance, shrewdly points out that there is another major American city that can boast of metro government, light rail, and an urban growth boundary, but that city—Miami—has never been credited with being smart about growth. In any case, the jury is still out on the Portland experiment. For one thing, the growth girdle has been let out whenever it has proven to be politically expedient. And given the law of supply and demand, it is reasonable to expect that Portland's UGB will inevitably put the squeeze on low-income residents of the city center. Even such Portland partisans as Richard Moe and Carter Wilkie, in their account of the revitalization of the neighborhood called Albina, concede the possibility that "longtime low-income residents of the neighborhood could be priced out of their community by Portland's escalating housing market."[71] They also recognize the possibility of sprawl-like development marring areas within the UGB, as well as the dangers of "leapfrog" development in remote areas that have heretofore been far outside Portland's socioeconomic gravitational pull.

There are other reasons to be wary of "smart growth." There is, for one thing, the remarkable capacity of a capitalistic economy to produce cheap knockoffs of designer products. Think of the way that Le Corbusier's Radiant City vision degenerated into the banality of Erieview, Riverside into Levittown, Fallingwater into the lowest-common-denominator '60s "rambler," and Wright's Usonian house into the "mobile home." Think of the phony canals of Almere-Haven, or, closer to home, of plastic window shutters and pop-off mullion grids. Curiously, Lewis Mumford seems to have anticipated such developments in his "law of cultural seepage,"[72] whereby innovations introduced by the elite gradually insinuate themselves into popular culture but are degraded in the process. If this law continues to have currency, it would seem to guarantee the proliferation of the accoutrements of, as opposed to the essence of, the New Urbanism—the gingerbread of Seaside, in other words, without any of Duany's communitarianism. Disney's investment in Celebration, Florida, may be regarded as a sure sign that this process is well along; as Moe and Wilkie report, Disney's "marketing research showed that more compact new communities built around traditional town centers could indeed appeal to potential home buyers."[73] In short, the triumph of the New Urbanism could result in a quintessential Peggy Lee moment ("Is that all there is?").

Also, the rhetoric of the New Urbanism is sure to be cynically appropriated by the growth industry and government. That is what is happening in Alexandria, Virginia, a close-in suburb of Washington experiencing a traumatic burst of infill development, fueled in part by the closing of a military installation and the recycling of old railroad yards. New residents were attracted in the 1990s to a site adjacent to Old Town and handy to the King Street Metro station by promises of a mixed-use, traditional town center. Suddenly it was announced that the city had lured to that site (from Crystal City, itself a good-enough-for-government-work Radiant City knockoff) the U.S. Patents and Trademarks Office (PTO), which was proposing construction of a building designed for 7,100 employees, two-thirds of whom drive to work. As planned, the complex is a classic megalith—according to the *Washington Post,* the fourth largest government building in the United States (after the Pentagon, the Ronald Reagan Building, and the Jacob Javits Center in Manhattan). Owing to security considerations—think Oklahoma City—the complex will be sited on a superblock and will have no underground parking; instead, there will be three aboveground parking garages designed to accommodate thirty-eight hundred cars. A careful reader of Jane Jacobs might observe that if government offices were woven into the fabric of the living city, on a conventional street grid and in standard row houses within a mixed-use district, they would be not only less inviting to potential terrorists, but far less deserving as targets. But the PTO will be informed by a different idea of good design. Street-level stores and restaurants will actually be outlawed, and the whole district will be deliberately cut off from, rather than served by, the grid of city streets. It promises to be precisely the type of big government box that deserves to be in a distant suburb surrounded by a parking lagoon. Inevitably, it is being touted by its advocates as enlightened "infill," or "smart growth," when what it really seems to be is a new source of much-needed revenue for a city with tax rates that are among the highest in Virginia.

What, in the end, are we to make of sprawl and its alternatives? In the first place, as we have seen, it would be wrong to think of sprawl as the product of "unregulated private effort" in residential and commercial construction. On the contrary, construction is one of the most heavily regulated industries in the United States; if developers seem to be deeply invested in local politics, and if politicians seem to be part of the growth industry, it is for the same reason that Mark Hanna and Tom Johnson were involved in municipal politics in turn-of-the-twentieth-century Cleveland. Far from being an expression of anarchy, suburbia was deliberately planned to look and to work the way it does.

In the second place, sprawl has its attractions. If nothing else, it has been a profoundly democratic phenomenon. After the end of World War II, housing was in short supply, the public acknowledged a substantial debt to returning GIs, the construction industry was ready to accommodate their needs on a large scale, and government was happy to oblige by providing whatever incentives it could, which turned out to be substantial. Sometimes the resulting "chaos" of American suburbia is characterized as the selling out of an incipient proletariat. From another perspective, though, it can be argued that the living conditions of millions of American families—who under-

stood themselves to be trading in the streetcar or bicycle for the automobile, the tenement for the suburban ranch, the icebox for the Frig-
idaire, a wage for a salary—were permanently upgraded by sprawl.
Think again of *It's a Wonderful Life* and the suburban development
in Bedford Falls that ultimately convinces George Bailey that his life
has been worthwhile. In trying to account for the dynamics of sprawl,
it is not necessary to factor anything mysterious (e.g., "false consciousness") or evil (e.g., white racism) into the equation. The high
crime rates, inferior schools, and escalating tax rates of the central
cities explain enough. Sprawl has its natural constituents, in short,
and there is no doubt in my mind that its momentum will be sustained well into the twenty-first century even if all the government
subsidies and tax incentives supporting it magically disappear.[74] As
Duany has argued, sprawl may represent a disassembling of the city,
but it is not without a certain elegance, judged on its own terms.[75]

Sprawl continues to be an agent of upward mobility and social
integration. Forget the supposed lily-white conformity of Pleasantville. Consider that between 1990 and 1998 the number of African
Americans in the suburbs increased by 41 percent, Hispanics by 58
percent, and Asians by 76 percent, compared with a 17 percent increase for non-Hispanic whites.[76] *Preservation* magazine, observing
that "America's suburban dream has global appeal" and that today's
immigrants are "well briefed on the suburban dream before they get
here," documents the transformation: "Down-at-heel suburban strip
malls are once again occupied, offering the foods, goods, and services
demanded by this complex new ethnic mix. Cookie-cutter postwar
residential communities are being invigorated by the introduction of
mosques or Buddhist temples; by whole neighborhoods of Vietnam-
ese Catholics, enterprising Koreans, or Asian Indians; or by refugees
from the wars of the tail end of the century: Kurds, Somalis, Bosni-
ans."[77] In short, today's African Americans and immigrants—from
Mexico, Central America, the Caribbean, and the far corners of Asia
and Africa—are jostling for the privilege of being bourgeoisified, not
for the putative right to experience a touchy-feely multicultural nir-
vana. The indifference of these newly middle-classified Americans
to the New Urbanism, inner-city gentrification, and downtown funfairs is entirely justified. Sprawl serves their interest far more than the
growth girdles and other market restraints of "smart growth," and
more even than the urbane visions of enlightened planners such as
Duany and Calthorpe.

There is, finally, something eerily familiar about the rhetoric being employed in the war against suburban growth. The fact is that "sprawl"—like its predecessor, "blight"—is, in the end, an epithet, not an analytical term. As for the ballyhooed "smart growth," it is not at all clear what's so smart about it, and one wonders who would be its managers, and why anyone should expect them to be any smarter than their predecessors who ripped up the trolley tracks that we would like to have back, drove wooden stakes (read: interstate highways) through the hearts of our cities, boasted that they had ironed the bugs out of public housing, and were the very architects of sprawl. One wonders, too, how smart it is to assume that if we can avoid being raped we will remain virgins forever. Real-world options are seldom binary. Citizens of northern Virginia discovered this truth when they fought Jack Kent Cooke's mid-1990s campaign to build a stadium for his Redskins in the Potomac Yards corridor near Ronald Reagan National Airport. Eventually the good guys won, but it turned out that their victory over Cooke cleared the way for construction of a "big box" retail strip that rounded up the usual suspects—Target, Old Navy, Staples, Barnes & Noble, the Sports Authority, et al. And so it goes.

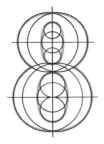

WHEN
GOVERNMENT
DARES TO
DREAM

FRANCE, THROUGH A FEW BASIC
principles of urban design, taught the modern world everything it knows about state
sovereignty. The echoes from Paris and Versailles still reverberate—albeit faintly, in some
cases—at sites as disparate and widely dispersed as Quebec City, Detroit, Port-au-
Prince, and Washington, D.C., parvenus all.
But the world also learned from France the
limits of royal absolutism. Tocqueville, for example, was astounded by the uselessness of
royal edicts in the war against urban expansion: "Six times during his reign Louis XIV
tried to check the growth of Paris, yet all-
powerful as he proved himself in many other
fields, he failed in this."[1]

Given this experience, the French government has sometimes been willing to settle for
managing urban growth, rather than outlawing it. This is one reason that Peter Hall has
referred to the French capital as "the city of
perpetual public works."[2] Certainly, Hall's
characterization aptly describes the city as it
was administered by Baron Georges-Eugène
Haussmann, prefect under Napoleon III and
the man largely responsible for Paris as most
of us know it. Haussmann constructed grand
boulevards and annexed suburbs. He completed projects begun by his predecessors,
including "the continuation of the Rue de
Rivoli, the completion of the Louvre, a new

north-south axis, the Halles Centrales." He built aqueducts that more than doubled the city's water supply, and he doubled the length of the water mains. He installed sanitary sewers to supplement a system in which fifty teams of men and horses removed sewage at night. He quadrupled the length of the city's stormwater sewers and presciently made provision within them "for water mains, and later, for electricity, telegraph, and telephone wires, and for pneumatic tubes carrying letters." He built parks and nearly doubled the number of trees in the city, from fifty thousand to ninety-five thousand. Most notably, "there was the transformation of the two great Bois."[3] Lewis Mumford gives Haussmann full credit for the Bois de Boulogne and the Bois de Vincennes, invariably described as the "two great lungs" of the city.[4]

Lungs or no lungs, Haussmann's legacy remains controversial. It has often been argued that his motives were essentially counterrevolutionary—that by "cutting great swaths, too broad to be blocked by barricades, through working-class districts," he effectively broke up the proletariat "into *quartiers* geographically isolated from one another."[5] Haussmann denied that these were his intentions, and scholars such as Donald Olsen have mounted a persuasive case in his defense. Sigfried Giedion heaped extravagant praise on Haussmann, recognizing him as the prototype of the modernist city planner for having dared "to change the entire aspect of a great city, a city which had been revered for hundreds of years as the center of the civilized world. To build a new Paris—attacking all aspects of the problem simultaneously—was an operation still unequaled in scale. The indomitable courage of the Préfet de la Seine has also remained unequaled. Haussmann allowed no group to block his schemes: in his transformation of Paris he cut directly into the body of the city."[6]

In France, the tradition of state planning lives on. During the last third of the twentieth century, most Americans were unaware that a plan of Haussmannesque proportions was being implemented by the central government of France, which, since World War II, "has followed a model of indicative planning which is the Haussmann model writ large, and which relies on huge public works—motorways, the Parisian RER system, the TGV—as a trigger and a guide to the investment decisions of the private sector. This system, originating in the immediate post-war years and associated with the name of Jean Monnet, reached its high point in the Gaullist era of the 1960s; and in many ways, Gaullism was a reincarnation of the Second Empire:

an all-powerful president, with a faithful and supremely confident army of professional functionaries."[7] The head of President de Gaulle's army of functionaries was Paul Delouvrier, who in only seven years accomplished "for the suburbs of Paris what Haussmann had done over one hundred years earlier for the city; and the polycentric structure of the region today—its five new towns, its three circumferential motorways, its five RER lines—is the lineal successor to Haussmann's works."[8]

The "deconcentration" of state power[9] was all the rage in the late 1960s, and French technocrats thought that the unrestrained growth of the Paris region—projected to increase the total population from eight to twenty million people by the end of the twentieth century—would necessarily occur at the expense of the rest of the country. French officials also thought such rapid growth would, if unregulated, result in the kind of physical and aesthetic chaos that breeds human alienation, what the French call *urbanisme sauvage*. And so a plan was devised to manage growth along two corridors, both running roughly east to west, about thirty kilometers north and south of the historic center of Paris.[10] Adopted in 1965, the point of the Paris Regional Plan, or Schéma-Directeur, was to manage the growth of the Paris region.

Using state power to acquire land, suppress real estate speculation, and provide incentives for private investment, the plan adopted for the Paris region had a number of interesting features. One was historic preservation. It was thought that proper development of the suburbs—the *banlieus*—would concentrate growth on the outskirts, meaning that the historic heart of the city could be preserved as a cultural center and tourist attraction. A second motive had to do with relating the Isle-de-France more successfully to the rest of the country. This was to be achieved by means of an extensive regional rail network—the RER—that would fill the gap between the national, high-speed railroads on the one hand and the local Paris Métro on the other. Finally, there were to be strategically situated "new towns" that would in effect be growth nodes conceived not as mere satellites of Paris, but as viable communities in their own right. The five development hubs were Cergy-Pontoise, Melun-Senart, St. Quentín-des-Yvelínes, Marne la Vallée, and Evry New Town. The last of these, situated about twenty-five miles south and east of Paris, was arguably the most original and ambitious.

At the outset, Evry New Town was divided into three sectors

according to land use. The northernmost part of the parcel was essentially suburban and tied to Paris both economically and culturally. The southernmost part was a provincial town called Corbeil-Essonnes, which had its own history quite distinct from Paris but which had fallen on hard times economically. Between the two was an agricultural belt on a wide plateau. At the time the Schéma-Directeur was adopted, there were about 150,000 people already living within this area. The plan called for growth to about 235,000 by 1975 and to 500,000 by the year 2000. It was thought that this type of measured growth, imposed throughout the whole region by the master plan, would hold the population of greater Paris to under fourteen million by the end of the century, it being taken for granted that inhibiting the growth of Paris would fuel growth in other parts of the country.

The owners of agricultural land on the site chosen for Evry New Town had hoped to negotiate the sale of their land at highly inflated prices. The French parliament, however, passed measures that allowed the state to intervene and acquire the land at a low price. Then a regional planning authority, called the Établissement Public d'Aménagement, or EPA, was created to devise a master plan and prepare the land for development. It must be emphasized that Evry New Town was conceived as a city, not as a suburb. The point was to appeal to those of the French who wished "to rediscover urban life and to escape from the boredom of 'suburb dormitories.'"[11] Residential developments at Evry (see figs. 39 and 40) demonstrate how dramatically the Paris Regional Plan departs from the romanticism of the Anglo-American "new towns" movement.

One of the economies of planned communities is that infrastructure can be installed from the outset, with extra room built in to accommodate growth. Care was taken to weave Evry New Town into the greater Paris transportation system. Since rail lines already ran down the Seine valley, easy access to Paris was assured. A cavernous rail station was installed early on, when it seemed all out of proportion with the embryonic new town it was intended to serve. Evry was connected to two important national highways running nearby, as well as to a regional bus system that uses seventeen kilometers of dedicated bus lanes. A shopping center was planned that would bring people from all over the region to the center of the New Town; to ensure its success, state subsidies lured the major department stores and banks. A hospital, one of the first amenities in Evry, had 450 beds

FIGURE 39
Evry I, the Pyramids, an award-winning housing development in Evry New Town, France. Construction began in 1973; this photograph was taken in 1980. The bridge is a dedicated bus route. Note pedestrian overpass, far right.

FIGURE 40
Tenement chic, 1980: Evry New Town would never be mistaken for Letchworth.

in place by 1977. An athletic park was designed to function as a regional sports complex. A suburban park, including forests and game preserves for leisure and weekend activities, was part of the basic package. The national government anointed Evry New Town as the capital of Essonnes, and so a parcel was set aside for the buildings of the prefecture. The Roman Catholic Church chose Evry, perhaps in part as a response to the presence of two synagogues and a mosque, as the site of a new cathedral. A branch of the University of Paris was to be located in the urban center of Evry New Town, part of which the city planners christened the agora (its planners no doubt had visited Lelystad).

This explicit reference to the center of civic life in the ancient Greek polis expressed the hope of the planners that Evry would develop a vital civic heart. According to James M. Rubenstein, "The most innovative concept in the design of the new towns is the creation of important town centers. The French say they are trying to build 'animated' town centers, a concept that corresponds to the French ideal of urban life. The French do not admire the bucolic green image of the British garden city. Their idea of a true city involves a lot of bustle and excitement in a man-made environment. Animated centers are those where a lot of activity takes place. Many people are on the streets performing a variety of roles. All of the major functions in life would be concentrated in the town center including apartments, jobs, and leisure facilities."[12] This should be understood in quite a literal way. As André Darmagnac, one of the planners of Evry

FIGURE 41

Where have all the animators gone? Public space at Evry New Town, 1983. According to official literature of the time, the agora is the place for "spontaneous and self-controlled initiatives" that provide citizens "many opportunities to share social experiences and leadership."

New Town, has explained, in the early 1970s teams of "animators" were hired by all the new towns.[13] Their activities were "very diverse, ranging from all kinds of entertainment, to initiations in the principal art forms, to activities for furnishing and decorating homes, and the loan of audio-visual equipment. The goal of such action is not to provide activities, but to create a solid social tissue."[14]

Not surprisingly, the provision of a lively town center was considered too important to be left to the private sector, and so, "in contrast to the rest of the new town, the town center is not privately owned; the EPA retains ownership of the land and leases it to private developers. This arrangement permits the EPA to control the character of the town center—which largely determines the overall visual image of the new town—and to secure much of the profit that accompanies the conversion of rural land for intensive urban use."[15]

From an early-twenty-first-century perspective, there are several things to be said about Evry New Town. The first is to observe that there are plenty of slips 'twixt cup and lip. For example, as we have seen, Evry was projected to have a population of 500,000 by the turn of the century; as it turns out, it has closer to 230,000, meaning presumably that there is a great deal of sprawl and *urbanisme sauvage* that Evry has not been able to contain.

Second, there are some serious design problems. As Rubenstein has noted, the town centers of the French new towns "require very complex designs, such as multilevel megastructures. Buildings are joined by pedestrian decks and underground garages. Individual buildings house more than one function. For example, the so-called 'agora' at Evry contains the shopping center and community recreational center within the same building."[16] But multifunctional, multilayered, indoor-outdoor space often is very confusing, and that certainly is the case at Evry. The overall plan of the new town may be impressive from the air, but on the ground there is no rhyme or reason to it. The absence of a street grid contributes to a sense of formlessness, as there are no intersections, and the segregated pathways and bus lanes add to the visual din. Too often, it seems as if there is no there there—or if there is, that you can't get there from here. And multifunctionality sometimes generates questions about whether one has actually reached one's destination. (Is this empty plaza the agora? In the absence of conspicuous "animation," how can one be sure?) To aid pedestrians in distress, Evry has had a sophisticated signage system, but that is less helpful, especially in a multilayered facility, than an intelligible layout (if you find yourself on the wrong level, how do you go about finding the stairs?). The reader who has visited the Barbican in London will recall that this multilayered, multifunctional space has had to install permanent yellow lines on the pavement—the urban equivalent of Arthur Murray's dancing feet—to reinforce signage that attempts to shepherd pedestrians through a dispiriting, exhausting city-within-a-city.

At Evry, the agora itself is infinitely disappointing. On the three occasions that I have visited Evry over the past twenty years, there has never been any sign of life, civic or otherwise, in that place. Or, to put it another way, there is no more life at the heart of Evry New Town than there is outside any shopping mall, recreation center, or suburban commuter rail station. The original planners claimed that what was special about Evry was to be found in its public life, especially at the agora. But in my last visit to the agora, in 1998, I found that the signage, and even the pavement, is badly in need of repair, and evidence of neglect and vandalism is rampant.

In truth, the planners' original vision of Evry New Town contained a great deal that was affecting, and even the architectural whims were not without an element of charm. In one neighborhood, called Le Dragon, the pedestrian was led through a passage designed to resemble a dragon's mouth. But in the condition in which I found this precinct in 1998, with Le Dragon littered with shopping carts—fugitives from the *hypermarche*—the designers' playful conceit seemed a lot less endearing.[17] The housing development known as the Pyramids continues to be one of the visual treats of Evry New Town. While this modular-looking precinct appears to be still flourishing, there is now a McDonald's directly across the street. Granting that there is an argument for having a McDonald's next door, isn't it the case that the private sector is perfectly capable—all *too* capable, most people would say—of providing that particular amenity? It forces one to ask what the EPA has achieved in Evry New Town that private enterprise could not have done on its own.

I am prepared to be persuaded that Evry New Town has succeeded in providing affordable housing for the working class; and that, as we saw in chapter 7, is no mean feat. Even if that is so, Evry New Town stands as yet another cautionary tale about the limits of planning. As Lloyd Rodwin has argued, urban planners are quick to "point an accusing finger at the market mechanism and the need to correct its inadequacies or to substitute new mechanisms" for market forces.

"What is often ignored," however, "are the limited capabilities of urban planners. In the past, it has been all too easy for them to assume that they could correct the inadequacies of the market or that they could create new mechanisms that would function more adequately. It is this assumption that makes the period when urban planners get significant status and power such a risky one for the profession. For then city planners must show that they can make matters better, or at least not worse; which is precisely what they all too often may not

FIGURE 42
Evidence of vandalism on the pedestrian deck adjacent to the agora and Evry-Courcouronnes railroad station, 1998.

be able to ensure, and for all sorts of reasons, some good, some bad. The situation today is critical because the failings are becoming embarrassingly obvious."[18]

The limits of state planning are also on display in Washington, D.C., one of America's major links—through Major Pierre Charles L'Enfant primarily, but also through Olmsted, Daniel Burnham, and more recently Senator Daniel Patrick Moynihan—to European city planning in the grand style. One need only consult a map of downtown Washington to learn how a capital city should look, that is, how it should radiate authority by commanding the attention, and the resources, of a far-flung nation. And one need only walk across the Mall to see the way the baroque mind managed "to organize space, make it continuous, reduce it to measure and order, and to extend the limits of magnitude, embracing the extremely distant and the extremely minute; finally, to associate space with motion and time."[19]

Baroque regimentation (take a peek back at fig. 1) represented a radical departure from medieval aesthetics (see fig. 43). In marked contrast to the medieval town, "which one must slowly walk through to appreciate its never ending transformations of mass and silhouette, its intricate and surprising details, one can take in a baroque town almost at a glance. Even what one does not see one can easily extrapolate in one's imagination, once the guiding lines are established."[20] Thus, anyone who has seen the monuments of Washington, D.C., has some sense of what power in general, and absolute power in particular, is all about. Anyone who has driven around Dupont Circle has little difficulty imagining what Paris might be like. The American who has seen the Mall and the city's various squares, or Daniel Burnham's Union Station, has had a glimpse, at least, of Versailles and baroque Rome.[21]

In Washington, implementation of the original L'Enfant plan, as appropriated and adapted by Andrew Ellicott, got off to a slow start. The early city, sometimes referred to as Washingtonople, seemed impossibly pretentious. For example, the Irish poet Thomas Moore, who visited the city in 1804, wrote of

This embryo capital, where fancy sees
Squares in morasses, obelisks in trees;
Which second-sighted seers, ev'n now, adorn
With shrines unbuilt, and heroes yet unborn,
Though naught but woods and Jefferson they see,
Where streets should run and sages ought to be.[22]

When Charles Dickens visited Washington in 1842, things were essentially the same. Dickens found "spacious avenues that begin in nothing and lead nowhere; streets a mile long that only want houses, roads, and inhabitants; public buildings that need only a public to be complete, and ornaments of great thoroughfares that need only great thoroughfares to ornament."[23] It is astounding, in fact, how recently Washington was a sleepy town, full of Southern efficiency and Northern charm, and how dramatically it was transformed by the emergence of big government under President Franklin Delano Roosevelt.[24] It says something about Lewis Mumford that he regarded D.C. as too faint-hearted a celebration of the state. For example, he praised L'Enfant's setting aside of certain parcels for federal offices and other public and quasi-public buildings, but castigated L'Enfant's heirs for their restraint: "Surely, a wise, foresighted government would . . . have acquired the whole District of Columbia by purchase, and would have rented, not sold, the land essential to its development as a national capital. Without public control of the land itself, Major L'Enfant's plan was defeated before he had even come within sight of the opposing army."[25] Le Corbusier himself never made a more forceful statement on behalf of state planning.

The expansion of government in the twentieth century has rendered Washington, D.C., a pilgrimage site, a monument to the state and the collectivist ethos. Most of the pilgrimage destinations—the White House, the Capitol, the Supreme Court Building, the Federal Bureau of Investigation, the Pentagon—honor branches or agencies of government. Others are dedicated to particular citizens, public officials, or military leaders, many of whom made the supreme sacrifice; Arlington Cemetery, the Vietnam Memorial, and Ford's Theater come instantly to mind. Most

FIGURE 44
In the late sixteenth century, Pope Sixtus V introduced planning principles that favored a new kind of vista. The avenues radiating from the Piazza del Popolo (below), the work of his mid seventeenth-century successor, Pope Alexander VII, led pilgrims to the major sacred and profane monuments of Rome. This became the prototype of the European capital city.

FIGURE 43
A medieval urban vista (Chartres).

families and tour groups also gravitate to the Mall and its array of museums.

Despite all that there is to see and do in the nation's capital, my hunch is that for many a tourist the single most compelling experience Washington has to offer is one of its newest and ostensibly most utilitarian landmarks, an urban amenity that, like so many institutions established to promote convenience, has come to be appreciated for its formal qualities. Considering that it cost $10 billion to build and consumes another $300 million annually to operate, perhaps it deserves to be Washington's chief tourist attraction. I refer to the Washington Metro.

There is much to be said on its behalf. For one thing, its name, an explicit reference to the city that was Major L'Enfant's inspiration, is a way of acknowledging and preserving an important antecedent. Functionally, the Metro is a fast, efficient, reasonably quiet, clean, and safe means of transportation providing access to a number of important sites in the city and to points of entry and egress, including Ronald Reagan National Airport and Union Station. More than that, the Metro is ultimately a democratic experience—infinitely more so than a motorcade of limousines with darkened windows traversing Pennsylvania Avenue—and more inspirational than gazing at the U.S. Constitution through translucent glass at the National Archives. Among Washington attractions, the Metro alone offers some of the cheap thrills available at Disney World or Busch Gardens. Kids can only *see* the Spirit of St. Louis at the Air and Space Museum, or money being printed at the Bureau of Engraving and Printing. But they can *ride* the Metro.

Tourists may think that Metro is extremely punctual, and so it is, most of the time. Every train is on a tight schedule, although those schedules are not published. I am reminded of this when I miss, by less than a minute most days, my Yellow Line connection at L'Enfant Plaza; I have learned to cool my heels until the next one comes along six minutes later. Tourists are rightly impressed by the relative absence of graffiti and litter in the Metro system. Metro's planners—Harry Weese was the chief architect—cleverly made many wall surfaces inaccessible to spray paint, and trash bins and newspaper-recycling containers are regularly emptied. Strategically placed cameras create the impression—one suspects it is largely an illusion—of unobtrusive surveillance. The absence of public restrooms perhaps contributes to a sense that everyone should be on the move, that this is no place to lurk or loiter. Vagrants receive a gentle but firm bum's rush.

As wondrous as it is, Metro has its downside. For one thing, it generally conveys a false impression of its own centrality to the lives of most Washingtonians. Fully half of the people who ride mass transit in the Washington metropolitan area are dependent on Metrobuses, which are about as glamorous and efficient as buses in any other city. The problem, as with any rail system, is that vast tracts of land lie in-

FIGURE 45
A Red Line train, Metro Center station, Washington, D.C. Metro managers often express wonder that it takes so long for passengers to debouch and board.

conveniently between the various Metrorail lines. Washington Cathedral, Adams Morgan, Tyson's Corner, Dulles Airport, and Old Town Alexandria are among the many destinations without direct subway links. Some other places were deliberately bypassed by Metro, for whatever reason, while Georgetown held itself aloof. Then, too, Metro does not begin to extend to the limits of the metropolitan area, which now encompasses virtually everything inside a four-cornered frame extending from Annapolis to Frederick and from Leesburg to Quantico. And Metro is not inexpensive, especially for those (not tourists) who must commute during rush hour. From my inside-the-Beltway home, approximately seven miles from the Mall, it costs $3.70 per day to ride the subway, on top of the $2.00 fare charged by the Alexandria Transit Company for the connector bus that takes me to Braddock Road station.

There are maintenance issues. Like any large-scale facility or system, Metro is vulnerable to massive breakdowns; when one thing goes wrong, there is a chain reaction. Even when nothing in particular has gone wrong, it seems to be extremely difficult for Metro to keep its cars in service. That may be one reason why rush-hour trains are invariably too short, and therefore overcrowded; most days, I have to stand on the Blue Line between Braddock Road and Farragut West, a trip of some twenty minutes. What kind of incentive is that for people to take public transportation, rather than driving into the city?

Some escalators and elevators seem to require constant servicing; at the Federal Triangle station, one can expect a third of the escalators to be stationary at any given time. Some Metro escalators are permanently shut down because they need to be used at all times for traffic going in both directions; there is one such escalator at the Pentagon. And so every day thousands of commuters are required to execute awkward little mincing maneuvers at the top and bottom where the steps are uneven. One wonders, why don't they just rip that escalator up and install an old-fashioned staircase? One wonders, too, what it is about department-store escalators and elevators that makes them so much more reliable than Metro equipment. One answer to that question is that many of Metro's escalators are exposed to rain, sleet, and snow, allowing water to seep into wiring and gearboxes. Until recently, when the policy was changed, Metro never built canopies over its outdoor escalators; the argument against canopies was based strictly on aesthetics. Water, as a matter of fact, poses a grave threat to the entire system, especially the Red Line. The *Washington Post* reports that 1.25 billion gallons of water are pumped out of the subways every month.[26]

But the real downside of Metro, which also may not be immediately apparent to tourists, has to do with its social dimensions. At rush hour, trains are extremely crowded, which means that one must expect to stand, to be jostled in a crowd, and to be exposed to other people's germs and hygiene lapses. These things are unpleasant, but tolerable. Less tolerable are the bad manners on permanent display. Inevitably, there are the People Who Insist on Standing in Front of the Door, who seem oblivious to the fact that they are preventing people from entering or exiting. It turns out that most of these folks are also People Who Step onto the Train and Immediately Stop, re-

gardless of how many people are behind them and intent on board-
ing. That's how the People Who Insist on Standing in Front of the
Door got there in the first place.[27]

The willingness of the Japanese to deploy staff to shove commuters
onto their "bullet trains," a simple solution that is unthinkable in the
West, speaks volumes about cultural differences. But it also serves to
underscore the point that every transit system, no matter how rational
and scientific, has to anticipate the subversive tendencies of its customers. The People Who Insist on Standing in Front of the Door and
the People Who Step onto the Train and Immediately Stop will always
find allies among the People Who Sit in the Aisle Seat and Put Their
Bags on the Window Seat to Discourage Anyone Else from Claiming It (an argument for seating around the perimeter, as in New York
and London, as opposed to Metro's pew-style seating); the People
Who Blithely Ignore the Signs That Say "Seats Reserved for Elderly
or Handicapped Passengers"; and the People Who Try Repeatedly to
Get through the Turnstile with Insufficient Fare, never thinking to
step aside to let others pass while they attend to their farecard problems. I will not deign to speak of the People Who Stand Two Abreast
on the Escalator, or the People Who Share, through Cheap Earphones,
Their Taste in Music, Invariably Bad, with Everyone Else on the Train.
Recently, Metro has been fighting back with a schizophrenic campaign that combines high-tech electronic signage ("Be a Nice Rider")
with a "zero tolerance" policy that seems to require the handcuffing
of pre-teens who smuggle French fries into the system.

Human nature as it manifests itself in the Washington Metro is
not particularly attractive. But it is comforting to think that the very
qualities that can prove endlessly exasperating on the Metro are, as
we saw in the introduction to this book, responsible for the feckless
glory of Pessac—that is, for the constructive vandalism perpetrated
by its occupants on Le Corbusier's little house for proles. I do not
mean to suggest that the Washington Metro has been a failure. Rather,
I mean to draw attention to the way that Metro invites us to engage
in "dreaming the rational city"[28] while simultaneously mocking those
dreams. It is no wonder that clever commuters have devised other
means of getting in and out of the city.

In the mid-1970s, when energy consciousness was at its zenith,
both the state and federal governments encouraged carpooling by restricting access to certain commuting corridors. The express lanes
of northern Virginia's Shirley Highway, for example, are designated

HOV-3, meaning that only "high-occupancy vehicles"—defined in this case as carrying three (at times it has been four) occupants—are allowed access. The incentive lay in the fact that during rush hour, the regular lanes of Shirley Highway resemble an elongated parking lot extending from the District of Columbia south to Dale City and beyond. In the mornings the limited-access express lanes are open only to northbound HOV-3 vehicles. Drivers entering the express lanes at Springfield cannot exit until the Pentagon, some nine miles to the north. At midday the express lanes are closed to all traffic. Then in the evening they are opened to southbound traffic. Naturally, the HOV-3 rule has proved a boon to the mannequin industry.

Another unanticipated consequence of HOV regulations is the Springfield Meat Market—some call it "slugging"—an informal mechanism in use throughout the Washington metropolitan area for matching drivers in need of warm bodies with commuters without wheels. I have a colleague who commutes daily by this means. Let's call her Elizabeth. Each morning, she leaves her Springfield home at precisely 6:25. For early birds like Elizabeth, the traffic on the connector roads is not so bad; ordinarily, it takes only about ten minutes for her to reach the commuter parking lot in Springfield Plaza. There she gets out of her car, walks to the adjacent parking lot of Long John Silver's, and queues up in the "slug line" of riders heading for the vicinity of Fourteenth Street and Constitution Avenue, N.W. There is a separate line that serves the part of town accessed by Memorial Bridge.

Elizabeth's destination is Twelfth Street and Pennsylvania Avenue. If the line is long, she will gladly accept a ride to Fourteenth and Pennsylvania, then walk the final two blocks. On such days the drivers pass by the line slowly, windows down, calling out their destinations and negotiating from a position of decreasing strength as they approach the end of the line; sometimes they agree to deliver to the doorstep. On days when there is a dearth of riders—"no meat," drivers lament— motorists park their cars and hustle riders as best they can. Some prowl through the movie-theater parking lot. Elizabeth usually arrives at work by 7:00—by Washington standards, an incredibly fast commute.

Habitués of this institution have never been able to agree about its essential nature. Liberals, shrinking from the element of anarchy at its heart, prefer to think of it as improvised carpooling, which they deem acceptable, if inferior to state-owned and -operated mass transit. Free marketeers, relishing that same element of anarchy, see "slug-

ging" less as carpooling than as a form of hitchhiking. The key point
is that there has grown up a kind of "slug culture" that has been well
described by Francis Fukuyama: "The slugs have established an elaborate set of rules over the years. Neither cars nor passengers may jump
the line; passengers have the right to refuse to get into a particular
car; smoking and the exchange of money are forbidden; slug etiquette
demands that conversations stay away from controversial issues like
sex, religion, and politics. The process is remarkably orderly. In the
past thirteen years, there have been only two criminal incidents, both
occurring on dark winter mornings when few people were waiting.
As a result, no one will leave a woman alone on a slug line."[29]

It is understood that the driver maintains strict control over the
car radio or cassette player; riders must not complain about the driver's taste in music, although they may exercise some control over the
volume. Riders must not second-guess the motorist's driving skills,
or his or her tactics for avoiding snarled traffic. Southbound passengers are obliged, in other words, to ignore a driver's calamitous deci-
sion to stay on the express lanes past the Edsall Road exit instead of
transferring to the regular Shirley Highway lanes. Likewise, riders are
expected to respond impassively to the driver who, realizing too late
that he or she should have exited at Edsall, tries dangerously to access
the regular lanes through a break in the guardrail reserved for the
highway patrol and other emergency vehicles.

The slugs, in short, have "created social capital." The institution
"emerged spontaneously in the ecological niche created by the government mandate, a bit of social order created from the bottom up
by people pursuing their own private interests in getting to work."[30]
One needn't be a thoroughgoing libertarian to think that the difference between human nature as manifested on the Metro and in the
Springfield Meat Market derives from the fact that the latter institution is built on the privately owned automobile, where property
rights may be asserted, while the former is based on "public" ownership, an abstraction that discourages any individual shareholder from
actually exercising property rights.

The afternoon Meat Market springs to life daily, when HOV restrictions take force at 3:30, across from the Museum of American
History at Fourteenth Street and Constitution Avenue, N.W. As there
is no place to park at that location, drivers are obliged, if riders are
scarce, simply to sit at the curb lane of Fourteenth Street until riders
materialize. When, as on most days, riders stand in a long queue,

motorists drive past slowly, calling out "Bob's" (actually it's now a Shoney's, but old habits die hard) if their final destination is Springfield, or, if they are going as far as Burke, "Rolling Valley," where there is another commuter parking area. Since she has a car to pick up at Springfield Plaza, Elizabeth is a Bob's person.

The afternoon slug line is very different from the morning version, mainly because of the attitude of the District government toward a strictly informal and suburb-serving institution (not that it doesn't serve the District by reducing demand for parking spaces). Official indifference turns to outright hostility when afternoon riders are scarce, at which time the line of vehicles idling at the curb on Fourteenth Street tends to back up onto Constitution Avenue. On such occasions the D.C. police can be counted on to hand out tickets liberally. A large part of the problem is that drivers waiting for riders to turn up don't move up far enough, a problem

FIGURE 46
Bob's or Rolling Valley? The "slug line" at Fourteenth Street and Constitution Avenue, N.W., part of Washington's "vernacular landscape."

that could be solved simply by installing a strategically placed sign— "Slug Line Begins Here"—to move the cars farther toward the southern end of the block and away from the intersection. That would keep the traffic on Constitution Avenue moving. But it would also require that the District officially recognize the legitimacy of slugging, which, no doubt on the advice of its attorneys, it is loath to do. So the slug line persists, but as a kind of urban Taiwan.

And that segue brings us to Washington's Old Post Office Building (OPO), a Pennsylvania Avenue landmark designed by the Chicago architect Willoughby J. Edbrooke, the man responsible for the U.S. Government building at the World's Columbian Exposition in Chicago, 1893.[31] By the time the building was completed in 1899, the Romanesque Revival style was already going out of fashion, and it was definitely incompatible with the City Beautiful groupings of the McMillan Commission that revived, just a few years later, L'Enfant's original vision of a baroque capital. Still, as the OPO was brand-new, it was tolerated for a while. Two decades later, when Secretary of the Treasury Andrew W. Mellon commissioned the Federal Triangle project, the OPO's days seemed numbered. But by the time the Federal Triangle project was winding down in the late 1930s, so was popular enthusiasm for the classicism of the City Beautiful movement, and the OPO was spared again. By the 1950s the Old Post Office was a certified derelict, and so it remained through the 1960s, when revitalization plans called for completion of the Federal Triangle (i.e., demolition of the OPO). But the building survived long enough to be rescued by the historic preservation movement in the 1970s, and at that point the Old Post Office "was transformed into a model of the federal government's efforts to create multi-use, publicly accessible federal government buildings. The firm of Arthur Cotton Moore/ Associates designed the rehabilitation of the Old Post Office, reopening its covered center court, upgrading office space around the perimeter for federal government cultural and arts programs, and placing a two-level shopping arcade at the ground floor."[32] It has been said that in its reincarnation as a "festival marketplace," the OPO was "Rousified"—a reference to the celebrated developer of Baltimore's Harborplace.

Several upscale restaurants and boutiques were among the original tenants in the OPO's commercial area—the Pavilion—but they didn't last. One by one, the sit-down restaurants—first Maxim's, then Fitch, Fox, and Brown, then Blossoms, then Hunan—moved out. A stationery store and fancy card shop were replaced by stores selling flags and leather goods, reflecting a change, not for the better, in the Pavilion's clientele. Gradually the food court in the OPO, so conveniently located vis-à-vis the Smithsonian museums and other attractions on the Mall, evolved as the noontime destination of high school tour groups; eventually, the *only* purpose being served by the Pavilion at the Old Post Office was to provide lunch for adolescent tourists. That was unfortunate, since, as Roberta Brandes Gratz has written, "any place left primarily to tourists ceases to be a real place and eventually loses its appeal even to tourists."[33]

The lease changed hands. In the early 1990s, at great expense and breakneck speed, a steel-and-glass east atrium was added to the OPO. But that addition housed mainly fast-food joints as well, and after a couple of years they clearly were cannibalizing one another. Suddenly the east atrium, which won at least one architectural award, was quietly closed. In recent years there have been rumors about new tenants— a major bookstore, a cinema complex—but still the east atrium lies padlocked and vacant, along with the space in the Pavilion once occupied by the four sit-down restaurants. More recently still, it has been rumored that the federal offices would be moved out of the OPO to make way for a hotel.

What went wrong? Unquestionably, the building itself poses a

FIGURE 47
At the time of its construction, the Old Post Office at Twelfth Street and Pennsylvania Avenue, N.W., Washington, D.C., was surrounded by living urban tissue. Now it is a Romanesque fortress in a sea of neoclassical government office buildings. This photograph was taken in 1894.

challenge. It is something of a castle keep—all granite, with formidable, largely windowless doors that sit up high and back from the street. There is no visual access to the interior. At one point the management of the building, in an attempt to control traffic and reduce heating and cooling costs, sought to restrict access by removing the brass handles from a number of the doors, an odd thing for merchants dependent on walk-in trade to do. There never has been much

creative thinking about how customers might be lured in from the
street.

As an office building the Old Post Office is a disaster. The roof
leaked for years, and air quality is low. The plumbing is archaic. The
elevators are safe, but slow and eccentric. Employees of several small
cultural agencies regard the food court as a mixed blessing: "While
tourists and office workers alike benefit from the food services in
the shopping arcade, this function also produces an odoriferous pall
throughout the interior."[34] Worse than the smells is the noise. And
worse yet are the historic preservation laws cited by the General Services Administration, properly or improperly, to account for its inability to make improvements. Inevitably, the OPO has been embroiled
in local (and, considering that it's Washington, national) politics.[35]
In spite of everything, the OPO has apparently inspired the development of the nearby Reagan Building, which similarly combines
government offices with a basement-level food court—one that is in
direct competition with the emporium in the OPO. With all due respect to Senator Moynihan, the genius behind Pennsylvania Avenue
development, this was not a good idea.

But perhaps the most serious problem with the Old Post Office is
that it is only superficially a multipurpose district. There really are
only two uses to which this structure is put: it provides office space
and midday fast food. Those two uses are barely integrated with one
another. How could they be? There needs to be another overlay of re-
inforcing use patterns—sometimes called "coupling"—which is what
the developers who attempted to attract a movie-theater complex or
a megabookstore had in mind. They had the right idea. In addition,
something needs to be done to connect the internal commercial activity to the street.[36]

As Jane Jacobs taught us years ago, every great city needs aged
buildings. Preserving the Old Post Office seemed like a good idea at
the time. But someone should have considered the possibility that
a public-private partnership could manage to combine the *worst* of
both worlds.

THE BRITISH LIBRARY

From Great Planning Disaster to Almost All Right

CONNOISSEURS OF THE LITERATURE of Big Plans—like most arcane genres, it is an acquired taste—have a special place in their pantheon for Peter Hall's *Great Planning Disasters,* a book that manages to be professionally responsible and slightly irreverent at the same time.[1] Hall's interest lies primarily with out-and-out disasters, such as London's third airport, San Francisco's BART system,[2] and the Anglo-French Concorde. At the time he was writing, the British Library seemed a borderline case.

Here is the gist of the story. The British Library, a vast collection organized around a gift to the nation by George III, was for over a century administered by the British Museum and housed in its legendary Round Reading Room in Bloomsbury. As early as the 1930s, it appeared that some thought needed to be given to the library's expansion. Severe bomb damage inflicted by the Germans in World War II gave impetus to the idea of acquiring a large parcel of land just south of the British Museum on Great Russell Street. That plan seemed to have many virtues, one being that it conformed to Patrick Abercrombie's postwar master plan for the County of London, which called for turning Bloomsbury "into a national education and research precinct."[3] Readers who recall from chapter 3 Jane Jacobs's observations about cultural districts uncontaminated by other uses will recognize the Bloomsbury plan as a single-minded monolith in the making, but in fact no one objected to the idea on those grounds. Objections were raised on other grounds—that old standby, the NIMBY reflex—to the proposal to clear the area around the museum, a complex and vibrant neighborhood of varied uses, many of them museum-related (there were between 1,000 and 1,500 permanent residents, along with many secondhand bookstores, restaurants, pubs, and other businesses).

The trustees of the museum—a group of Old Boys that included such worthies as Lord Eccles, Sir Kenneth Clark, and the Archbishop of Canterbury—were inclined to think of themselves as stewards of a national treasure. Naturally, they regarded the intense, persistent, and eloquent opposition to the Bloomsbury project, spearheaded by the Holborn Chamber of Commerce, the Holborn Borough Council, and the local M.P., Mrs. Lena Jeger, as gross interference in their internal affairs. And so, in 1963, the trustees commissioned Sir Leslie Martin and Colin St. John Wilson to draw up plans for the new library at the Great Russell Street site. But in 1965, a new Labour government that was far less receptive to the Old Boys was installed at Westminster. The subsequent reorganization of the Greater London Council transferred jurisdiction over the museum and its surrounding neighborhood to the new Borough of Camden, which "immediately took over Holborn's implacable opposition to the scheme."[4] Suddenly, the Bloomsbury site seemed problematical.

Two things occurred in the early 1970s—the administrative separation of the library from the museum, and the discovery of a promising new site—that were to prove crucial. The creation of a separate library board meant that the fates of library and museum were no longer inextricably wedded. The parcel in question was the old Somers Town goods yard near St. Pancras station, the site of a notorious Dickensian slum that had been "rendered derelict by containerization and the end of the coal trade."[5] Within walking distance of Bloomsbury, accessible by Underground, and involving the displacement of no businesses or residents, the St. Pancras site was a no-brainer. "Thus," Hall writes, "at the end of a saga extending over thirty years, it seemed, miraculously, that everyone was satisfied—though not to the same degree. The conservationists had saved their corner of Bloomsbury. The residents would live in peace. The bookshops and curio shops would continue to delight visitors to the museum, who were growing in number year by year. The users of the libraries would get a superb complex of buildings, maximally accessible from all parts of London and from much of Britain. Even the National Library Board was consoled by the offer of a virtually immediate start to the complex for which everyone had waited so long."[6]

Meanwhile, the comeback of the Tories at both the local and national level complicated matters, as did the appointment in 1970 of Lord Eccles as the new Minister for the Arts and his later assumption of the duties of chairman of the new British Library Authority. An election in 1974 ushered in another Labour government, which finalized plans for a national library on the St. Pancras site. The design for the new library, unveiled in March 1978 by Wilson—Sir Leslie having long since thrown in the towel—was described by Hall as "a highly imaginative one with red brick and massive overhanging slate roofs, providing an apt foil to the neighboring Gothic fantasy of St. Pancras Station."[7] It is hard not to be impressed by the sheer audacity of a project that featured ten million handmade bricks, "the biggest basement ever built for peacetime purposes,"[8] more than three hundred kilometers of shelving,[9] and the first new clock tower on the London skyline since World War II.[10] Moving a library from Bloomsbury to St. Pancras, particularly one with 150 million separate items,[11] while continuing to provide regular readers' services, is an enormous project that is still under way as this is written; so far, it has proceeded with dispatch. Long before the facility was officially opened by the Queen on June 25, 1998, bringing to a close what Wilson has called his "Thirty Years War,"[12] people were "already speaking of the British Library as a success."[13]

Perhaps the biggest challenges were the political ones. Once the St. Pancras site had been secured and the architectural plans unveiled, the British Library ran into the twin-bladed buzz saw of Margaret Thatcher and the Prince of Wales. The Thatcherites objected not only to the costs associated with "the largest civil building to be constructed in Europe this century,"[14] but also to the principle of subsidizing the chattering classes. For his part, Prince Charles was appalled by the building, which he famously described as a "dim collection of brick sheds" resembling an "academy for secret police."[15] He was not alone. The National Heritage Committee judged it "one of the ugliest buildings in the world . . . a Babylonian ziggurat seen through a funfair distorting mirror."[16] Former arts minister David Mellor deemed it "vile and horrible."[17] The unlikely image that sticks in my mind is of a Bhutanese aircraft carrier. But having said his piece, the Prince of Wales dutifully laid the cornerstone in 1982.

The exterior of the building remains controversial. As a good modernist architect, Wilson argues that buildings need to be designed from the inside out, and since the exterior is derivative, it is not to be judged according to the criteria that might be applied to, say, the Palazzo Farnese. That said, external form was not simply to be dictated by internal function. The public space in front of the British Library, for example, was intended to serve both as a sanctuary for weary readers and as a link to the streets of London, and by extension to the capitals of Europe. According to Wilson, "The primary purpose of the Piazza enclosure is that it will allow the visiting reader to regain the tranquillity that was lost in the street and also to have a place in good weather in which to rest between spells of work. It is however also open in normal day-time hours to the general public: and since it is the only open public space in the neighbourhood and, furthermore, will lie adjacent to the proposed Channel Tunnel Terminal, it should take on the unique sense of a place of a rendez-vous not only for the Library but also to visitors to and from the Continent."[18] Green window awnings repeat a motif from the reading rooms, where the personal reading lamps are trim, trapezoidal solids imparting a dash of color, geometry, and Art Deco flair to the interior. There is a nautical theme to this building, expressed through a kind of prow that it extends toward its dock on Euston Street, as well as through features that Wilson refers to as "portholes."[19] Other rounded features, not unlike the medallions punctuating a Renaissance arcade, carry on the nautical motif—an architect's conceit, to be sure, but one that is not entirely inappropriate, given the role of the Royal Navy in generating the nation's wealth. The use of brick, at any rate, was quite self-conscious: "Brick was chosen as the facing material both because it is the one material that in this climate improves rather than degenerates in appearance over time but also to orchestrate the Library on a broad scale with St Pancras whose bricks come from the same source in Leicestershire. The colours for the metal sun louvres

FIGURE 48
The new British Library at St. Pancras, 1998.

and trim to the ground floor panels and columns were also selected as common to both buildings."[20] The fact is that Wilson, modernist or no, understands that a national library is not simply a machine for storing and regurgitating books. "There are certain types of building," he writes, "over which there hovers an aura of myth. The most transcendent of all, the cathedral, is grounded in the sacred so that both form and pattern of use are fused in the language of ritual. But there is one type of building which is profane yet in fulfilling its proper role touches the hem of the sacred: the great library. One has only to think of what crowds into the mind when we recall the destruction of the Library in Alexandria or, akin to that fire, the blasphemy that underlay the burning of the books by Nazi decree, for one to be made aware that the library and what it houses embodies and protects the freedom and diversity of the human spirit in a way that borders on the sacred."[21]

The interior, meanwhile, is a functional and aesthetic triumph. All the book ordering is done electronically. A light comes on at the reader's desk whenever materials have arrived. Pickup at the Issue Desk is simple and convenient. Materials stored on site are delivered within forty-five minutes. The fact is, however, that thanks to cuts imposed by the Thatcher government as the costs escalated, the facility at St. Pancras "will account for only half of the British Library's activity."[22] Brian Lang, executive in charge of the library at the time of its opening, explains that while the St. Pancras facility "concentrates on providing direct access to readers, usually through primary sources in reading rooms," the library supplies "from Boston Spa in Yorkshire, 250 miles north of London, . . . well over four million items to readers around the world, as well as to other libraries and workplaces, by fax, photocopy, traditional mail, and directly from computer to computer."[23]

The furniture was designed with meticulous care. The chairs in the humanities rooms, for example, were intended to provide long-term comfort, inasmuch as studies have shown that humanists stay put and pore over their materials—unlike scientists, who tend not to alight for long in any one place. For security purposes, readers are required to check all extraneous items at the central cloakroom; accordingly, extra-wide chair backs were cleverly designed to discourage the draping of jackets. The desks are of generous size. There are no windows at eye level, but one does not feel cut off from nature; thunderstorms, for example, are clearly audible from within. Most of the light is natural, but it is diffuse, so there is no glare. The personal lamps at each desk were designed to be turned on for reading, off for computer use. The services have been installed in such a way as to accommodate future technological change. The library has adequate staffing; efficient but humane auxiliary services, including security; and a comfortable physical plant.

The architect has persuasively addressed some of the concerns of his heritage-minded critics. Wilson insists that he is working out of a tradition within modernism that can be traced back to Ruskin and the English Free School, as well as to Frank Lloyd Wright. He writes that in designing the British Library,

we have drawn widely upon this tradition not only in the adoption of organic forms that are responsive to growth and change but also in the repertoire of sensuous materials that are particularly responsive to human presence and touch—leather, marble, wood and bronze. We touch, hear and smell a building as much as we see it and furthermore what we do see in terms of weight and texture, density or transparency transmits explicit resonances of a body language that is common to us all but all too seldom consciously addressed. It is a tradition that unlike the hard-line modernist obsession with "progress" never sought to cut itself off from the past or deny itself allusion to precedent and always retained a blood relationship with painting, sculpture and hand-crafts in an age increasingly committed to mechanical reproduction.[24]

A good case in point is the architect's handling of the king's library, "a six-floor tower of bronze and glass to display the leather and vellum bindings of George III's collection."[25] Instead of interring the collection in a vault deep within the library's bowels, Wilson has put the books (holy relics at the altar of his secular cathedral) on conspicuous display in the very center of the building, all the while shielding them from the sun.

Of course, Wilson's handling of the king's library is all about aesthetics and symbolism, rather than function. As a matter of fact, a large part of the British Library's appeal lies in the fact that high-quality—that is, expensive—materials have been used throughout, with a heavy emphasis on brass, leather, ebony, and travertine. As Wendy Law-Yone has written, "readers—many of them die-hard devotees of the sumptuous old Round Reading Room in the British Museum—seem unable to resist the quiet, functional yet opulent appeal of a split-level reading room with soaring ceilings, varied spaces, and soothing materials: American oak tables and chairs, sage carpets, and table tops of matching leather."[26]

There are nits to pick, but they have much more to do with the structure itself than with the functioning of the library it houses. As urban space, the piazza in front of the British Library is not at all successful. It is extremely wide, and not so inviting as to draw pedestrians in from the street. A coffee shop embedded in the complex lacks a proper visual connection to both piazza and street. In truth, the library seems unlikely ever to be an important part of the London cityscape—in the way that the Pompidou Center is in Paris, for example.[27] Max Page, writing in *Preservation,* faults the library precisely on these grounds: "This is a monk's library and not an emporium of ideas. The city, of noise but also of inspiration, has been shut out."[28] In addition, Wilson seems altogether too glib in claiming descent from the English Free School and in his friendly nod toward St. Pancras. While others have praised the architect for the way the library defers to its neighbor, I have always thought the two piles of bricks warily turn their shoulders away from each other like musclebound prizefighters at the weigh-in.[29]

On the inside, too, there are design problems. Consider the entrance to the library's cafeteria. The reader in search of a midday snack or a jolt of caffeine is encouraged by the sight of diners seated in the refectory, just a few steps away from Humanities Reading Room I. One is naturally drawn to a turnstile that would seem to be the point of entry, except that the sign says "Way Out." The impression that this is not to be used as an entrance to the cafeteria may be reinforced by people who are actually using the turnstile as an exit from the dining area. Thus, one searches for the entrance. Eventually that search is abandoned, and one returns to the original, "Way Out" turnstile. The reader at this point might look for a place to insert his or her identification card to open the gate. But there is no such slot. Next, one pushes gently on the gate—which gives way.

I suspect I am not the only reader who has then found himself a cup of tea and a strategically situated table to enjoy the spectacle of others confounded by this turnstile. It soon becomes apparent that library patrons are using their identification cards to activate the gates as they leave the cafeteria—that is, as they enter the part of the library restricted to those who have been issued reader's cards. And then one realizes that the turnstile is a two-way device that offers free access to the cafeteria while requiring IDs for access back into the restricted

FIGURE 50
View down Judd Street and across Euston Road of the British Library (left) and St. Pancras Station, 1998.

area. From the security guard's perspective, this turnstile may represent a "way out," but what the ordinary reader is looking for is a "way in."

This confusing signage could be easily corrected, and no doubt will be. Perhaps it already has been. The point is not that a billion-dollar library has been badly designed. The point, rather, is that recognizing and planning for such contingencies is next to impossible. There is a reason that the planners of college campuses prudently wait for students to beat their footpaths before paving the walkways.

During the process of construction, the project experienced more than its fair share of snafus, including faulty shelving, a leaky roof, and rapidly accelerating costs. The total cost of £511 million is either five or fifty times over budget, depending on what one wishes to use as a reference point. Thanks to the Thatcher-imposed budget reductions, the need for expansion is already evident. Law-Yone has written that by the time the British Library is more or less complete, it will have "gone through more than two decades of start-and-stop planning, building, tearing down, rebuilding, etc., and five times as much money as projected. After major cutbacks and canceled building phases, it will also end up with space for less than half the books envisioned."[30]

Given the way that politics intruded on the planning process, the brute fact of the library's presence at St. Pancras seems almost a miracle. Hall, from the vantage point of the late 1970s, was struck by the pivotal role of the National Library Board. Its creation meant that for the first time, a public authority existed that had the welfare of the library, rather than the museum, as its primary responsibility; that these institutions often spoke though Lord Eccles wearing different hats only serves to prove Hall's point. Beyond that, for Hall the main lesson seems to be that "it may sometimes pay to wait for the unexpected."[31] There were, in this case, two wholly unanticipated developments: a souring of the public's attitude toward urban renewal and the availability of the perfect site.

A political scientist may perhaps be forgiven for adding to Hall's account a further observation: the British Library objectifies the virtues of a political system that is consensus-driven nationally and in which an important role is still reserved for local government. The result, of course, is that public policy issues forth slowly, incrementally, rather than in cataclysmic spasms. In the case of the British Library, the involvement of those directly affected in the debate over location, and the difficulty of reaching closure on that and many other issues, provided sufficient time for the intervention of serendipity. In addition, it meant that the architect was far more tractable than he would have been if his patrons had been armed with the power to ratify his judgments with peremptory edicts. In the early 1980s, Wilson's response to criticism of his design was animated, but never intransigent; he made all necessary changes. It may be significant that, as a metaphor for his brand of modernism, Wilson borrows T. S. Eliot's tribute to the English language, which he said possessed "the greatest capacity for changing, and yet remaining itself."[32] In sum, the British Library may be regarded as a monument to the arts associated with "muddling through."

Consider the alternative. In the last decade of the twentieth century, the opposite of muddling through by means of democratic consensus-building—government by fiat—was on conspicuous display in the controversy over the new French National Library (Bibliothèque de France) in the Paris quarter of Tolbiac. There, in the spring of 1995, the library was inaugurated—despite the fact that there were no books in it at the time—just as French president François Mitterrand was leaving office.

Like its counterpart at St. Pancras, the French National Library is often described in terms of crunched numbers: constructed in 19 months, it contains "10-million books, 600,000 hours of tape, 1.2 million pictures in an image bank, all stored among four 264-foot-high towers and 430,000 sq ft of reading rooms in a $1.6 billion building."[33] Books are delivered in 15 minutes via 5 miles of conveyor belts.[34] The architect, the young and little-known Dominique Perrault, had in mind a tribute to emptiness—an exercise in the "aesthetics of the void." One insightful student of architecture has argued that the point of such exercises is to encourage a kind of absent-mindedness and the suspension of the faculties associated with criticism: "The critical attention is absorbed by involving the observer in a sort of mere game, *divertissement, imagerie:* the city as a non-functioning fun-fair, full of persuasive images, replete with signs and more and more empty of meaning, that has as its symbolic monuments the Lincoln Center and New York World Fair, on one side; the Scandinavian *new-town centers* (from Vallingby to Farsta), and the projects for the restructuration of Paris on the other. The *emphasis on the void* is the recurring structure of this new urban rhetoric" (emphasis in the original).[35]

The design of the Bibliothèque de France, which has been likened to "an overturned table with its legs in the air,"[36] generated instant opposition, which led Jacques Chirac, then mayor of Paris, to personally ask President Mitterrand to revise the project. When Chirac moved to stop work, the response of Mitterrand's Minister of Culture, Jack Lang, was to confiscate the site. A commission was appointed to review the situation; among other things, it sent a team of inspectors to the new British Library. But by this time (1992), Perrault's building was a fait accompli.

Though planning for a building of this size ordinarily takes at least a year, the competition for the library was opened on March 8, 1989, and Perrault's design was chosen on July 26, 1989, when the government was still planning to house no more than three to five million books in the new building and to leave the rest at the Rue de Richelieu. It was only later, on August 2, that a government ruling came down after Perrault's design had been selected: all but one hundred thousand of the eleven million books would be moved to Tolbiac, with plans to store twenty million more books during the next century. (In the present plan, the rue de Richelieu library will house an arts research center.) In any case the design competition was not re-opened: if construction was to become irreversible before the next election, when a neo-Gaullist majority might suspend it, there was no time to consider new plans.[37]

The former head of the Bibliothèque Nationale, Georges Le Rider, has referred to Perrault's plan as "spectacularly bad,"[38] primarily because of the temperature and climate-control issues posed by the glass towers. Claire Downey, writing in *Architectural Record,* insists that Perrault intended it as a "paradox" that books would be placed in the towers and the readers underground, and she argues that many French people approve the idea of the written word rising above people. "What they find less acceptable," according to Downey,

is the idea of precious books being baked in glass boxes. Perrault insists that his idea of transparency was greatly misunderstood. "I never said that the building would be completely transparent," he stresses. What he hoped, he says, was that there would be a sense of the towers filling up over time. Actually, the towers will be full on opening day, with offices now taking up their lower seven floors. For protection, the new glass facades of the book-storage floors are lined with permanently

closed, vertical wood shutters. The opacity undermines Perrault's origi-
nal premise. Rather than witness the library's gradual accumulation of
books, views in are obscured. The architect fought to maintain his
design, which, at least from the outside, gradually lost its reason for
being.[39]

Patrice Higonnet, arguing that the books were "clearly designed
not to be used, but to be seen," charges that the new Bibliothèque de

FIGURE 51
View from across
the Seine of the
French National
Library, 1998.

France is "a threat to French culture" and that it is "hostile to books,
hostile to people, hostile to the city of Paris." Perrault's design, "a
throwback to a once-popular modern style that has now become stale
and widely discredited," is a "librarian's nightmare," insofar as it "in-
tends to store the BN's collection in glass towers far removed from
the reading room, with obvious possible risks for the preservation
and delivery of books."[40]

Objections were also raised to the way Perrault handled the Tolbiac site, which at eighteen acres is more than twice the size of the St.
Pancras site of the new British Library. Considering that Perrault was
given "the last great open space in Paris,"[41] there was no particular
reason why he had to build Corbusian towers. In addition, his composition "resolutely turns its back on the Seine, which runs directly

in front of the site. Its reading rooms look instead onto a huge, sunken

inner courtyard the size of the Palais Royal, which will be planted to
simulate the forest of Fontainebleau. Instead of echoing the facing
building of the Ministry of Finance, which is in part built over the
Seine, Perrault's plan arrogantly refers only to itself. It will rest on a
huge, wind-swept slab of concrete the size of the Place de la Concorde. Its tiny, unmarked entrances will baffle visitors. Its glass walls
extend right down to the ground: there is no provision here for any
sort of interaction between pedestrian and building."[42]

Downey, who tries hard to be fair, describes the relationship between the library and its urban setting as follows:

> Situated on the less-affluent eastern edge of Paris, in a neighborhood
> cut off from the Seine by train tracks, barges, and light industry, the
> BNF is the focal point of the Seine Rive Gauche development. On over
> 321 acres, with 74 acres gained by building on top of the tracks, will be
> built 9.2 million sq ft of office space, 5.38 million sq ft of residential,
> and 3.76 million sq ft of commercial, all to create a gateway to the
> river front. From 1987 until the present, dozens of local and interna-
> tional architects submitted proposals for the area, until a single, fairly
> classic government master plan was selected. Its two key features—the
> creation of the broad Avenue de France along the southern limit of the
> site, and the development of the river front with walkways and park
> area to the north. Underway is the housing, arranged in traditional
> Parisian ilot (or small island) blocks, which give priority to the unified
> street façade, hiding ample interior courtyards. Grouped around the
> library and along the Seine, each housing block, designed in city
> competition, follows the master plan with little relation to the library.
> As Perrault points out, urban zone and library have two different
> clients—city and state—who didn't work together.[43]

The reviews are now in, and they are uniformly bad. Le Figaro's
architecture critic, for example, has referred to it as a giant folly,
"worthy of Kim Il Sung."[44] To make matters worse, the library has
been plagued by personnel problems: "The day after the inaugural
ceremonies, the staff at the existing National Library went on strike
to protest low wages and insufficient personnel to run the new complex."[45] Higonnet's conclusion is hard to resist: "In Perrault's building, form follows function only if it is understood that the function
is political."[46] The French National Library was conceived as one

of President Mitterrand's *grand projets,* and that is how it will be remembered, for better or worse.[47]

The new Bibliothèque de France has to go down as one of the great planning disasters of all time, one that makes the Thirty Years' War over the British Library seem like a rollicking good time. That said, it must be conceded that the Brits have jumped out to an early lead in the race for greatest planning disaster of the early twenty-first century.[48] It is the Millennium Dome, an idea that originated in John Major's Conservative cabinet—specifically, with Michael Heseltine[49]—but that was eagerly adopted by Tony Blair's culture minister, Peter Mandelson. The idea boiled down to celebrating the dawn of the year 2000 in a domed stadium—Richard Rogers Partnership, architects—on the Thames at Greenwich: "Twice the size of Britain's biggest football stadium, the dome will cost £758m to construct— £400m of which will come from the lottery, with the rest supposed to be provided by private sponsors and commercial sales. In other words, the British government will be spending the equivalent of 12% of its annual defence budget on a calendar event whose meaning and importance none of those involved can, it seems, convincingly summarise."[50] A somewhat incredulous Richard Jenkyns spelled it out in the pages of the *New York Review of Books:*

> *Peter Mandelson, Prime Minister Tony Blair's fixer, spin doctor in chief, and Minister for the Millennium, recently appeared before the members of a House of Commons select committee to tell them the purpose of the dome which the British government is currently building at Greenwich at a cost of one and a quarter billion dollars, the most lavish spending on the forthcoming year 2000 anywhere on the planet, although the costs of the Roman Catholic Church for its Jubilee year in Rome may come close to it. "It's a chance for people to think about their society, and hopefully improve it," he said. The chief attraction, he added, would be an interactive computer game called surfball.*
>
> *This is not to be the only delight. We are also promised the thrill of an enormous steel ball drawn to earth by a giant magnet, an intriguing prospect for those of us who had supposed that large metal objects were drawn to earth by gravity. In addition, according to the original plans, visitors would also be able to walk inside the model of a man, a hundred and fifty feet high, learning how the body works—or most of the body, since the man was to have no genital organs. The plan has*

since been modified: the figure will now recline, and be more than 300 feet long. It is not yet determined whether it will be male, female, or "genderless."

This is not the first time that New Labour has adopted this some-what unhappy symbolism. . . . Stephen Bayley, then creative director of the Millennium Exhibition, wrote in a recent article that it would contain "thought-provoking exhibits and experiences which blur the distinction between education and entertainment whose accumulative effect is to equip the individual visitor with liberating insights into the present and future condition of this world." Sounds fun, doesn't it? It also sounds extremely vague. On another occasion he told an inter-viewer, "I am the project's creative conscience. My task is to make sure the display is stimulating. If I have my way, it will be about sex, man-ners, music, cinema, architecture, sport, shopping." He has since flounced out of his job, claiming that Mandelson could not live up to these lofty standards. What we seem likely to get is a mixture of funfair and earnest didacticism. An eight-year-old boy has recently been appointed to advise the committee on its proposed exhibits.[51]

In short, a master plan was drawn up by the government and cor-porate leaders, including some of Britain's most celebrated architects, that will, to the extent that commoners can be lured to an ongoing "festival" extending from Kew to Greenwich, shape twenty-first-cen-tury London. Among the main attractions are the London Eye, or Millennium Wheel, and Sir Norman Foster's pedestrian bridge, a "blade of light" designed to take tourists across the Thames to the new Tate Modern, but closed as this is written due to its being exces-sively wobbly.[52] Thus, we have, in the new London, "the painful spec-tacle of courtiers trying to entertain their subjects. . . . In the past the royal court would not have worried about this. They'd have hired Handel to write music for their firework display and floated up and down the Thames on a royal barge, showing off. That wouldn't do in these democratic times with the people's prime minister."[53]

Drawing inspiration, perhaps, from the lessons of the British Li-brary, *The Economist* held out hope for a happy ending: "Mr Blair has castigated doubters, which would seem to include most of Britain's press, left and right, as 'cynics' who are 'rubbishing' an idea that will be the 'envy of the world'. Confounding the mockers, Britain's mil-lennium may yet prove to be a cracking success. Good parties are

FIGURE 52
The Millennium Dome under construction, Greenwich, England, 1998.

often the least expected ones."[54] But the dour Jenkyns, while noting that he has loved funfairs throughout his adult life, wondered "if this one may not be a little too childish for me."[55]

Early in 2000, after its "disastrous opening" on New Year's Eve, James Fenton found himself marooned at the Millennium Dome. "I had been alone in the Work Zone, alone in the Learning Zone and the Faith Zone and the Prayer Room. The Mind Zone and the Body Zone (where spermatozoa dance on film through an overhead vagina) had been sparsely populated." The problem derives from the fact that the Dome's "infotainment" is completely devoid of content: "Learning for life is key. We are living in a time of immense change. We are heading for gridlock. It pays to pray." Who needs a preachy funfair? Fenton pronounced it "a flop."[56] Its epitaph has been written by Andreas Whittam Smith: "The Dome will shortly close. It is now, officially, a disaster. And the enquiries into what happened have already begun. But I don't believe there is any great secret to be discovered. We already know the cause. It was hubris. Both Mr Major's government and Mr Blair's presumed too much."[57]

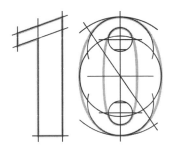

WITH ITS
"DOORS SET
WIDE TO
THE CITY"

JANE JACOBS'S *The Death and Life of Great American Cities* is widely recognized as one of the most influential books of our time. Its contribution consisted mainly in exposing the hubris of master planners and in directing attention toward such apparently prosaic questions as why cities need old buildings, mixed-use districts, and lively streets more than they need downtown funfairs. A successful urban district, Jacobs argues, "must serve more than one primary function; preferably more than two. These must insure the presence of people who go outdoors on different schedules and are in the place for different purposes, but who are able to use many facilities in common."[1] Ideally, the population density should be high, new construction should be respectful of old buildings, and residential and commercial uses should be interwoven, rather than mindlessly separated.

Given the putative influence of Jacobs's book, it is curious that certain aspects of *The Death and Life* have been, in the four decades since its publication, blithely and almost universally ignored. One of these is her indictment of urban universities for their "turf protection" proclivities. Jacobs cites by way of example the University of Chicago's policy—long abandoned, one trusts—of "loosing police dogs every night to patrol its campus and hold at bay any human being." An extreme case, to be sure. But Jacobs suggests that even when their policies are essentially benign, universities tend to undermine urban vitality by their mere physical presence; as monolithic, single-purpose districts, they generate the kinds of "border vacuums" that can "tear a city to tatters."[2] She claims that universities, at least at the time she was writing in the early 1960s, were oblivious to such issues: "Big universities, so far as I can see, have given no thought or imagination to the unique establishments they are. Typically they either pretend to be cloistered or countrified places, nostalgically denying their transplantation, or else they pretend to be office buildings. (Of course they are neither.)"[3]

It is hard to account for the neglect of this issue. A cynic might suspect that the contemporary university's robust appetite for land, money, and power has had a chilling effect on academic scholarship. But it could also be that when it comes to university grounds,[4] Americans have simply lost the ability to imagine alternatives to a small handful of dominant archetypes, most of which—the distinctive Oxford cloister, Mr. Jefferson's "academical village" in Charlottesville, Olmsted's Stanford, or the Radiant City campuses of our own day— aspire to be compounds distinct from, rather than integrated into, their host cities. Thus, it may be useful by way of contrast to examine the experience of the University of St. Andrews, a nearly six-hundred-year-old Scottish university that claims not to have a campus at all, but to be virtually synonymous with its town.[5]

When Christianity was spreading into the British Isles, its toehold in the Kingdom of Fife was Kilrymont, a fishing village on the North Sea between the Firth of Forth and the Firth of Tay. Physically, the town that was to become the Scottish equivalent of Canterbury[6] was a simple little oval with three streets running east and west, "converging upon the cathedral, and connected with one another by narrow wynds [i.e., alleys].[7] Southgait, Merkatgait, and Northgait—now anglicized to South Street, Market Street, and North Street—were the broad thoroughfares; and a fourth, Swallowgait, commenced near the castle."[8]

Kilrymont first appears in the historical record at the end of the sixth century when an Irish missionary known as St. Regulus, or St. Rule, came to convert the local heathens. The good St. Rule was not, alas, destined to become the patron saint of Scotland, for "at some time between the year 732 and the year 761, Bishop Acca, a Northumbrian exiled from Hexham, fled northward to the Picts of Fife with his great treasure: an arm-bone and some finger-bones of St. Andrew the Apostle."[9] The Culdees of Kilrymont assumed responsibility for the holy relics, and by the twelfth century the town had been rechristened St. Andrews.

Spiritually, the university that was founded in 1411, and recognized by papal bull in 1413, was, according to R. G. Cant, little more than an extension of the monastery that stood upon the "Kirkhill" overlooking the sea.[10] But, as Alan B. Cobban has argued, the development of the medieval university went hand in hand with the urbanization of European society.[11] And so it is significant that the first college, St. Salvator's, was built not adjacent to the church compound, but in town, it being the stated intention of Bishop James Kennedy that St. Salvator's Church be "in the very forefront of his college, with its doors set wide to the city."[12] The whole point was "inviting the townsfolk in, for this was no mere college chapel, but a splendid house of God where all might take the sacraments and listen to the preaching of the masters and learn how Reason confirms Faith."[13]

This integrationist approach to university architecture may reflect the influence in Scotland of the continental university—the University of Paris in particular. Paul Venable Turner explains that, in contradistinction to the English concept of universities as "communities in themselves" that tended to turn their backs to the city, Scottish universities were "more urban in character, or at least less dominant over their urban environments. Partly as a result of this (and also because of a greater reliance on European models of education), the Scottish schools were less collegiate than the English, in that the English ideal of a tightly regulated college community did not hold sway. Scottish students were freer to live in town rather than at their colleges, and in this way their lives were more like those of continental students. Architecturally, this meant that fewer collegiate buildings were required."[14]

FIGURE 53
The town of St. Salvator's (left), a college with its doors set wide to the town, as seen from College Street, St. Andrews, Scotland.

The town into which the university insinuated itself would originally have been built of wood. "The early tenements of St. Andrews," Kirk writes, "were mean enough—timbered dwellings, or wattle and daub. Not until wood became scarcer in Fife, and cathedral and monastic buildings provided a convenient quarry, did St. Andrews complete its present aspect of sturdy stone houses."[15] The oldest structure in town is St. Rule's Tower, the campanile of an ancient church—later replaced by a cathedral, the eerie ruins of which live on as the main attraction on the Kirkhill. Other surviving antiquities include a ponderous castle; several city gates, especially the West Port; the market at the east end of Market Street; the quadrangle at St. Mary's College; Blackfriar's Chapel; and the precinct known as Louden's Close, where "the cobbled edging, wall lamp, pantiled roof and dormers all capture the character of the old town."[16]

Other colleges followed after St. Salvator's. St. Leonard's, an "appendage of the Priory," was a going concern by the mid-sixteenth century.[17] St. Mary's College was founded by Archbishop James Beaton in 1538. The colleges helped to ground the university in material reality—medieval universities tended toward the ethereal—but they detracted from any sense of the whole university.[18]

Early on, Scotland's King James I attempted to move the university to his intended capital at Perth, an idea that was to be disinterred later on, as we shall see. But at the time of James's death in 1437, the burgh was "at the apex of its prosperity. A dense population dwelt in the three principal streets and the wynds and closes; there was a Tolbooth [a town hall with customs offices and prison cells], and a Cross in the market square, and a Fish Cross near the cathedral end of North Street, where the fisherfolk congregated. Vessels like Bishop Kennedy's great barge called St. Salvator lay alongside St. Andrews quay. Several fortified gates protected the entrances to the town."[19] The tolbooth was destined to be the place where heretics were executed by officials who simultaneously exercised ecclesiastical and civil authority. Not that this succeeded in suppressing dissent. In fact, St. Leonard's College became so receptive to Reformed doctrines in the early sixteenth century that "'to drink of St. Leonard's well' became a synonym for the adoption of Protestantism in St. Andrews and beyond."[20] No one seems to know for sure whether John Knox studied at the university, but it was at Holy Trinity Church—the *town* kirk—that Knox argued his case against orthodoxy. By 1560, Protestantism had triumphed, and if it is possible to capture in a single image the essence of the Reformation in Scotland, it would be an urban image: Knox's agitated parishioners setting out through the streets of St. Andrews to sack the cathedral.

The little Roman Catholic university was by no means ruined by

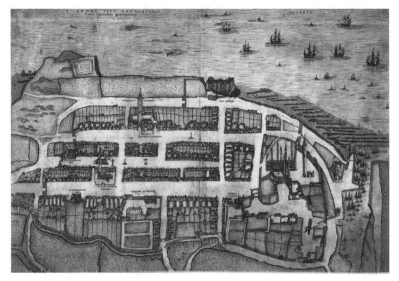

FIGURE 54

Bird's-eye view of St. Andrews, circa 1580. Close inspection of this scene reveals the religious compound on the Kirkhill overlooking the harbor (on the right, or east side of town), including the cathedral, St. Rule's Tower, and adjacent priories. Other landmarks include the castle (center, top), tolbooth and town kirk (both near the market, town center), Dominican and Franciscan friaries (west side of town), and three colleges: St. Salvator's (on North Street), St. Leonard's, and St. Mary's.

the Reformation.[21] By the time of the royal visit of 1617, the great strength of the university "lay in the fact that St. Andrews had once more become the ecclesiastical capital of Scotland, and by express royal injunction was also to be the chief centre of the educational life of the country."[22] Interestingly, one consequence of the Reformation was that town and gown were now more apt to pray together, rather than separately: "Ever since the Reformation, the old practice of corporate worship had been abandoned in the colleges. Morning and evening prayers were still held, but for public worship the usual practice was for St Salvator's and St Mary's to attend at the Town Kirk, and although the members of St Leonard's still worshipped in their own College Kirk, they did so because it was also their parish church."[23]

During the crisis of 1638, "both university and town were persuaded, with few exceptions, to sign 'the National Covenant.'" The subsequent reforms dictated that students "were to wear their gowns both in college and in the streets. For ordinary conversation Latin was still prescribed. 'Lawfull recreations,' such as golf and archery, were encouraged, but dicing and 'carding' prohibited." It was further decreed that the regents could marry, the result being that eventually "most of the masters married and set up house in the town, an arrangement which had a great deal to do with the eventual abandonment of the residential system as a whole."[24]

The Revolution of 1689 had lasting, almost entirely negative consequences for St. Andrews. The university had joined the Scottish bishops in issuing "a very laudatory Address to the King (James VII) just before William of Orange landed in England." As a consequence, "one of the first acts" of the new regime in 1690 was "to descend on St. Andrews and purge the university of almost all its senior members." The archbishopric and the ecclesiastical primacy of the city were swept away once and for all, and after that the university enjoyed "no preferential treatment such as it had enjoyed under both Reformers and Covenanters."[25]

Relations between town and university deteriorated despite the mutual enjoyment of certain sports.[26] A particularly revealing incident occurred in 1690 in the aftermath of an assault on a townsman by a university servant. In the ensuing ruckus, the chancellor, a gentleman named John, Earl of Tullibardine, exhumed James I's radical proposal of removing the university to Perth. Tullibardine's brief for the move was a litany not of Perth's virtues, but of St. Andrews's vices. Cant's is a classic account of town-gown paranoia: "Rarely has there been a more libellous attack on any city. The place was in a remote corner. Victuals were dear, other necessities unobtainable. The water supply was inadequate and unwholesome, the air 'thin and piercing,' so that old men coming to the place were 'instantly cut off.' The young fared no better, for epidemics throve on the herring guts and middens which littered the streets. Worst of all, the inhabitants were brutish, quarrelsome, and unscrupulous, with a particular aversion to learning and learned men."[27] The most remarkable part of this story is that although Perth made "a generous offer," it was finally rejected by the St. Andrews masters, who apparently expected Perth not merely to provide commensurate facilities but to build "an exact reproduction, of the traditional form of the university in St Andrews"[28]—which, considering the physical integration of colleges and town, was tantamount to asking for a new *Perth*.

During the Jacobite rising of 1715,[29] the university was "more than a little mixed in its loyalties. St Leonard's was regarded by good Whigs as a particular hotbed of sedition."[30] The Hanoverian regime responded predictably: while the universities in Edinburgh and Glasgow were treated to government largess, the neglected St. Andrews was left to stagger on alone. Later in the century, Dr. Johnson wrote in his *Journey to the Western Islands of Scotland* that in St. Andrews he had found "an university declining, a college alienated, and a church profaned and hastening to the ground."[31] The "alienated" college was St. Leonard's: "In 1754, the detached portion of the college site in the Priory was feued to William Imrie of Dunmoor, and in 1772 the main site, with the college buildings and gardens, was sold by the professors of the United College to one of their colleagues (Robert Watson) for £200 and a yearly feu-duty of £10. Professor Watson may well have thought it a bargain. It is not often that one can buy a complete college for so little."[32]

By the late eighteenth century, the masters of the university "are found complaining that although rooms in college had recently been repaired and fitted up for use by students, most of them lodged in the town."[33] When common tables were given up in 1820,[34] students had no choice but to resort to the private sector; this resulted in an institution called "the bunks." "It may be," concludes the ever-cautious Cant, "that the students were better off in private lodgings."[35]

The town itself "sank nearly into its grave during the Enlightenment, being reduced at one time to a sixth of its medieval population; its university was drained of spirit and substance; trade dwindled; and fishing disappeared for thirty-five years."[36] Various pageants and civic rituals, vestiges of medievalism that had once symbolized the sharing of a common life, gradually dissolved. "The archers' matches at the Bow Butts, with their processions and their Silver Arrow,"[37] for instance, were abandoned in 1754.[38] By 1807, even the annual Cat Race seems to have lost its charm.[39] Later in the nineteenth century, the university felt it had to act to suppress the Kate Kennedy celebration, a raucous affair that, because it took place in the streets of town, was deemed by the authorities "as much a public scandal as an academic misdemeanour."[40]

That town and gown shared an enthusiasm for "gowff" is evident from the fact that the university had always specifically exempted it, "along with archery from any list of prohibited pastimes."[41] This was fortuitous, since the patronage of William IV was to transform the humble golf club founded in the middle of the eighteenth century, "at the nadir of St. Andrews' fortunes,"[42] into the storied Royal and Ancient. The town expanded and added some graceful "Georgian" touches. Growth proved a mixed blessing, however, unleashing as it did Major Hugh Lyon Playfair, who, beginning with his appointment to the office of provost in 1842, displayed an astonishing "proclivity for dinging things down."[43] According to Kirk, Playfair knocked off Gothic porches, paved cobblestone streets, demolished the ancient Tolbooth, "flung down" the medieval arch in front of St. Salvator's Church, cleared the "fisherfolk's quarter," and "Victorianized" the names of streets and alleys.[44] Playfair seems to have been the Robert Moses of Scotland.

A tourism boom that began in earnest in the 1880s set the stage for the revival of the university, which had been legally reinvented by an 1858 act of Parliament. Still, as late in the day as 1876 there were no more than 130 students enrolled. Various schemes were advanced with a view to "reviving collegiate residence and so attracting back to St Andrews the sons of 'persons of the higher ranks' of Scottish society who had formerly come there but who now went instead to the two ancient English universities."[45] Two major innovations[46] were to contribute much to the university's revival. One was the admission of women, at first through a certificate scheme known as the L.L.A. (Lady Literate in Arts). The other was the foundation of University College, Dundee (Queen's College), for the purpose of offering professional training in a number of fields, including medicine.[47] Yet again, St. Andrews University was shedding its skin. By the early years of the twentieth century, the university was as heavily dependent on the munificence of Andrew Carnegie and the British Parliament as it had ever been on the Roman Catholic Church or the Scottish Crown.

Cant credits James Colquhoun Irvine, principal between 1921 and 1952, with leaving the university "very much stronger than he found it,"[48] although Sir Kenneth Dover, the great classicist, reports in his notorious memoirs that many regarded Irvine as the agent of virulent "anglification."[49] In any event, a number of dormitories were constructed, and by the early 1950s the student body exceeded two thousand, about eight hundred of whom were enrolled at Dundee. The relationship between the two campuses was never satisfactorily resolved, however, which led inexorably to the creation, in 1967, of a separate University of Dundee. It is probably not a coincidence that the loss of its Dundee college occurred at the precise moment that the university embarked on "a building programme of unprecedented scale and comprehension" on the edge of St. Andrews.[50]

Most of this construction took place on the North Haugh, a sixty-seven-acre parcel near the Old Course. Mathematics, physics, and chemistry were accommodated in new buildings at this location, along with an ill-starred coed dormitory, Andrew Melville Hall.[51] The North Haugh is, alas, a campus, a low-density area where none but students dwell. There is no commercial activity in this part of town, no industrial activity. While it is not unattractive, it would be hard to find a better example of what Jacobs calls the Great Blight of Dullness.[52] More to the point, the North Haugh represents a repudiation of Bishop Kennedy's policy of having the university's doors set wide to the city—a policy that helps to account not only for the university's survival, but also for some of the vicissitudes of its checkered past. Today, about two-thirds of St. Andrews students live in residence halls, many of them on the North Haugh.[53]

This modernist campus, to put it in terms imported into the field of urban planning from mathematical set theory, threatens to render St. Andrews more of a tree and less of a semi-lattice. Christopher Alexander has explained that a tree is an oversimplified structure where "no piece of any unit is ever connected to other units, except through the medium of that unit as a whole." Alexander perceives that the isolated university campus is one result of tree-like thinking, where a line is drawn in the city so that "everything within the boundary is university, and everything outside is non-university."[54] Alexander argues that the more natural alternative[55] is the intricate overlapping pattern of the semi-lattice:

Take Cambridge University, for instance. At certain points Trinity Street is physically almost indistinguishable from Trinity College. One pedestrian crossover in the street is literally part of the college. The buildings on the street, though they contain stores and coffee shops and banks at ground level, contain undergraduates' rooms in their upper stories. In many cases the actual fabric of the street buildings melts into the fabric of the old college buildings so that one cannot be altered without the other.

There will always be many systems of activity where university life and city life overlap: pub-crawling, coffee-drinking, the movies, walking from place to place. In some senses whole departments may be actively involved in the life of the city's inhabitants (the hospital-cum-medical school is an example). In Cambridge, a natural city where

WITH ITS "DOORS SET WIDE TO THE CITY"

university and city have grown together gradually, the physical units overlap because they are the physical residues of city systems and university systems which overlap.[56]

Sir Kenneth Dover has observed that town-gown relations have been notably healthier at St. Andrews than at Oxford; at the former institution, the "characteristically Scottish spirit of courteous and humorous egalitarianism dissolved the glue which at Oxford had kept class boundaries in place." Elaborating, Dover notes the "more relaxed ambience (and lower standards, if you will) of St. Andrews" and contrasts the exclusivity of High Table at Balliol College, Oxford, with the St. Andrews Staff Club, of which "not only university staff" but also their spouses are "members on an equal footing."[57] While Dover argues that the different cultures of Oxford and St. Andrews reflect differences in national character, one wonders whether the whole truth has something to do with the contrasting physical plants—that is, with exclusionist proclivities reflected in or reinforced by Oxford's introspective cloisters and with the more permeable boundaries of the San Andrean "semi-lattice."

And yet, all things considered, the University of St. Andrews must be considered something of a "lost cause,"[58] failing as it did first as a bulwark of Roman Catholic orthodoxy,[59] and then again in its Jacobite incarnation as the Scottish Oxford.[60] The university may yet fail as a British institution, as all Scotland is being put to new tests in the Age of Devolution.[61] Perhaps it can capitalize on Prince William's stated intention of matriculating at St. Andrews in the fall of 2001; the admissions office reports a surge of applications by American women.

Any institution that can manage to survive nearly six hundred years of turmoil and grief must have something going for it. That something has often been the town with which St. Andrews University has been so closely identified. Having its "doors set wide to the city"— architecturally at St. Salvator's Church, doctrinally at St. Leonard's— might have helped the university escape ruin during the Reformation. Similarly, after the Restoration, the demise of corporate worship in the colleges, in favor of attendance at the town kirk, might have had something to do with the fact that in its daily life the university was largely unaffected by "whether Episcopacy or Presbyterianism was in the ascendant."[62] As for the aborted move to Perth after the Glorious Revolution, that strange episode may be a measure of the university's lingering affection for the old burgh. For, notwithstanding all the complaints about anti-intellectualism and herring guts, the masters' absurd notion that their suitors in Perth ought to have been willing to duplicate the St. Andrews physical plant is simply inexplicable save in terms of deep-seated loyalty to place. On the other hand, the same stodginess might have been at the root of the twentieth-century university's failure to attend to the proper development of University College, Dundee. A genuine extension of the university to Dundee seems to have been as unthinkable in the twentieth century as transporting it to Perth had been two centuries and more earlier.

As for the town, prior to its becoming the Mecca of golf, St. Andrews had little going for it aside from fishing and higher education. It is clear in retrospect that one of the town's luckiest breaks was having to endure a two-hundred-year-long economic depression, one of the consequences of which was that there was so much medieval detritus remaining in St. Andrews when it awoke from its torpor early in the nineteenth century that not even Major Playfair could ding it all down. A ready supply of old buildings is a hidden benefit of long-term economic stagnation, for, as Jacobs has taught us, aged buildings diversify the housing stock, invite diverse uses, and even contribute an element of the picturesque; in all these ways, aged buildings engender urban vitality.

FIGURE 55
Pier walk, St. Andrews, with view of St. Rule's Tower (left) and the ruined cathedral on the Kirkhill. Courtesy of the University of St. Andrews.

In the lively streets of stony St. Andrews, there is a kind of dance that goes on—Jacobs's "ballet of the streets," featuring ordinary people running errands, tourists gawking at the sights, students shuffling off to class, professors scurrying to the bank or pub. Activity may be spawned at various times by churches, schools, health care facilities, a theater, a cinema, and countless restaurants and bars. Thanks largely to the welfare state, there is no part of the town that is particularly splendid, but neither is there urban squalor. There are traces of a lingering provincialism: St. Andrews has a Woolworth's, but no Benetton; at the Chinese restaurant, entrees are served with a choice of steamed rice or "chips." It is not uncommon on North Street to see a golfer swaggering toward the Old Course, bag slung over the shoulder and cleats clattering on the cobbles. There is even some industrial activity—golf-related, for the most part—"pleasantly tucked away in closes and behind houses."[63] Certain ceremonies draw university students and faculty members into the streets. After church services on Sundays, for example, there occurs at the harbor a ritual in which university students, their red gowns billowing in the wind, waves crashing on both sides, precariously negotiate a long, narrow pier extending into the sea.[64]

No one could possibly choreograph such vitality, although, as we have seen, there are ways of setting the stage architecturally and seeing to it that urban space is "open-minded," rather than "single-minded." As Andres Duany and Elizabeth Plater-Zyberk could testify on the basis of their experience at Seaside, a seacoast is a precious natural resource. A golf course, too, can be an urban amenity. But it helps to have a university, particularly one that does not aspire to be a fortress, a cloister, a City Beautiful, or a Radiant City, and one that is prepared to share a common fate with its town.

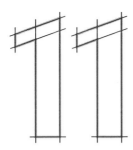

SIMCITY AND OUR TOWN

YEARS AGO, WHEN ROBERT CARO'S magisterial biography of Robert Moses was first published, I remember reading it with mixed emotions.[1] On the one hand, it reinforced every lesson I tried to convey in my course on urban politics. On the other hand, it taught those lessons so vividly, in a way that was so engaging, that it made my conventional textbooks and lectures seem hopelessly abstract and lifeless. There was only one thing to do: throw out the old texts and make *The Power Broker* the centerpiece of the course. I redesigned everything from scratch.

Many years later, in the early 1990s, one of the students in my course on the history of city planning ambled up after class. "Have you ever played sin city?" I thought I heard him ask. He quickly set me straight—"*Sim-City*" he said, enunciating carefully—and then offered a demonstration, during which I was reminded of Caro's book. Here we go again, I thought to myself as I purchased the Windows version of the game.[2]

SimCity, created by Will Wright, is described in the user's manual as a computer simulation that allows you "to design, manage and maintain the city of your dreams."[3] The point of the simulation is to duplicate, by massive and virtually instantaneous numbers-crunching, the real world of urban politics in which land-use decisions are made, as well as the results of those decisions. As Paul Starr has put it, the "hidden curriculum" of SimCity is "the management of complex systems based on 'intelligent scanning' of streams of constantly changing information."[4]

SimCity is all about land use, so it is significant that zoning is the first and most fundamental act. Land is designated for either residential, commercial, or industrial use; actual construction is done on behalf of the residents—the "Sims"—by the software. While the zones are fairly small, there is an incentive—if only because it requires less in the way of tedious mouse-clicking—to clump zones together, making for large, single-use districts. While this may quite accurately simulate conditions in real cities, and while zoning was considered a "progressive" concept through most of the twentieth century, it frustrates the player whose idea of urban utopia consists of the small, mixed-use areas that so many of us have enjoyed in Europe and in the pages of Lewis Mumford, Jane Jacobs and J. B. Jackson. Jacobs, as we have seen, argues that healthy urban tissue is characterized by density, complexity, and adaptability and that zoning is anathema to all three. Zoning, according to Jacobs, leads naturally to Cyclone fences, security gatehouses, "redlining," and all the other accoutrements of social stratification and segregation (by class if not by race). The ubiquity of zoning and bulldozing in SimCity bespeaks a simplistic (albeit quintessentially American) approach to public works in general and urban renewal in particular.

In addition, the Sims share America's love affair with the automobile. In fact, the Sims are adamant on the subject of roads, and will use them regardless of their origins or destinations. And the software recognizes a principle that Jacobs lamented years ago: if you build it, they will drive. As Johnny L. Wilson explains, "Even a casual SimCity player will soon learn what urban planners and traffic engineers have been discovering for the last few decades—the strategy of widening existing streets and building new major and secondary highways is not a viable solution to traffic congestion. All this street widening and major construction simply serves to invite even more traffic onto the expanded street network."[5]

If the automobile is endemic to SimCity, it is not the mode of transportation preferred by the creators of the simulation; as in real life, the citizens are car-happy and the planners are obsessed with mass transit. Mark Schone quotes Will Wright to the effect that the game is based largely on a few straightforward premises, such as "mass transit is good."[6] It doesn't take long for players to recognize this and to respond by laying track from the outset. This might be a good strategy for playing the game, but it is completely unrealistic. In the real world, and particularly in the United States, subways and metro systems have been built by mature cities, and thus—to the extent that right-of-ways have had to be acquired and buildings demolished to make way for mass transit—at great expense. But only mature cities have the *need* for mass transit.

SimCity has many virtues, not least of which is that it is fun to play—and that may be why many commentators have been impressed by its pedagogical potential. Most of the problems associated with the original SimCity—those, at least, that were in principle soluble—have been addressed by its several upgrades. In SimCity 2000, for example, zoning became far more subtle, allowing for some mixture of uses. You can build bus depots and expressways. You can found a college, a zoo, or a marina. Municipal finance is more sophisticated, involving the floating of bond issues and requiring the payment of interest. You can legalize gambling, if you like, provided you can get it through the city council. You can build a military base, tunnels, elementary schools—even one of Paolo Soleri's "arcologies." You can pass ordinances that address the quality of life in various ways. SimCity 2000 has its own climate, and weather reports can be monitored in the newspapers: "The different papers (once your city is big enough to have more than one) will have different angles on stories, so you may want to read through more than one."[7] In sum, to quote a reviewer who admits to being "addicted" to the original game:

SimCity 2000 *has enough new features to justify readdiction. Now, time itself becomes a factor: As new technologies, such as desalinization and fusion power, are invented, the tools to use them pop up in your toolbox. The terrain (completely editable) has hills and valleys, and you can zoom into and completely rotate the 3-D model of your city. You have to dig in the dirt to lay pipes and construct subways. Your constituent Sims demand education and health care, and their IQs drop if you don't build them enough libraries and museums. If they don't like where you laid the train tracks, the Sims will drive cars; if they don't like your judgment (or lack of it), they'll vote you out of office or move to a neighboring city.*[8]

One extraordinarily realistic feature of SimCity is the way it approximates the limits of political success in the real world. Novice SimCity players often perform as if the simulation were a race against the clock. It's not, although time marches on, as in real life. Nor is it a game that can be "won" in the way that one wins chess or Monopoly. Positive reinforcement comes in the form of winning the keys to the city, a statue, or a ticker-tape parade, which is achieved mainly by maintaining modest levels of security and prosperity[9] and by competent damage control. The mayor of SimCity, like New Haven's famous Mayor Lee, must be content with victories that are far from total.[10] And even unqualified success raises the question of what one does for an encore. Does one create a new SimCity and start all over again? Does one graduate to SimEarth or The Sims—and is that really a higher office? Or does one continue to play at being mayor until one finally manages to fail, à la Teddy Kollek? In the real world, too, political success is elusive and contingent.

SimCity is far from perfect. For one thing, it is maddeningly complex. As Schone has written with reference to SimCity 2000, "programming any more real-world variables into the simulation might make it unplayable."[11] There continues to be a "bias against mixed use development";[12] the mayor is still unrealistically omnipotent; some social issues are dealt with in a hopelessly simplistic manner. Crime rates, for instance, instantly plummet with the construction of a police station. Would that it were that simple. Moreover, there are problems inherent in both versions of the simulation that would be far more difficult to address than any of these, and that may severely limit its pedagogical potential. Of these, I wish to focus on three: SimCity's exaggeration of the role of state planning in urban development, its neglect of one of the most salient features of American urban life (race), and its underestimation of the *social*—as opposed to the *material*—dimensions of city life.

In general, SimCity overstates the role of the state; it is hard, for example, to imagine a more naïvely statist proposition than that the mayor, rather than the developer, should be the star of the show. More specifically, the role of the state in managing urban growth is exaggerated. As Schone has put it, "Wright's toy [i.e., SimCity] overstates the importance of urban planners and underplays the role of developers, pressure groups, preservationists, etc."[13] It is undeniable that growth is more orderly when strict controls are placed on private enterprise. In Europe, as we saw in chapter 8, the New Towns movement has guaranteed the success of certain communities, thus allowing them the luxury of early investment in expensive infrastructure. At Evry New Town, for example, the train station seemed completely out of scale during the early years of development—a colossus in a Lilliputian world. Two decades of state-planned and -subsidized development has since justified the original scale of the project; Evry New Town has grown into its train station the way that a puppy grows into its paws.

Planning ahead *is* in many ways economical. If the success of your city is guaranteed by the state, why not bury the power lines as soon as the site has been cleared from forest or desert, or reclaimed from the sea? Why not just build a nuclear power plant instead of starting with coal? Another case in point—one in which Will Wright might find inspiration—is the Pneumatic Refuse Conveying (PRC) System that has been implemented in several of the new planned communities outside Stockholm.[14] Of course, the builders of real American cities—cities that can fail—have not generally had the luxury of burying their power lines or laying track for their light rail systems at the moment when it would have been most economical. For in the United States, the success of particular cities has seldom been assured. At all stages of the life cycle, our cities are subject to market forces and engaged in heated competition with their municipal rivals. Whether one views this as the rigors of healthy capitalism or dysfunctional chaos, the consequences are on display everywhere. The American landscape is littered with failed New Jerusalems and Zion Cities. Every Kansas City has its Leavenworth; every Chicago, a Superior, Wisconsin;[15] every Tower City, a lakefront union depot.

Mark Schone is surely right to note that the single most curious, and least realistic, feature of SimCity is the absence of race and ethnicity, which he attributes to Will Wright's wish to "avoid controversy"[16]—a profitable instinct for a capitalist. But the result is that the player for whom rich cultural diversity, the economic equality of the races, and no discernible pattern of residential segregation by race or ethnic group are the sine qua non of utopia would play SimCity in vain. Since the Sims come in only one racial flavor, there can be no map to show the distribution of different races through the city, and no way to correlate race with income; by definition, there can be no race riots among the canned disaster scenarios.[17]

It is not clear, however, that the absence of race actually impairs SimCity as a simulator of urban development, and that is interesting in and of itself. Schone asserts that the racial homogeneity of the Sims means that it is impossible to simulate "inner-city decay," which he characterizes as a function of "white flight" exacerbated by "city-hating suburbanites" and Reaganomics, an ideology in which "cities didn't matter."[18] Maybe. But the hypothesis built into SimCity—in which inner cities can, but will not inevitably, decay—is that when government spends more than it takes in, taxes have to rise, which means that investment declines and the tax base erodes, resulting in increasing joblessness and added pressure on government. People without choices—meaning people without skills—end up being concentrated in those few places where they can afford to dwell. Those places become "blighted"; in my version of the original SimCity, blight appears as a rust-colored smudge that spreads like crabgrass. It's a vicious circle, fully accounted for in SimCity without any reference to race or racism. The full implications of the political incorrectness of this aspect of the computer simulation have not gone unnoticed by those who believe racism is the primary engine of inner-city decay. Schone, for example, shrewdly observes that at some point in the 1970s, causal modeling was abandoned by the planning profession because "they didn't like what the sophisticated models told them."[19]

FIGURE 56
A tour guide demonstrates the Pneumatic Refuse Conveying System in a new town outside Stockholm.

My hunch is that many professional city planners, and probably many scholars as well, came to urban studies out of an interest in architecture and with more or less well developed aesthetic sensibilities. For most of us, utopian yearnings manifest themselves in visions of buildings; as Jane Jacobs puts it, cities are "thoroughly physical places." To be sure, Plato is persuasive when he demonstrates that building a city—if only mentally, or linguistically—requires asking about the meaning of justice and the good. But for most of us, any ideal city we might conjure up in our fevered imagination—Eutopia, Amaurote, Erewhon, Oz, or Broadacre City—is conceived as a built environment, much more so than as a set of laws, customs, or socioeconomic structures. The power of these architectonic visions is such that we are easily led to believe that judgments about cities, and about whether they are good or bad places to live, are essentially aesthetic. But our estimate of imperial Rome should be based as much on the character of Caligula as on the formal properties of the Forum of Trajan. And Renaissance Florence on Savonarola no less than on Brunelleschi. To anyone who would suggest that in the postmodern age we have outgrown simple-minded architectural determinism, I would cite J. B. Jackson's account of downtown "revitalization" in Dallas, Houston, Denver, Oklahoma City, and Little Rock: "I have the feeling that this expensive facelifting affected the rest of the city very little. Architecture buffs enjoy the results, and so do tourists, but if you are a resident of the city or merely on your way to work, you see the display in a different light."[20] There are not a few among us who, despite Jane Jacobs's powerful indictment of "Radiant Garden City Beautiful," still believe that a city *is* its skyline.[21]

Cities are more than just bricks and mortar, and they are more than just bricks and mortar over time. Lewis Mumford made this point brilliantly in his treatment of the medieval city, which was, he contended, "above all things, in its busy turbulent life, a stage for the ceremonies of the Church."[22] We have seen that remnants of this survive here and there—for example, in the "pier walk" at St. Andrews. But the point also is applicable—*mutatis mutandis*—to the modern American city. For example, Witold Rybczynski reminds us that our sense of place, our "actual sense of physical belonging, is not mainly conditioned by architecture and urban design but by shared daily, weekly, or seasonal events, that is, by a sense of time. . . . Spaces are identified not so much by their physical features as by the events that take—and took—place in them. One might say, following Jackson, that the homecoming game matters more than the stadium, the parade more than the street, the fair more than the fairground."[23] Of course, it is not always so easy to untangle the meaning of these events from architectural evidence—and that is particularly so in the case of ancient or remote civilizations, as we saw in chapters 1 and 2. Nor would it be fair for our descendants to judge us on the basis of the archaeological evidence—Styrofoam and all—alone. The point has been made famously, and hilariously, in David Macaulay's *Motel of the Mysteries.*[24]

In addition to its "edifice complex," SimCity assumes that when people set out to build their dream city, they have the option of starting from scratch. But in the real world, as we have repeatedly seen, the city is in certain respects immaterial. It is a cultural, even spiritual construct, and we do not have the option of jettisoning our cultural inheritance by just clicking on a tabula rasa icon. In fact, I would be inclined to argue that great urban space begins with a willingness to accommodate, rather than obliterate, the cultural detritus of the past. I would argue, too, that this is the secret of some of the world's most beautiful and successful cities, and that Lewis Mumford was right to insist on the power of aesthetics—that cities can, after all, be works of art. Even Jacobs concedes as much, whether she knows it or not, in her moving account of the ballet of the streets.

Florence, to take the case that Mumford cites first in his diatribe about Jacobs's "schoolgirl howlers," ordinarily is thought of as a Renaissance city. Indeed, most of us are first drawn to Tuscany by the glories of the Quattrocento. Our tour guides reinforce that prejudice by directing us to the famous works of the Renaissance masters—the paintings and works of sculpture in the Uffizi and the Bargello, and also works of architecture, such as Brunelleschi's dome. Eventually, we discover inspired cityscape, such as the Piazza della Santissima Annunziata. But somewhere along the way we learn that it was the *medieval* Commune that "laid down the precise relationship that was to exist between public and private spaces, regulating the streets and placing limits on the height and projection of the houses."[25] Sooner or later, we figure out that the greatness of the Renaissance masters has something to do with the fact that their work was not in any sense a repudiation of medieval form, but rather an extension of it. And we are reminded of a lesson Mumford tried valiantly to teach us: "Not merely were the ambitions of the new urban planners of the sixteenth century still limited and modest: it was this very modesty that brought out what was best in the old order as well as the new."[26] Eventually, we come to cherish Florence as a palimpsest, a medieval city constructed on an ancient grid—the Romans called the town Florentia—with Renaissance adornments, some of which refuse to conform to the chronology that we imbibed from Janson or Gombrich. That in turn reminds us of Mumford's objections to the nomenclature of the Renaissance: "To call these fifteenth- and sixteenth-century changes a 're-birth' is to misunderstand both the impulse and the result. We are dealing rather with a kind of geometric clarification of the spirit that had been going on for many generations, and that sought, not a wholesale change, but a piecemeal modification of the historic city."[27]

A good example is the Loggia dei Lanzi, opposite the Palazzo della

Signoria and part of the frame surrounding the city's most important public square. Our *Blue Guide* tells us that it is a "graceful structure" used by a guard of German Lancers in their public ceremonies, and that within it we may now find important works of sculpture, such as Benvenuto Cellini's famous Perseus with the head of Medusa. We read that with its "three lofty semicircular arches," it "anticipates the Renaissance."[28] But it is Mumford who brings the point home: "The Loggia dei Lanzi in Florence . . . was completed in 1387. Though by calendar it belongs to the Middle Ages, in form it is definitely 'renascence'—open, serene, with its three round arches and its classic columns. A rebirth? No: a purification, an attempt to get back to the starting point, as a painter might paint over the smudged colors and confused forms of his canvas to recover the lines of his original sketch." This is why Mumford insists that "there is no renascence city," only "patches of renascence order."[29] And it is why R. W. B. Lewis can with justice assert that the Loggia dei Lanzi "became what Leon Battista Alberti . . . would say every loggia should be: the chief adornment of the piazza, which is in turn the chief adornment of the city."[30]

An even better example is the church called Santa Maria Novella. Again, we can learn from our *Blue Guide* that it is a cruciform church in the basilica style, meaning that there are side aisles, each with its own roof, flanking the nave, which is surmounted by a higher gable roof. The structure itself was complete by 1348, but work on the facade, which was begun around 1300, languished for a century and a half. In 1456 the project was continued by Giovani Bertini, working from designs by Alberti. In characteristic *Blue Guide* deadpan, we are informed that "the use of scrolls to connect the nave and aisles was an innovation that has since become familiar through its excessive employment in Baroque buildings."[31]

Far more important than the point about baroque excess is the fact that Alberti, famous as a student of classical antiquity, was not overweening in his ambitions. The Dominicans had left him with some Romanesque arches, and also with some of the pointed arches associated with the more recent French style, known derisively as the Gothic. In building materials, too, Santa Maria Novella indulged the prevalent Tuscan taste for green, pink, and white stone. Instead of calling in a fleet of medieval bulldozers to create a clean slate for himself, Alberti showed how a master works within the constraints imposed by tradition. Rather than resisting the medieval vocabulary of his predecessors, he appropriated it, then used it in a celebration of classical ideals. Those volutes, or scrolls, on the corners of the facade, which link the rooflines as well as the upper with the lower story, introduce something entirely novel—an essay in unity adorning a trinitarian shrine, and as such a juxtaposition of the human and the divine, truth and mystery, right reason and religious passion.

The entire city of Florence exudes this spirit. Ultimately, we learn that the genius behind Florentine urban form is not one of the Renaissance masters but the relatively unknown Arnolfo da Cambio.

FIGURE 57
The church of Santa Maria Novella, Florence. Alberti's innovative facade builds on the work of his predecessors, in no way repudiating their ideas or sensibilities.

Under Arnolfo's direction, or with his advice, the late-thirteenth-century city undertook the construction of a fifth set of circumferential walls, built a new town hall on the Piazza Signoria, and reoriented the civic center. A new cathedral, called Santa Maria del Fiore, was constructed near the ancient Baptistery; later, the "Duomo" would be adorned by Giotto's Campanile and then surmounted by Brunelleschi's famous dome.[32] Leonardo Benevolo elaborates:

Two new squares were opened up: the Piazza del Duomo (Cathedral Square), formed by pulling down an old palace opposite the Baptistery, and the Piazza della Signoria, on the site of the houses of the Uberto family, which had been destroyed following the defeat of the Ghibellines. The two centres were joined by the Via dei Calzaioli, which was subsequently widened in the fourteenth century, and half way along it, in 1290, Arnolfo built the loggia of the cornmarket, the modern Or San Michele. 1287 was the year in which the Lungarno was built along the right bank of the river, while in 1294 the meadow of the Ognissanti became a public thoroughfare, and in 1292 the district and parish boundaries of the newly laid-out city were fixed.[33]

Florentine beauty stems directly from its willingness to innovate without repudiating its cultural heritage. Arnolfo's city is a dynamic, rather than a static, work of art, emblematic of the distinction between civic pride and hubris.

It is the spirit of Arnolfo, and of his successors, that has been wanting in the modern age. Our conception of city planning, a vestige of baroque regimentation and display, has been destructive of urban order, and it has alienated us from the things we most want to know about the city. For so long as we imagine ourselves building utopias on clean slates—the SimCity conceit—for so long will we wonder why Sparta had no need of city walls; why the Venetians even now cling tenaciously to their lagoon; why, "when the worst has been said about urban Rome, one further word must be added: to the end men loved her."[34] For so long, too, will we eagerly accede to the latest construction project appealing to our noblest civic impulses, while standing in mystified awe before the Ozymandian wrecks that already litter our urban landscape.

NOTES

EPIGRAPH

Daniel Burnham's immortal words were in fact cobbled together by his friends and biographers after his death in 1912. See Charles Moore, *Daniel H. Burnham, Architect, Planner of Cities*, vol. 2 (Boston: Houghton Mifflin, 1921), 147. On the problematizing of the "Make no little plans" motto, see Henry H. Saylor, "'Make No Little Plans': Daniel Burnham Thought It, but Did He Say It?" *Journal, American Institute of Architects* 27 (March 1957): 95–99; and Thomas S. Hines, *Burnham of Chicago: Architect and Planner* (Chicago: University of Chicago Press, 1979), 401.

INTRODUCTION

1. Lewis Mumford, *The City in History* (New York: Harcourt, Brace and World, 1961), 172.

2. See, for instance, the account in Robert A. Caro, *The Power Broker: Robert Moses and the Fall of New York* (New York: Vintage, 1975), 895–919. Caro reports that Moses considered Mumford not just a crank, but "an outspoken revolutionary" (471), a charge that contains a soupçon of truth.

3. Mumford, *The City in History*, 521.

4. Jane Jacobs, *The Death and Life of Great American Cities* (New York: Vintage, 1961).

5. See Robert Venturi, Denise Scott Brown, and Steven Izenour, *Learning from Las Vegas: The Forgotten Symbolism of Architectural Form* (Cambridge: MIT Press, 1972). Helen Lefkowitz Horowitz argues that John Brinckerhoff Jackson anticipated Venturi's Las Vegas insights by about sixteen years. See Jackson's *Landscape in Sight: Looking at America*, ed. Horowitz (New Haven: Yale University Press, 1997), xxv.

6. George Bernard Shaw's famous epitaph for the founder of the Garden City movement.

7. Lewis Mumford, *The Urban Prospect* (New York: Harcourt, Brace and World, 1968), 189. See the account of this spitting match in Donald L. Miller, *Lewis Mumford: A Life* (New York: Weidenfeld and Nicolson, 1989), 473–77.

8. Mumford, *The Urban Prospect*, 194. Mumford neglected to mention that many of his fifty years in New York were logged in the minuscule Hudson River valley communities of Amenia and Leedsville.

9. Ibid., 198.

10. Ibid., 203.

11. Jane Jacobs, *Death and Life,* 30. There is an ancient Akkadian oath—"If a city street makes people murmur, that city's god will have mercy on it"—that conveys something akin to this thought. *If a City Is Set on a Height: The Akkadian Omen Series Šumma Alu ina Melê Šakin,* ed. Sally M. Freedman, vol. 1, tablets 1–21 (Philadelphia: Occasional Publications of the Samuel Noah Kramer Fund, 1998), 31.

12. Jane Jacobs, *Death and Life,* 30, 60–61. For many years, mainstream city planners and architects have resisted the lessons of *The Death and Life,* but that is beginning to change, as indicated by the presentation to Jacobs of the Vincent Scully Prize at the National Building Museum, November 11, 2000.

13. Mumford, *The Urban Prospect,* 190.

14. Mumford, *The City in History,* 296.

15. Jane Jacobs, *Death and Life,* 95–96.

16. Wolfgang Braunfels, *Urban Design in Western Europe: Regime and Architecture, 900–1900,* trans. Kenneth J. Northcott (Chicago: University of Chicago Press, 1988), 368.

17. Ibid.

18. Jackson, *Landscape in Sight,* 224.

19. Mumford, *The City in History,* 392.

20. Braunfels, *Urban Design,* 368.

21. If human beings seem to be programmed to both create and subvert Big Plans, it may be because they are "congenitally indisposed to accept reality as it is." Yi-Fu Tuan, *Escapism* (Baltimore: Johns Hopkins University Press, 1998), 6.

22. Aleksandr I. Solzhenitsyn, *The Gulag Archipelago, 1918–1956: An Experiment in Literary Investigation, I–II,* trans. Thomas P. Whitney (New York: Harper and Row, 1973), 69–70.

23. Jackson, *Landscape in Sight,* 246.

24. Wolf Von Eckardt, *Back to the Drawing Board!* (Washington, D.C.: New Republic Books, 1978), 67.

25. From the Web site of Dirk Wright: <http://www.kreative.net/wright/hickoryclusterweb/hc2intro.html>.

26. Lois M. Baron, "A Rebuilding Community, in Many Ways," *Washington Post,* January 15, 2000.

27. Jamey Gambrell, "The Wonder of the Soviet World," *New York Review of Books* 41 (December 22, 1994): 30, 33.

28. Italo Calvino, *Invisible Cities,* trans. William Weaver (San Diego: Harcourt Brace Jovanovich, 1974), 32.

29. Naomi Rogers, *Dirt and Disease: Polio before FDR* (New Brunswick, N.J.: Rutgers University Press, 1992).

CHAPTER ONE A FUNNY THING HAPPENED
ON THE WAY TO TRAJAN'S FORUM

1. James E. Packer, *The Insulae of Imperial Ostia,* Memoirs of the American Academy in Rome, vol. 31 (Rome, 1971).

2. Georgina Masson, *Fodor's Rome: A Companion Guide,* 2d ed. (New York: David McKay Co., 1971), 373.

3. James E. Packer, *The Forum of Trajan in Rome: A Study of the Monuments,*

with architectural reconstructions by Kevin Lee Sarring and James E. Packer, additional artwork by Gilbert Gorski, 5 vols. (Berkeley: University of California Press, 1997), 1:xxiii. See also James E. Packer, "Trajan's Glorious Forum," *Archaeology* 51 (January/February 1998): 32–41.

4. Quoted in Peter Monaghan, "Reconstructing Trajan's Forum," *Chronicle of Higher Education,* June 6, 1997.

5. Joseph Rykwert, "Trajan's Mall," *Los Angeles Times,* May 25, 1997.

6. Ammianus Marcellinus, quoted in Packer, *Forum of Trajan,* 1:xxiii.

7. Rykwert, "Trajan's Mall."

8. Garry Wills, review of *The Forum of Trajan in Rome: A Study of the Monuments,* by James E. Packer, *Preservation* 49 (May/June 1997): 119.

9. Monaghan, "Reconstructing Trajan's Forum." The virtual-reality model is "on the uSim urban simulation system, an interactive virtual reality system with real-time kinetic and sound capabilities." Diane Favro with Dean Abernathy, "A Columnar Experience: Virtual Reality of Trajan's Forum," *CRM* 21 (1998): 23.

10. James E. Packer, one-page synopsis of a lecture, "Restoring Trajan's Forum: A Three-Dimensional Approach for the Early Twenty-first Century," delivered at the Center for Advanced Study in the Visual Arts, National Gallery of Art, December 3, 1997.

11. Sharon Waxman, "Rebooting Ruins of Ancient Rome," *Washington Post,* January 11, 1998.

12. This is Packer's characterization, quoted in Waxman, "Rebooting Ruins of Ancient Rome."

13. Ibid.

14. Packer also explained that the computer model was a useful research tool and showed how it had helped him clarify some thorny construction issues.

15. Waxman, "Rebooting Ruins of Ancient Rome."

16. Packer, *Forum of Trajan,* 1:259, 260, 272–73.

17. Ibid., 1:274.

18. Waxman, "Rebooting Ruins of Ancient Rome."

19. Ibid.

20. From the interpretive essay accompanying *The Republic of Plato,* trans. Allen Bloom (New York: Basic Books, 1968), 402.

21. Kenneth Burke, *A Rhetoric of Motives* (Berkeley: University of California Press, 1969), 87.

22. Masson, *Fodor's Rome,* 373–74.

23. Trajan's Market fared better than the Forum because at some point it was occupied by squatters. In addition to serving the cause of historic preservation, this kind of "making do" would have "eased the poverty and sordor of the transitional period between the fifth and the tenth, or in Rome's case, the fifteenth century." Mumford, *The City in History,* at plate 15.

24. Masson, *Fodor's Rome,* 23.

25. Ibid.

26. Leonard Barkan, *Unearthing the Past: Archaeology and Aesthetics in the Making of Renaissance Culture* (New Haven: Yale University Press, 1999), xxx.

27. Masson, *Fodor's Rome,* 116.

28. Ibid., 347.

29. Evelyn Waugh, *Brideshead Revisited: The Sacred and Profane Memories of Captain Charles Ryder* (Boston: Little, Brown, 1944), 226.

30. No book teaches this lesson more memorably than R. W. B. Lewis's *The City of Florence* (New York: Henry Holt, 1995).

31. Jane Jacobs, *Death and Life*, 150–51.

32. Packer, *Forum of Trajan*, vol. 1, chap. 5.

33. Ibid., 268, 276.

34. The quotations in this paragraph are taken from a press release, "The Getty Center—Architectural Description," published on the Getty's Web site: <http://www.getty.edu/>. See also Martin Filler, "The Big Rock Candy Mountain," *New York Review of Books* 46 (December 18, 1997): 29–34.

CHAPTER TWO THE "HIDDEN CITIES" OF ANCIENT NORTH AMERICA

1. H. M. Brackenridge, *Views of Louisiana, together with a Journal of a Voyage up the Missouri River in 1811* (Pittsburgh: Cramer, Spear and Eichbaum, 1814), 187.

2. Roger G. Kennedy, *Hidden Cities: The Discovery and Loss of Ancient North American Civilization* (New York: Free Press, 1994). Kennedy is a former director of the U.S. Park Service.

3. Cahokia is a much-studied site. Some of the most important studies of the mound complex are those of Melvin L. Fowler; see, for example, "A Pre-Columbian Urban Center on the Mississippi," *Scientific American* 233 (1975): 92–101; "The Cahokia Atlas: A Historical Atlas of Cahokia Archaeology," Studies in Illinois Archaeology, no. 6 (Springfield: Illinois Historic Preservation Agency, 1989); and "Mound 72 and Early Mississippian at Cahokia," in James B. Stoltman, ed., *New Perspectives on Cahokia: Views from the Periphery*, Monographs in World Archaeology, no. 2 (Madison: Prehistory Press, 1991). The classic study of urban issues remains Patricia J. O'Brien, "Urbanism, Cahokia and Middle Mississippian," *Archaeology* 25 (1972): 188–97. A more sober account of many of the issues treated by O'Brien is provided by George R. Milner, *The Cahokian Chiefdom: The Archaeology of a Mississippian Society* (Washington, D.C.: Smithsonian Institution Press, 1998).

4. The most important nonarchitectural artifacts come from the Caddoan site of Spiro, in Oklahoma, which has been described as "the King Tutankamen's *[sic]* tomb of the Eastern United States." William N. Morgan, *Prehistoric Architecture in the Eastern United States* (Cambridge: MIT Press, 1980), 102.

5. Stuart J. Fiedel's estimate is thirty thousand. *Prehistory of the Americas*, 2d ed. (Cambridge: Cambridge University Press, 1992), 254. But others strike a cautionary note; Rinita Dalan of Minnesota State University, Moorhead, for example, would put the figure closer to three thousand. Dalan and her colleagues are preparing a study of Cahokia based on a landscape approach that involves comparison of the mound complex with the public architecture of other cultures.

6. *Cahokia: City of the Sun* (Collinsville, Ill.: Cahokia Mounds Museum Society, 1992), 19, 66. But it has also been argued that "existing data are compatible with an alternative model for a structurally simpler society, one that was not as politically centralized, economically differentiated, heavily populated, or aggressively expansionistic as commonly thought." Milner, *The Cahokian Chiefdom*, 176.

7. The word *plaza*, like *pueblo*, has currency despite Spanish connotations that create a certain amount of confusion. In this essay, unless otherwise indicated, both

words should be understood as referring to indigenous urban forms, not to the Spanish colonial heritage in North America.

8. William Bartram, *The Travels of William Bartram,* ed. Francis Harper (1791; New Haven: Yale University Press, 1958), 331.

9. James Anderson, "A Cahokia Palisade Sequence," in Melvin L. Fowler, ed., *Explorations in Cahokia Archaeology,* Illinois Archaeological Survey, bulletin 7 (Urbana: Illinois Archaeological Survey, 1977), 89–99. As Cahokia developed into a mature Mississippian chiefdom, housing, which had traditionally been grouped around courtyards, came to be organized more by mound-and-plaza units, which are arguably indicative of increased social stratification.

10. Timothy R. Pauketat, *The Ascent of Chiefs: Cahokia and Mississippian Politics in Native North America* (Tuscaloosa: University of Alabama Press, 1994), 87.

11. Warren L. Wittry, "The American Woodhenge," in Fowler, *Explorations in Cahokia Archaeology,* 43–48.

12. Fiedel, *Prehistory of the Americas,* 257.

13. See Gaetano Mosca, *The Ruling Class,* trans. Hannah D. Kahn (New York: McGraw-Hill, 1939).

14. Le Page du Pratz, *The History of Louisiana, or of the Western Part of Virginia and Carolina, in Two Volumes* (London: T. Becket and P. A. DeHondt, 1768), 221. For an unusually insightful and unsentimental critique of European accounts of early contact with the Natchez and other Indians, see Jon Muller, *Mississippian Political Economy* (New York: Plenum Press, 1997), 55–116.

15. Du Pratz, *History of Louisiana,* 147. Francis Jennings has formulated the highly unorthodox theory that the historic Natchez were actually descendants of Toltec colonizers who invaded sometime between A.D. 700 and 900. Jennings argues that the Great Sun himself was a post-Spanish-conquest émigré from Teotihuacán. See his *The Founders of America: How Indians Discovered the Land, Pioneered in It, and Created Great Classical Civilization; How They Were Plunged into a Dark Age by Invasion and Conquest; and How They Are Reviving* (New York: W. W. Norton and Co., 1993), 64.

16. The engaging Le Page du Pratz reports that the Natchez "are brought up in a most perfect submission to their sovereign; the authority which their princes exercise over them is absolutely despotic, and can be compared to nothing but that of the first Ottoman emperors." *History of Louisiana,* 184. Then again, it stands to reason that an eighteenth-century Frenchman might have been a connoisseur of royal absolutism. Similarly, Muller observes with some amusement that English explorers were wont to describe Indian methods of governance in terms that can only be called parliamentary. Muller, *Mississippian Political Economy,* 271.

17. John A. Walthall, *Prehistoric Indians of the Southeast: Archaeology of Alabama and the Middle South* (University: University of Alabama Press, 1980), 216.

18. Intriguingly, Anna C. Roosevelt has noted that "earth causeways that run between habitation mounds also have been noted in the floodplains of both the middle Orinoco and the Bolivian Amazon." See Anna C. Roosevelt, "The Mounds of the Amazon," in Brian Fagan, ed., *The Oxford Companion to Archaeology* (Oxford: Oxford University Press, 1996), 484.

19. Morgan, *Prehistoric Architecture,* xxxii.

20. Fiedel, *Prehistory of the Americas,* 260–61.

21. Lynne Sebastian, *The Chaco Anasazi: Sociopolitical Evolution in the Prehistoric Southwest* (Cambridge: Cambridge University Press, 1992), 9.

22. Stephen H. Lekson, "Chacoan Phenomenon," in Fagan, *The Oxford Companion to Archaeology,* 129. Jonathan E. Reyman has made a persuasive case that "two exterior corner windows at Pueblo Bonito were used to record the winter solstice sunrise," a hypothesis that he derived in part from ethnographic sources. Jonathan E. Reyman, "Astronomy, Architecture, and Adaptation at Pueblo Bonito," *Science* 193 (September 1976): 961.

23. Fiedel, *Prehistory of the Americas,* 217.

24. Ibid.

25. Charles L. Redman, "The Comparative Context of Social Complexity," in Patricia L. Crown and W. James Judge, eds., *Chaco and Hohokam: Prehistoric Regional Systems in the American Southwest* (Santa Fe: School of American Research Press, 1991), 289–90.

26. Sebastian, *The Chaco Anasazi,* 20.

27. Fiedel, *Prehistory of the Americas,* 218.

28. See John M. Fritz, "Paleopsychology Today: Ideational Systems and Human Adaptations in Prehistory," in Charles L. Redman et al., eds., *Social Archaeology: Beyond Subsistence and Dating* (New York: Academic Press, 1978), 37–59. Fritz also is coauthor of a book on the Hindu royal city of Vijayanagara, the geometric pattern for which was informed by the mandala, with the result that the city is laid out "according to the cardinal directions and in harmony with the movement of heavenly bodies such as the sun, moon, and planets." John M. Fritz and George Mitchell, with photographs by John Gollings, *City of Victory: Vijayanagara* (New York: Aperture, 1991), 15.

29. Redman, "Comparative Context of Social Complexity," 280–81.

30. See the discussion in Fiedel, *Prehistory of the Americas,* 219–21.

31. Sebastian, *The Chaco Anasazi,* 129, 130.

32. Ibid., 131.

33. Mumford maintains that it was family rivalries that turned the skylines of San Gimignano, Lucca, and Bologna into "bristling urban pin-cushions." Mumford, *The City in History,* 378.

34. Sebastian notes that as late as the thirteenth century there was some new construction, but the sites were small, and "many of those on Chacra Mesa have a defensive look to them." Sebastian, *The Chaco Anasazi,* 140. Interestingly, Neal Salisbury notes that when Cahokia was at its peak, during the late twelfth and early thirteenth centuries, "even then laborers were fortifying Cahokia's major earthworks against attack." Neal Salisbury, "The Indians' Old World: Native Americans and the Coming of Europeans," *William and Mary Quarterly* 52 (July 1996): 445.

35. Heather Pringle, "North America's Wars," *Science* 279 (March 27, 1998): 2040.

36. Fiedel, *Prehistory of the Americas,* 209–10.

37. Paul R. Fish, "The Hohokam: 1,000 Years of Prehistory in the Sonoran Desert," in Linda S. Cordell and George J. Gumerman, eds., *Dynamics of Southwest History* (Washington, D.C.: Smithsonian Institution Press, 1989), 21.

38. David A. Gregory, "Form and Variation in Hohokam Settlement Patterns," in Crown and Judge, *Chaco and Hohokam,* 166.

39. David R. Wilcox and Charles Sternberg, *Hohokam Ballcourts and Their Interpretation,* Arizona State Museum Archaeological Series, no. 160 (Tucson: University of Arizona, 1983).

40. Gregory, "Form and Variation," 167.

41. Ibid.

42. David R. Wilcox, "Hohokam Social Complexity," in Crown and Judge, *Chaco and Hohokam,* 267.

43. Gregory, "Form and Variation," 168.

44. Pringle, "North America's Wars," 2038.

45. Ibid.

46. Salisbury, "The Indians' Old World," 435–58. Salisbury relies on Donald Bahr et al., *The Short Swift Time of Gods on Earth: The Hohokam Chronicles* (Berkeley: University of California Press, 1994).

47. See, for example, Lawrence Keeley, *War before Civilization* (New York: Oxford University Press, 1996).

48. See A. Gibbons, "Archaeologists Rediscover Cannibals," *Science* 277 (August 1, 1997): 635–37. See also Lynn Flinn, Christy G. Turner II, and Alan Brew, "Additional Evidence for Cannibalism in the Southwest: The Case of LA 4528," *American Antiquity* 41 (July 1976): 308–18.

49. According to Fiedel, "the Adena culture in the Ohio Valley was transformed into the Hopewell culture." Fiedel, *Prehistory of the Americas,* 240.

50. Ibid., 241.

51. Morgan, *Prehistoric Architecture,* 20.

52. See Clarence H. Webb, *The Poverty Point Culture,* Geoscience and Man, vol. 17 (Baton Rouge: Louisiana State University School of Geoscience, 1982); Jon L. Gibson, "Poverty Point: The First North American Chiefdom," *Archaeology* 27 (1974): 97–105; Jon Muller, "The Southeast," in J. D. Jennings, ed., *Ancient North Americans* (San Francisco: Freeman, 1983), 373–419; Kathleen M. Byrd, ed., *The Poverty Point Culture. Local Manifestations, Subsistence Practices, and Trade Networks,* Geoscience and Man, vol. 29 (Baton Rouge: Louisiana State University School of Geoscience, 1991); and Jon L. Gibson, *Poverty Point: A Terminal Archaic Culture of the Lower Mississippi Valley,* 2d ed. (Baton Rouge: Louisiana Archaeological Survey and Antiquities Commission, May 1996).

53. Gibson reports evidence of a possible "woodhenge" on the western side of the plaza. Gibson, *Poverty Point: A Terminal Archaic Culture,* 11.

54. See Brian M. Fagan, *Ancient North America: The Archaeology of a Continent,* 2d ed. (London: Thames and Hudson, 1995), 440. See also Muller, *Mississippian Political Economy,* 273–75.

55. Webb, *The Poverty Point Culture,* 19, 12.

56. Ibid., 12, 67.

57. Fagan, *Ancient North America,* 396.

58. See Joe W. Saunders, Thurman Allen, and Roger T. Saucier, "Four Archaic? Mound Complexes in Northeast Louisiana," *Southeastern Archaeology* 13 (winter 1994): 134–53.

59. Joe W. Saunders et al., "A Mound Complex in Louisiana at 5400–5000 Years before the Present," *Science* 277 (September 19, 1997): 1796.

60. Ibid., 1798–99.

61. Morgan, *Prehistoric Architecture,* 4. For an interesting account of the first systematic studies of shell middens, see Bruce G. Trigger, *Native Shell Mounds of North America: Early Studies* (New York: Garland, 1986).

62. Fiedel, *Prehistory of the Americas,* 96, 76.

63. Certainly more than Lewis Mumford ever imagined. Only four of the 567

pages of *The City in History* are devoted to the ancient New World, and those pages deal exclusively with Mesoamerica and Peru.

64. See V. Gordon Childe, *Man Makes Himself* (London: Watts and Co., 1936); and Bruce G. Trigger, *Gordon Childe: Revolutions in Archaeology* (London: Thames and Hudson, 1980). See also the useful commentary on the "urban revolution" concept in Robert McCormick Adams, *The Evolution of Urban Society* (Chicago: Aldine, 1966), 1-37.

65. O'Brien, "Urbanism, Cahokia and Middle Mississippian," 189.

66. Ibid., 196, 197.

67. Mumford, *The City in History*, 93, 5. Mumford certainly would have held Cahokia to the same high standards that he applied to his own native city of New York, which he considered a "conurbation"—his term for cancerous urban overgrowth.

68. David J. Meltzer, introduction to *Ancient Monuments of the Mississippi Valley*, by Ephraim G. Squier and Edwin H. Davis (1848; Washington, D.C.: Smithsonian Institution Press, 1998), 69.

69. Ibid., 80.

70. Morgan, *Prehistoric Architecture,* xii.

71. Ibid.

72. See the reconstructions at the CERHAS Web site: <http://www.earthworks.uc.edu>.

73. Esther Pasztory, *Teotihuacan: An Experiment in Living* (Norman: University of Oklahoma Press, 1997), 26.

CHAPTER THREE CLEVELAND AS CITY BEAUTIFUL

1. John W. Reps, *The Making of Urban America: A History of City Planning in the United States* (Princeton: Princeton University Press, 1965), 15–19.

2. W. A. Morris, *The Frankpledge System* (New York: Longman's, Green and Co., 1910).

3. John R. Stilgoe, *Common Landscape of America, 1580 to 1845* (New Haven: Yale University Press, 1982), 12, 3. Stilgoe writes that landscape is "shaped land, land modified for permanent human occupation, for dwelling, agriculture, manufacturing, government, worship, and for pleasure" (3).

4. In fact, it has been argued that what we think of as the quintessential New England town, with white clapboard houses, church, and town hall clustered around a village green, is more a product of early-nineteenth-century commercialism (and the Romantic reaction to it) than of medieval Europe. See Joseph S. Wood, with a contribution by Michael P. Steinitz, *The New England Village* (Baltimore: Johns Hopkins University Press, 1997). Wood argues, contrary to conventional wisdom, that "from the beginning of settlement in the late 1620s, New Englanders avoided nucleation whenever they could" (115).

5. See Kenneth A. Lockridge, *A New England Town: The First Hundred Years* (New York: W. W. Norton and Co., 1970).

6. Jackson, *Landscape in Sight,* 83–84, 85–86.

7. Stilgoe, *Common Landscape of America,* 44.

8. Harlan Hatcher, *The Western Reserve: The Story of New Connecticut in Ohio* (Cleveland: World Publishing Co., 1949).

9. Stilgoe, *Common Landscape of America*, 45.

10. A number of such cases have been researched by the Illiam College Center for Regional Studies.

11. See Reps, *Making of Urban America*, 227–39.

12. Burke Aaron Hinsdale, *The Old Northwest* (New York: T. MacCoun, 1888), 390.

13. At least the Western Reserve was spared the likes of General William ("I am Denver") Larimer and George Francis Train, the moving force behind the Credit Foncier and a certified lunatic. See Charles N. Glaab and A. Theodore Brown, *A History of Urban America*, 2d ed. (New York: Macmillan, 1976), 99–119.

14. William Ganson Rose, *Cleveland: The Making of a City* (Cleveland: World Publishing Co., 1950), 88–220.

15. Richard Hofstadter, *The Age of Reform* (New York: Alfred A. Knopf, 1955).

16. Peter Witt, *Cleveland before St. Peter: A Handful of Hot Stuff* (Cleveland, 1899).

17. Robert L. Briggs, *The Progressive Era in Cleveland, Ohio: Tom L. Johnson's Administration, 1901–1909* (Chicago: University of Chicago Press, 1961). See also Tom L. Johnson, *My Story* (New York: B. W. Huebsch, 1913).

18. Thomas Edward Felt, "The Rise of Mark Hanna" (Ph.D. diss., Michigan State University, 1960).

19. This narrative stems mainly from such popular accounts of the "traction war" as George E. Condon's *Cleveland: The Best-Kept Secret* (New York: Doubleday and Co., 1967), 152–76. Condon, in truth, is positively restrained compared to Elroy McKendree Avery, who considers comparing Mayor Johnson, on the day the three-cent fare went into effect, to "Caesar coming back from the wars with captive kings and princes in his train, or . . . Achilles dragging the body of the slain Hector three times around the walls of the ancient Troy"—then rejects those comparisons in favor of Columbus on the day he "rode through the crowded streets of Barcelona and into the presence of the waiting Ferdinand and Isabella." See Avery's *A History of Cleveland and Its Environs*, vol. 1 (Chicago: Lewis Publishing Co., 1918), 101.

20. Peter G. Filene, "An Obituary for 'The Progressive Movement,'" *American Quarterly* 22 (1970): 20–34. Class has been making a scholarly comeback recently; for an application of class analysis to Cleveland politics, see Shelton Stromquist, "The Crucible of Class: Cleveland Politics and the Origins of Municipal Reform in the Progressive Era," *Journal of Urban History* 23 (January 1997): 192–220.

21. "The Government of American Cities," *The Forum* 10 (December 1890): 357–72.

22. Peter Witt to William Allen White, August 24, 1908, Peter Witt Papers, Western Reserve Historical Society, Cleveland.

23. Joseph Lincoln Steffens, *The Struggle for Self-Government*, ed. David W. Noble (1906; New York: Johnson Reprint Corporation, 1968), 183.

24. Rose, *Cleveland*, 681.

25. See Candace Wheeler, "A Dream City," *Harper's Magazine* 86 (May 1893): 832.

26. For the story behind the "quotation," see Hines, *Burnham of Chicago*, 401.

27. Frederic C. Howe, *The Confessions of a Reformer* (New York: Charles Scribner's Sons, 1925), 113–14.

28. Jackson, *Landscape in Sight*, 239.

29. In addition to Hines's treatment of "the paradox of Progressive architecture" in Cleveland (*Burnham of Chicago*, 158–73), see Eric Johannesen, *Cleveland Architecture, 1876–1976* (Cleveland: Western Reserve Historical Society, 1979), 71–76. Useful discussions of the City Beautiful movement are to be found in Richard E. Foglesong, *Planning the Capitalist City: The Colonial Era to the 1920s* (Princeton: Princeton University Press, 1986), chap. 5; and William H. Wilson, *The City Beautiful Movement* (Baltimore: Johns Hopkins University Press, 1989).

30. *The Group Plan of the Public Buildings of the City of Cleveland,* Report made to the Honorable Tom L. Johnson, Mayor, and to the Honorable Board of Public Service by Daniel H. Burnham, John M. Carrere, Arnold W. Brunner, Board of Supervision (New York: Cheltenham Press, August 1903), 1. The definitive study is Walter C. Leedy Jr., "Cleveland's Struggle for Self-Identity: Aesthetics, Economics, and Politics," in Richard Guy Wilson and Sidney K. Robinson, eds., *Modern Architecture in America: Visions and Revisions* (Ames: Iowa State University Press, 1991), 74–105.

31. Frederic C. Howe, "Plans for a City Beautiful," *Harper's Weekly* 48 (April 23, 1904): 626. Howe, a longtime progressive (Ida M. Tarbell, author of the celebrated *History of the Standard Oil Company* [New York: McClure Phillips and Co., 1905], had been his Sunday-school teacher in Meadville, Pennsylvania), was anything but a disinterested observer, of course. In fact, he was one of Johnson's chief propagandists. As for Howe's $10 to $15 million price tag for the Group Plan, Rose calculated its cost, as of 1946, as $41,361,075 (*Cleveland,* 630). That was before the extensive improvements of the early 1960s, which cost at least $17 million. Concerning the reference to Napoleon III, Burnham is said to have kept Haussmann's plans for Paris constantly at his side. See George Kriehl, "The City Beautiful," *Municipal Affairs* 3 (December 1899): 594.

32. *Group Plan,* 3.

33. Wheeler, "A Dream City," 832.

34. "Indorse Group Plan Scheme," *Plain Dealer,* August 19, 1903; "Have Little to Say," *Plain Dealer,* August 19, 1903.

35. See chapter 4 for a very brief account based largely on Ian S. Haberman's *The Van Sweringens of Cleveland: The Biography of an Empire* (Cleveland: Western Reserve Historical Society, 1979). See also Leedy's account in "Cleveland's Struggle for Self-Identity."

36. Lewis Mumford, "The Garden City Idea and Modern Planning," introduction to *Garden Cities of To-morrow,* by Ebenezer Howard (London: Faber and Faber, 1945), 37.

37. Joseph L. Wagner and Christine J. Jindra, "Hanna Fountains Mall Proposed as Hyatt Site," *Plain Dealer,* February 14, 1980.

38. See Jackson, *Landscape in Sight,* 19–29.

39. Even Leedy, who admires the Group Plan for teaching lessons "about how successful urban imagery could function," concedes that "because the major buildings on the mall have their main entrances on the side streets, because of the overwhelming, monumental scale of the mall itself, and because of its location, the mall only obliquely affects the lives of Clevelanders." Leedy, "Cleveland's Struggle for Self-Identity," 101, 100.

40. Jane Jacobs, *Death and Life,* 185.

41. Quoted in ibid., 173.

42. Jackson, *Landscape in Sight,* 38.

43. Jane Jacobs, *Death and Life*, 169.

44. See "Shaping the Future: Making an Urban District Extraordinary," at <http://www.universitycircle.org/shape/book/>.

45. Jane Jacobs, *Death and Life*, 258, 259, 261.

CHAPTER FOUR UTOPIAN VISIONS ON THE CRABGRASS FRONTIER

1. *Peaceful Shaker Village* (Cleveland: Van Sweringen Co., 1927), unpaginated.

2. *The Heritage of the Shakers* (Cleveland: Van Sweringen Co., 1923), 48.

3. *Peaceful Shaker Village.*

4. Haberman, *The Van Sweringens of Cleveland*, 31–49.

5. Johannesen, *Cleveland Architecture*, 177–83. See also "New City within a City," *Plain Dealer*, June 29, 1930; and H. D. Jouett, "Cleveland Railroads Dedicate Union Terminal," *Civil Engineering* 1 (November 1930): 77–82.

6. Bruce E. Lynch, "A Study in Regional Planning: Shaker Heights, the Garden Suburb in America" (master's thesis, University of Illinois, 1978), 63.

7. *The Heritage of the Shakers*, 48.

8. Joseph G. Blake, "The Van Sweringen Development in Cleveland" (bachelor's thesis, University of Notre Dame, 1968), 19. See also Patricia J. Forgac, "The Physical Development of Shaker Heights" (master's thesis, Kent State University, 1981), 20–28.

9. This has never been verified, according to Forgac, Heritage Director of the City of Shaker Heights. Another unsubstantiated account has the Van Sweringens sending Gallimore to England for a crash course in town planning. In any event, Leedy has discovered the use of English place names in Euclid Heights during the 1890s.

10. Quoted in Reps, *The Making of Urban America*, 410. Tacoma was a variation on a theme that Olmsted perfected in Riverside, Illinois. See chap. 40 of Witold Rybczynski's *A Clearing in the Distance: Frederick Law Olmsted and America in the Nineteenth Century* (New York: Scribner, 1999). Philip Langdon, who argues that curvilinear street plans are unintelligible, has written that a Chicago architect claims that "if you ask anyone in Chicago whether he's been to Riverside, he'll say, 'Once—I got lost.'" Philip Langdon, *A Better Place to Live: Reshaping the American Suburb* (Amherst: University of Massachusetts Press, 1994), 39.

11. Ebenezer Howard, *Garden Cities of To-morrow*, ed. F. J. Osborn, introductory essay by Lewis Mumford (1898; Cambridge: MIT Press, 1965), 52. For an excellent summary of the Garden City vision, see Robert Fishman, *Urban Utopias in the Twentieth Century: Ebenezer Howard, Frank Lloyd Wright, and Le Corbusier* (New York: Basic Books, 1977), 23–88. For the ideas espoused by the Regional Planning Association of America, see especially Lewis Mumford, *Sticks and Stones: A Study of American Architecture and Civilization* (New York: W. W. Norton and Co., 1924).

12. There is a very useful discussion of these issues in Peter Wojtowicz, *Lewis Mumford and American Modernism: Eutopian Theories for Architecture and Urban Planning* (Cambridge: Cambridge University Press, 1996), chap. 4.

13. *Peaceful Shaker Village.*

14. Ibid.

15. Ibid.

16. Haberman, *The Van Sweringens of Cleveland,* 16–17. Some would say that that marriage has not to this day been consummated.

17. *Peaceful Shaker Village.*

18. *The Heritage of the Shakers,* 33. Jane Jacobs, or even Hillary Rodham Clinton, could not have expressed better the role of the community in raising the child. Of course, Jacobs argued for "streets with eyes," a concept that requires high population densities, row houses, and narrow streets—all of which are anathema to suburbia. Jane Jacobs, *Death and Life,* 29–54.

19. *Shaker Village Standards,* 2d ed. (Cleveland: Van Sweringen Co., 1928), 5.

20. Lynch, "A Study in Regional Planning," 69.

21. Van Sweringen Company Deed Restrictions, Western Reserve Historical Society, sections 1, 2, 4, 6, 12.

22. Blake, "The Van Sweringen Development," 28–29.

23. Van Sweringen Company Deed Restrictions, section 5.

24. Blake, "The Van Sweringen Development," 29–30.

25. This applies with particular force to gated communities. See Edward J. Blakely and Mary Gail Snyder, *Fortress America: Gated Communities in the United States* (Washington, D.C.: Brookings Institution, 1997).

26. Eugenie Ladner Birch, "Radburn and the American Planning Movement: The Persistence of an Idea," *Journal of the American Planning Association* 46 (October 1980): 433.

27. See Langdon, *A Better Place to Live,* 91.

28. Frederick Steiner, *The Politics of New Town Planning: The Newfields, Ohio Story* (Athens: Ohio University Press, 1981), 6.

29. Jackson, *Landscape in Sight,* 222.

CHAPTER FIVE URBAN RENEWAL

1. They lost their fortune during the Great Depression.

2. "A Housing Program for the United States," address by Ernest J. Bohn, President, National Association of Housing Officials, at the opening of the Baltimore conference, October 9, 1934, Bohn papers, Case Western Reserve University Library.

3. "A New Deal in Local Government: Housing and Slum Clearance," transcript, published by the National Municipal League, of a National Broadcasting Company program featuring Ernest J. Bohn, president of the National Association of Housing Officials, and Sir Raymond Unwin, former president of the Royal Academy of Architects, August 28, 1934, Bohn papers.

4. *Annual Report of the Cleveland City Planning Commission, 1963,* written by Theodore Hall (Cleveland: City Planning Commission, 1963), 4.

5. Address by Ernest J. Bohn, Chairman, Joint Council–Civic Committee on Housing, over WHK, September 2, 1932, under the auspices of the American Institute of Architects, Bohn papers.

6. See John T. Howard, *What's Ahead for Cleveland?* (Cleveland: Regional Association of Cleveland, 1941), 22–23.

7. *Report of the Mayor's Advisory Committee on Planning Organization,* Walter L. Flory, Chairman, to the Honorable Frank J. Lausche, Mayor of the City of Cleveland (1942), 1.

8. Ibid., iii.

9. See Melville C. Branch, "Sins of City Planners," *Public Administration Review*, January/February 1982, 4.

10. *Cleveland Today . . . Tomorrow: The General Plan for Cleveland* (Cleveland: City Planning Commission, 1949). Probably the most remarkable thing about this document is its failure to anticipate that Cleveland would lose approximately 350,000 citizens during the succeeding thirty years, a statistic made the more impressive when one considers that even in 1949, with the city's population at a little over 900,000, about one-fifth of the land in Cleveland lay vacant.

11. David R. Goldfield and Blain A. Brownell, *Urban America: From Downtown to No Town* (Boston: Houghton Mifflin, 1979), 361.

12. Allan B. Jacobs, *Great Streets* (Cambridge: MIT Press, 1996), 311.

13. "Quick to Queue at Mall Models; Lines Throng at Operation Demonstrate," *Plain Dealer*, October 12, 1955.

14. "Planners See Slums Ended in Ten Years with U.S. Aid," *Cleveland Press*, June 9, 1955.

15. "Juvenile Delinquency? Housing Is No. 1 Answer," editorial, *Cleveland Press*, December 31, 1954.

16. "It's Too Early to Abandon the Public Housing Program," editorial, *Cleveland Press*, May 14, 1956. But it seems that somebody had to get the tenants in line: "Rep. Charles Vanik last night told residents of the Longwood urban renewal development that the hostility which some of them had been showing toward the project could hurt the urban renewal program throughout the country. The theme was emphasized by Ernest J. Bohn." "Longwooders Told Danger of Grumbling," *Plain Dealer*, February 14, 1959.

17. In retrospect, the level of naïveté on the subject of public housing is simply astounding. A recent study, for example, has revealed that up until 1965 there were exactly *two* articles critical of public housing published in leading periodicals. Both appeared in the *American Mercury*. See Scott Henderson, "'Tarred with the Exceptional Family': Public Housing and Popular Discourse, 1950–1990," *American Studies* 36 (spring 1995): 31–52.

18. For the lurid details of the Garden Valley story, see Todd Simon, "City Is Just Making New Slums, Councilman Charges," *Plain Dealer*, November 29, 1955; Richard Murway, "Dunlop Set on Garden Valley Plans," *Cleveland Press*, April 11, 1956; "Builder Sees No Profit for Twenty Years," *Plain Dealer*, May 4, 1956; "Garden Valley Rent Rises, Homes Aren't Even Built," *Cleveland News*, May 18, 1956; Richard Murway, "Interview Families for Garden Valley," *Cleveland Press*, January 4, 1957; Eugene Segal, "Dreams True; Old Slag Pile Is Now Home—First Family to Move to Garden Valley," *Plain Dealer*, February 23, 1957; Bob Siegel, "City's Problem: Where to Put 7,000 from Razed Slum?" *Cleveland Press*, March 2, 1957; Bob Siegel, "Garden Valley Is Paradise to First Tenants," *Cleveland Press*, March 5, 1957; "Builder Here Lashes Back at Critics," *Plain Dealer*, March 20, 1957; Bob Siegel, "Once-Proud Garden Valley Is Eyesore," *Cleveland Press*, July 8, 1959.

19. Mayor Ralph S. Locher, *Statement on Cleveland's Urban Renewal Program*, for the Special Committee on Housing, House Banking and Currency Committee, U.S. House of Representatives, October 24, 1963, 2.

20. *Erieview, Cleveland, Ohio: An Urban Renewal Plan for Downtown Cleveland* (New York: I. M. Pei and Associates, 1961), 2.

21. Ibid., 26.

22. Ibid., 2, 1, 18.

23. Ibid., 4, 2.

24. Ibid., 16.

25. Commissioner William L. Slayton, Federal Urban Renewal Agency, *Statement on Erieview,* made a part of the record of the U.S. Senate by Senator John Sparkman, September 12, 1963.

26. James M. Lister, Director of Urban Renewal and Housing, Cleveland, Ohio, statement before the Special Committee on Housing, House Banking and Currency Committee, U.S. House of Representatives, October 24, 1963, 1.

27. Comptroller General of the United States, letter addressed to the President of the Senate and the Speaker of the House of Representatives, June 28, 1963, 1.

28. Comptroller General of the United States, *Premature Approval of Large-Scale Demolition for Erieview Urban Renewal Project I, Cleveland, Ohio, by the Urban Renewal Administration, Housing and Home Finance Agency,* Report to the Congress of the United States, June 1963, 23, 29, 30.

29. Martin Anderson, *The Federal Bulldozer: A Critical Analysis of Urban Renewal, 1949–1962* (Cambridge: MIT Press, 1964). Anderson's book revealed that urban renewal had destroyed more low-income housing than it had built. It's hard to know exactly why such revelations were so startling. In 1901, George Bernard Shaw observed that outlawing slums meant that "you turn a great mass of people out into the streets without homes. Do you suppose that that sort of reform is popular with the very class of people you intend to benefit?" Quoted in Fishman, *Urban Utopias,* 61.

30. Herbert J. Gans, "The Failure of Urban Renewal," in James Q. Wilson, ed., *Urban Renewal: The Record and the Controversy* (Cambridge: MIT Press, 1966), 539.

31. Donald Sabath, "Hough Slum Battle Still at a Standstill," *Plain Dealer,* July 26, 1966. Hough was described by *Time* magazine as an area consisting of "some 60,000 Negroes . . . jammed into a two-square-mile warren of squat apartment houses and decaying mansions carved up into flats." "The Jungle and the City," *Time* 88 (July 29, 1966): 11. Such words as "jungle" and "warren" might reveal as much about *Time* in those days as they do about Hough.

32. *Annual Report of the Cleveland City Planning Commission, 1968* (Cleveland: City Planning Commission, 1968), 16.

33. Jackson, *Landscape in Sight,* 246.

34. *Erieview, Cleveland, Ohio,* 1.

35. A useful guide to such alterations is David Sucher, *City Comforts: How to Build an Urban Village* (Seattle: City Comforts Press, 1995).

36. George E. Condon, "Plans Clutter City Hall," *Plain Dealer,* July 27, 1966.

37. It turns out that "midway," understood as "a synonym for any area of a carnival or circus devoted to sideshows and other amusements," is yet another issue of the World's Columbian Exposition in Chicago; Olmsted conceived of the Midway Plaisance as the dark side of the Court of Honor. See Rybczynski, *A Clearing in the Distance,* 398.

38. *Civic Vision 2000 and Beyond,* vol. 1, *An Overview* (Cleveland: Cleveland Tomorrow, 1998), 28.

39. For the uninitiated, Cap'n Frank's was a seedy fish-house near Municipal Stadium that for many years served up what little consolation an Indians fan could find.

40. Dennis R. Judd and Susan S. Fainstein, eds., *The Tourist City* (New Haven:

Yale University Press, 1999). See also Elizabeth Strom, "Let's Put On a Show! Performing Arts and Urban Revitalization in Newark," *Journal of Urban Affairs* 21 (1999): 423–36.

41. Nan Ellin, *Postmodern Urbanism* (New York: Princeton Architectural Press, 1999), 84.

42. Blair Kamin, "Reinventing the Lakefront," part 1, "To Shape the Shoreline," *Chicago Tribune,* October 26, 1998.

43. Ibid.

44. Ibid.

45. See Edward C. Banfield's dated but still notorious *The Unheavenly City* (Boston: Little, Brown and Co., 1968).

46. Jane Jacobs, *Death and Life,* 291–317.

47. William Claiborne, "HUD, Chicago Ink Deal to Reconstruct Public Housing," *Washington Post,* February 6, 2000.

CHAPTER SIX THE STRANGE CAREER OF ADVOCACY PLANNING

1. *Erieview, Cleveland, Ohio,* 1. By almost any measure, Cleveland was shrinking, not growing, in the 1950s and 1960s.

2. John T. Howard, quoted in Mel Scott, *American City Planning since 1890* (Berkeley: University of California Press, 1969), 481.

3. Paul E. Peterson, *City Limits* (Chicago: University of Chicago Press, 1981), 25.

4. Scott, *American City Planning since 1890,* 615–16, 617.

5. *Cleveland Policy Planning Report* (Cleveland: City Planning Commission, 1975). The report was financed in part through a Comprehensive Planning Grant from HUD.

6. Ibid., 9.

7. Norman Krumholz, "A Retrospective View of Equity Planning, Cleveland, 1969–1979," *Journal of the American Planning Association* 48 (spring 1982): 165, 166.

8. Author's interview with Layton K. Washburn, June 30, 1982.

9. Krumholz, "Retrospective View," 166, 168.

10. Ibid., 168.

11. *Pre Application New Town: Warren's Ridge, Ohio* (Cleveland: City of Cleveland, 1971).

12. Krumholz, "Retrospective View," 170, 171, 173, 172.

13. Michael D. Sorkin, remarks in "Cities and Suburbs," a roundtable discussion, *Harvard Magazine* 102 (January/February 2000): 56.

14. Allan Jacobs and Donald Appleyard, "Toward an Urban Design Manifesto," *Journal of the American Planning Association* 53 (winter 1987): 112–20. Jacobs and Appleyard maintain that under the "positivist influence of social science," city planners "have lost their beliefs" (115).

15. Calvin Trillin, "A Reporter at Large (Kansas City, Mo.)," *The New Yorker,* September 26, 1983, 57.

16. Mark F. Bernstein observes that while "Cleveland's magnificent Jacobs Field may be sold out for every game," it is not generally known that "Cuyahoga County, which guarantees its debt, has already paid more than $23 million to cover arrears, and, according to Barron's, may have to pay $70 million more over the next 16

years." See Bernstein's "Sports Stadium Boondoggle," *The Public Interest,* no. 132 (summer 1998): 51.

17. Richard Moe and Carter Wilkie, *Changing Places: Rebuilding Community in the Age of Sprawl* (New York: Henry Holt and Co., 1997), 70.

18. Researchers at the Johns Hopkins University agree that the 1990s "comeback" of cities such as Cleveland and Baltimore is largely a myth. See "Policy Students Debunk the Myth of Urban Revival," in *The Gazette Online:* <http://www.jhu.edu/~gazette/1999/dec1399/13debunk.html>.

CHAPTER SEVEN TWO CHEERS FOR SPRAWL

1. Edward Bellamy, *Looking Backward, 2000–1887* (1888; Cleveland: World Publishing Co., 1945).

2. Fishman, *Urban Utopias,* 32–33.

3. Ibid., 32.

4. Bournville and Port Sunlight, in Mumford's opinion, "rivalled in comeliness the best of the later suburbs." Mumford, *The City in History,* 475.

5. Henry George, *Progress and Poverty* (New York, 1879).

6. Fishman, *Urban Utopias,* 46.

7. Ebenezer Howard, *Garden Cities of Tomorrow* (London, 1902).

8. Mumford, *The City in History,* 515.

9. Fishman, *Urban Utopias,* 44.

10. Mumford, *The City in History,* 515.

11. Fishman, *Urban Utopias,* 24.

12. These were the attractions of the "town-country magnet," according to the famous diagram in *Garden Cities of Tomorrow.*

13. Frank Lloyd Wright comes to mind. See Fishman (*Urban Utopias,* 89–160) on Wright's Broadacre City.

14. Mumford, *The City in History,* 518.

15. Ibid., 519.

16. Fishman, *Urban Utopias,* 57.

17. Mumford, *The City in History,* 522.

18. Fishman, *Urban Utopias,* 67–69.

19. See Mumford, *The City in History,* at plate 20.

20. Fishman, *Urban Utopias,* 74, 75.

21. Mumford, *The City in History,* 519.

22. Fishman, *Urban Utopias,* 62.

23. Richard T. LeGates and Frederic Stout, eds., *The City Reader* (London: Routledge, 1996), 433.

24. Fishman, *Urban Utopias,* 80.

25. Mumford, *The City in History,* at plate 51. The case against the Radburn cul-de-sac is made persuasively in chapter 2 of Langdon's *A Better Place to Live.*

26. Birch, "Radburn and the American Planning Movement," 424.

27. Le Corbusier, *The City of To-morrow and Its Planning,* trans. Frederick Etchells (New York: Payson and Clarke, 1929), 168. Garden Cities were appropriated by Le Corbusier and included in his larger vision of the City of Tomorrow.

28. Birch, "Radburn and the American Planning Movement," 437.

29. According to Stein, Tugwell "fervently believed in Ebenezer Howard's Gar-

den City." Clarence S. Stein, *Toward New Towns for America* (Cambridge: Technology Press, 1957), 120.

30. Ibid., 122.

31. Deborah Sheiman Shprentz, "Greenbelt, Maryland: Preservation of a Historic Planned Community," *CRM* 22 (1999): 53.

32. William H. Wilson, *Coming of Age: Urban America, 1915–1945* (New York: John Wiley, 1974), 160.

33. Ibid.

34. Christopher Alexander, "A City Is Not a Tree," parts 1 and 2, *The Architectural Forum* 122, no. 1 (April 1965): 58–62; no. 2 (May 1965): 58–61; quotation is on p. 59.

35. William H. Wilson, *Coming of Age*, 159.

36. Charles F. Lewis, Buhl Foundation report, June 30, 1955.

37. Ibid.

38. Mumford, *The City in History*, at plate 43.

39. Jane Jacobs, *Death and Life*, 64.

40. Stein, *Toward New Towns for America*, 80.

41. Ibid., 85.

42. Ibid.

43. Some critics of the time regarded suburban development as a means of liberation from the tyranny of bankers and robber barons. It is hard to imagine a better expression of this thought than the Frank Capra film *It's a Wonderful Life*.

44. *Chatham Village*, a brochure published by Chatham Village Homes Incorporated for prospective investors, n.d.

45. The seminal work is Gerald L. Burke, *The Making of Dutch Towns: A Study in Urban Development from the Tenth to the Seventeenth Centuries* (London: Cleauer-Hume Press, 1956).

46. See Peter Hall, *The World Cities*, 2d ed. (New York: McGraw-Hill, 1977), 87–117.

47. *Flevoland: Facts and Figures* (Lelystad, Netherlands: IJsselmeerpolders Development Authority, n.d.), 26.

48. Ibid. See also two books by Coenraad van der Wal: *Villages in the IJsselmeerpolders: From Slootdorp to Zeewolde* (Lelystad, Netherlands: IJsselmeerpolders Development Authority, 1985); and *In Praise of Common Sense: Planning the Ordinary: A Physical Planning History of the IJsselmeerpolders* (Rotterdam: 010 Publishers, 1997).

49. Ellin, *Postmodern Urbanism*, 61.

50. Quoted in P. Popham, "A Tunnel Visionary," *The Independent Magazine*, 1994. See also Espace Croisé, *Euralille: The Making of a New City Center* (New York: Princeton Architectural Press, 1996).

51. Peter Newman, "Mixed Use and Exclusion in the International City," in Andy Coupland, ed., *Reclaiming the City: Mixed Use Development* (London: E & FN Spon, 1997), 257.

52. Benjamin Forgey, "A Breath of That Old Town Atmosphere," *Washington Post*, March 13, 1999.

53. James Howard Kunstler, "Home from Nowhere," *Atlantic Monthly* 278 (September 1996): 43.

54. Peter Calthorpe, *The Next American Metropolis: Ecology, Community, and the American Dream* (New York: Princeton Architectural Press, 1993), 16.

55. Forgey, "A Breath of That Old Town Atmosphere."

56. Langdon, *A Better Place to Live*, 108–9.

57. James Howard Kunstler, *The Geography of Nowhere: The Rise and Decline of America's Man-Made Landscape* (New York: Simon and Schuster, 1993), 126–27.

58. See Kunstler's insightful treatment of the Seaside beach in *The Geography of Nowhere*, 256.

59. Kunstler, "Home from Nowhere," 61.

60. Sue Leeman, "Prince Charles Builds Dream Village in Hardy Country," *Standard-Times*, March 19, 1997.

61. New Urbanist communities are becoming major tourist destinations. Outside his Seaside house, Krier has posted a sign that reads, "We appreciate your interest in architecture but please do not disturb our guests."

62. Warren Hoge, "Welcome to Charleyville, a Princely Living Plan," *International Herald-Tribune*, June 18, 1998.

63. Ibid.

64. Leeman, "Prince Charles Builds Dream Village."

65. Hoge, "Welcome to Charleyville."

66. The New Urbanism owes much to the work of Sitte, the Austrian who, in his celebrated *Der Städtebau* (1889), "focused attention on the aesthetics of the nongeometric, accretive urban texture of many old cities. . . . Sitte's work did much to increase appreciation of the small-scale pedestrian environment, emphasizing the need for a variety of form, broken vistas, and a sense of intimate enclosure." Norma Evenson, *Paris: A Century of Change, 1878–1978* (New Haven: Yale University Press, 1979), 22.

67. Vincent Scully Jr., "Seaside and New Haven," in Alex Krieger, ed., *Andres Duany and Elizabeth Plater-Zyberk: Towns and Town-Making Principles* (New York: Rizzoli, 1991), 20.

68. Forgey, "A Breath of That Old Town Atmosphere." He also argues that the New Urbanism "is still too focused on the outer suburbs, and thus may be said to contribute to sprawl." Ibid.

69. Calthorpe, *The Next American Metropolis*, 16.

70. Langdon, *A Better Place to Live*, 209.

71. Moe and Wilkie, *Changing Places*, 226.

72. Mumford writes that "industrial production got its start in luxury wares for the court; and even mass production began, not in necessities, but in cheap imitations of upper-class luxury products, like eighteenth-century Birmingham jewelry or twentieth-century motorcars." Mumford, *The City in History*, 101.

73. Moe and Wilkie, *Changing Places*, 30.

74. See Pietro S. Nivola, "Make Way for Sprawl," *Washington Post*, June 1, 1999.

75. Such backpedaling is, according to one critic of the New Urbanism, "the sound of theorists mugged by a gang of brutal facts." Joel Garreau, "Up against the Sprawl," *Washington Post*, May 7, 2000.

76. Brad Edmondson, "Immigration Nation," *Preservation* 52 (January/February 2000): 32.

77. Ibid., 32, 31.

1. Alexis de Tocqueville, *The Old Regime and the French Revolution* (Garden City, N.Y.: Doubleday Anchor, 1955), 73.

2. Peter Hall, *Cities in Civilization* (New York: Pantheon, 1998), chap. 24.

3. Ibid., 717, 725, 726.

4. According to Mumford, "Haussmann's bold and masterly treatment" of air pollution and sanitation problems "must earn a respectful salute." Mumford, *The City in History,* 478. This tribute reveals Mumford to have been a master planner at heart. Jane Jacobs's view of the matter is quite different and typically iconoclastic: "The first necessity in understanding how cities and their parks influence each other is to jettison confusion between real uses and mythical uses—for example, the science-fiction nonsense that parks are 'the lungs of the city.' It takes about three acres of woods to absorb as much carbon dioxide as four people exude in breathing, cooking and heating. The oceans of air circulating about us, not parks, keep cities from suffocating." Jane Jacobs, *Death and Life,* 91.

5. See Donald J. Olsen, *The City as a Work of Art: London, Paris, Vienna* (New Haven: Yale University Press, 1986), 44.

6. Sigfried Giedion, *Space, Time, and Architecture: The Growth of a New Tradition,* 5th ed. (Cambridge: Harvard University Press, 1967), 775.

7. Hall, *Cities in Civilization,* 744.

8. Ibid., 745.

9. As an approach to administration, "deconcentration"—in contrast to decentralization—has been described as striking with the same hammer after choking up on the handle.

10. See Hall, *The World Cities,* 53–86.

11. A. Darmagnac, "Evry" (paper delivered at the IFHP, 33rd World Congress, Helsinki, 1976), 34. As Darmagnac put it, "The Evry project is frankly committed to this goal of recovering a true urban life" (29).

12. James M. Rubenstein, *The French New Towns* (Baltimore: Johns Hopkins University Press, 1978), 151.

13. The same mentality led to the hiring of mimes and fire-eaters to work the plaza outside the Pompidou Center.

14. Darmagnac, "Evry," 34.

15. Rubenstein, *The French New Towns,* 152.

16. Ibid.

17. On the other hand, such experiences are useful in shattering illusions about European cities; as Pogo might have put it, we have met the exemplar and they is us.

18. Lloyd Rodwin, "On the Illusions of City Planners," in Rodwin, ed., *Cities and City Planning* (New York: Plenum, 1981), 229.

19. Mumford, *The City in History,* 364.

20. Ibid., 390.

21. See Richard Krautheimer, *The Rome of Alexander VII* (Princeton: Princeton University Press, 1985), 114–25.

22. Quoted in Reps, *The Making of Urban America,* 257.

23. Quoted in Mumford, *The City in History,* 407.

24. The definitive study of this subject is John W. Reps's *Monumental Washington: The Planning and Development of the Capital Center* (Princeton: Princeton

University Press, 1967). But see also Carl Abbott, *Political Terrain: Washington, D.C., from Tidewater Town to Global Metropolis* (Chapel Hill: University of North Carolina Press, 1999).

25. Mumford, *The City in History*, 406.

26. Lyndsey Layton, "Water in Metro's Basement," *Washington Post*, July 13, 2000.

27. One suspects that the People Who Step onto the Train and Immediately Stop are among those who instinctively pull up the drawbridge to desirable suburban housing ("Stop the Sprawl!") as soon as they are safely across.

28. M. Christine Boyer, *Dreaming the Rational City: The Myth of American City Planning* (Cambridge: MIT Press, 1983).

29. Francis Fukuyama, *The Great Disruption: Human Culture and the Reconstitution of the Social Order* (New York: Free Press, 1999), 144.

30. Ibid.

31. See Antoinette J. Lee, *Architects to the Nation: The Rise and Decline of the Supervising Architect's Office* (New York: Oxford University Press, 2000), 149–55.

32. Pamela Scott and Antoinette J. Lee, *Buildings of the District of Columbia* (New York: Oxford University Press, 1993), 170.

33. Roberta Brandes Gratz, *The Living City: How Urban Residents Are Revitalizing America's Neighborhoods and Downtown Shopping Districts by Thinking Small in a Big Way* (New York: Simon and Schuster, 1989), 43.

34. Scott and Lee, *Buildings of the District of Columbia*, 170.

35. Mike Cleary, "Charges of Favoritism Halt Old Post Office Pavilion Negotiations," *Washington Times*, October 9, 1998.

36. Is downtown Washington ready for mimes and fire-eaters?

CHAPTER NINE THE BRITISH LIBRARY

1. Peter Hall, *Great Planning Disasters* (Berkeley: University of California Press, 1982).

2. Even Hall probably could not have imagined a project as ludicrous as the Los Angeles Subway. See Roger K. Lewis, "L.A. Subway Experience Can Help Get D.C. on Track," *Washington Post*, July 15, 2000.

3. Hall, *Great Planning Disasters*, 171.

4. Ibid., 176.

5. Ibid., 182.

6. Ibid., 183.

7. Ibid.

8. A remark attributed to Wilson in Robert Wernick, "Books, Books, Books, My Lord!" *Smithsonian* 28 (February 1998): 84.

9. *Welcome*, a brochure published by the British Library.

10. Ibid.

11. *Using the Reading Room*, a brochure published by the British Library, 4.

12. Colin St. John Wilson, *The Design and Construction of the British Library* (London: British Library, 1998), 7.

13. Wernick, "Books, Books, Books," 85.

14. *Welcome*.

15. Quoted in Wernick, "Books, Books, Books," 79.

16. Ibid.

17. Quoted in Wendy Law-Yone, "Letter from London," *Washington Post Book World,* March 1, 1998.

18. Colin St. John Wilson, *The Design and Construction of the British Library,* 39–41.

19. Martin Filler reminds us that Le Corbusier, too, "was entranced by the utilitarian forms of ocean liner superstructures" and observes that "his nautical references sail on into history at Meier's Getty." Martin Filler, "The Big Rock Candy Mountain," *New York Review of Books* 44 (December 18, 1997): 29. To this maritime fraternity should be added Paolo Soleri, who has claimed the passenger liner as "the closest ancestor of arcology. The common characteristics are compactness and definite boundary; the functional fullness of an organism designed for the care of many, if not most, of man's needs; a definite and unmistakable three-dimensionality." Paolo Soleri, "Arcology: The City in the Image of Man," in LeGates and Stout, *The City Reader,* 456.

20. Colin St. John Wilson, *The Design and Construction of the British Library,* 41.

21. Ibid., 7.

22. Brian Lang, "Bricks and Bytes: Libraries in Flux," *Daedalus* 125 (fall 1996): 224.

23. Ibid.

24. Colin St. John Wilson, *The Design and Construction of the British Library,* 18.

25. Ibid., 30.

26. Law-Yone, "Letter from London," 15.

27. The Pompidou Center is a dominating presence, for good or ill. Martin Filler has written that "twenty-two years after it opened, the Pompidou Center seems less an architectural landmark—its preposterous imagery of an oil refinery in the heart of the otherwise gracefully preserved Marais quarter remains as offensive as ever—than it does a milestone in the devolution of the art museum into populist fun fair." Martin Filler, "High Wire Acts," *New York Review of Books* 46 (February 4, 1999): 27–32.

28. Max Page, "Paradise Lost," *Preservation* 51 (May/June 1999): 61.

29. Page argues that the British Library's "red-brick-bunker façade shuts out the neighboring St. Pancras Station, one of London's last remaining monumental 19th-century train stations." Ibid.

30. Law-Yone, "Letter from London," 15.

31. Hall, *Great Planning Disasters,* 184.

32. Colin St. John Wilson, *The Design and Construction of the British Library,* 27.

33. Claire Downey, "The New Paris Library Reads Like an Open Book," *Architectural Record* 183 (December 1995): 19.

34. Ann Landi, "Great Books Program," *Art News* 94 (summer 1995): 61. The director of the Folger Shakespeare Library, Werner Gundersheimer, has written that the effectiveness of the new French National Library "will depend heavily on a variety of proved and unproved technologies all of which will have to work optimally almost all the time to deliver a specific book to a given reader." *Folger News,* autumn 1996, 2.

35. Manfredo Tafuri, *Theories and History of Architecture* (New York: Harper and Row, 1976), 96.

36. Patrice Higonnet, "Scandal on the Seine," *New York Review of Books* 38 (August 15, 1991): 32. See also Higonnet, "The Lamentable Library," *New York Review of Books* 39 (May 14, 1992): 43.

37. Higonnet, "Scandal on the Seine," 32.

38. Quoted in Higonnet, "The Lamentable Library," 43.

39. Downey, "New Paris Library," 19–21.

40. Higonnet, "Scandal on the Seine," 32.

41. Ibid.

42. Ibid.

43. Downey, "New Paris Library," 21.

44. Quoted in Landi, "Great Books Program," 61.

45. Ibid.

46. Higonnet, "Scandal on the Seine," 32.

47. One sensitive critic, Nan Ellin, has written that Mitterrand's projects "hark back to a traditional sense of monumentalism without being contextual or social[ly] responsive." See her *Postmodern Urbanism,* 50.

48. Although my hometown is conceding nothing in the sweepstakes. Construction will soon begin on a new Woodrow Wilson Bridge at Alexandria, Virginia, a *drawbridge* intended to ease congestion at a critical point on I-95, the main corridor between New York and Florida.

49. See Hall's *Cities and Civilization,* 908–16, for a discussion of Heseltine's role in the Thatcher Revolution.

50. "Zero-Based Celebrations," *The Economist,* April 18–24, 1998, 113.

51. Richard Jenkyns, review of *Questioning the Millennium: A Rationalist's Guide to a Precisely Arbitrary Countdown,* by Stephen Jay Gould, *New York Review of Books* 45 (May 28, 1998): 4.

52. Adam Sherwin, "Crowds Queue for a Walk on the Wobbly Side," *Times,* June 12, 2000.

53. Ros Coward, "Dome Alone," *The Guardian,* December 21, 1999.

54. "Zero-Based Celebrations," 113.

55. Jenkyns, review of *Questioning the Millennium,* 4. See also George Walden, "Cool Rules UK," *Times Literary Supplement,* no. 4967 (June 12, 1998): 14–15. Meanwhile, a competition has been held to develop the area around the Millennium Dome. See *Greenwich Peninsula: Investing in the Twenty-first Century* (London: Greenwich Peninsula Development Office, n.d.); or Richard Rogers, *Cities for a Small Planet* (London: Faber and Faber, 1997).

56. James Fenton, "London's New Left Bank," *New York Review of Books* 47 (July 20, 2000): 26.

57. Andreas Whittam Smith, "The Pride That Came before the Fall of the Dome," *Independent,* November 13, 2000.

CHAPTER TEN WITH ITS "DOORS SET WIDE TO THE CITY"

1. Jane Jacobs, *Death and Life,* 150.

2. Ibid., 48–50, 45, 264–65. Arterial highways, housing projects, and industrial parks are among the other "massive uses of special land" (265) that spawn border vacuums.

3. Ibid., 267.

4. The definitive work is Paul Venable Turner, *Campus: An American Planning Tradition,* 2d paperback ed. (Cambridge: MIT Press, 1995). It is quite a fascinating exercise to thumb through Turner's book looking not at the campuses themselves, but at the contexts into which they were set by their designers—looking at the frames, so to speak, rather than at the pictures. My personal favorite is plate 254, Mies van der Rohe's plan for Illinois Institute of Technology, which is actually a three-dimensional model superimposed on a photograph of the neighborhood— as if the presence of a megalithic campus would have no impact whatsoever on surrounding urban tissue. Like Almere-Haven, the Dutch new town, the IIT campus is now getting its own Rem Koolhaas makeover.

5. According to the *Prospectus* for 1996, St. Andrews "is not a campus university" (p. 7).

6. Russell Kirk, *St. Andrews* (London: B. T. Batsford, 1954), 24. St. Andrews and Canterbury enjoyed the special status of episcopal cities, but it was not at all unusual for a monastery to be the nucleus of a medieval town. Lewis Mumford famously argued that monasteries were the single most important force leading to the revival of urbanism in Europe after the tenth century. See Mumford, *The City in History,* 246–61.

7. Jane Jacobs argues that one sign of healthy urban tissue is the tendency of streets and alleys to proliferate, the result being a characteristically intricate—if not self-evidently rational—pattern. Jane Jacobs, *Death and Life,* 185.

8. Kirk, *St. Andrews,* 29. Swallowgait is now known as The Scores.

9. Ibid., 24.

10. Ronald Gordon Cant, *The University of St Andrews: A Short History* (St. Andrews: St. Andrews University Library, 1992).

11. Alan B. Cobban, *The Medieval English Universities: Oxford and Cambridge to c. 1500* (Berkeley: University of California Press, 1988), 2.

12. Ibid., 30.

13. Kirk, *St. Andrews,* 71.

14. Turner, *Campus,* 3, 15.

15. Kirk, *St. Andrews,* 30. The triumph of stone over wood—the English refer to it as the Great Rebuilding—came relatively late to Scotland. J. B. Jackson considered it a mixed blessing: "For all their squalor, medieval peasant dwellings had a remarkable flexibility and mobility—not only in that they could be taken down and reassembled elsewhere, but also in that they could easily change function and change tenants. If their life span was brief, it allowed for frequent replacement. When the old dwelling collapsed, the new one was apt to be better and was certain to be cleaner. Finally, the temporary nature of the dwelling, its negligible material value, meant that it could be lightheartedly abandoned when the crops failed, when war threatened, or when the local lord proved too demanding." Jackson, *Landscape in Sight,* 215–16.

16. John M. Pearson, *A Guided Walk round St. Andrews,* 2d rev. ed. (Leven, Fife: Levenmouth Printers, 1992), 39.

17. Cant, *The University of St. Andrews,* 37.

18. The autonomy of the colleges was an issue for centuries. It was not until the early seventeenth century, for example, that the creation of a common university library was achieved. An act of Parliament joined St. Salvator's and St. Leonard's in a "united college" in 1747. St. Mary's College, the faculty of divinity, successfully held out against consolidation until as late as 1953.

19. Kirk, *St. Andrews*, 85–86.

20. Cant, *The University of St. Andrews*, 49.

21. Turner argues that Oxford and Cambridge also "came through the period educationally strengthened." Turner, *Campus*, 15.

22. Cant, *The University of St. Andrews*, 74.

23. Ibid., 77.

24. Ibid., 78, 80–81, 82.

25. Ibid., 92, 91.

26. Witch burnings, for example. Kirk reports that some forty were burnt in Fife during the span of a few months in 1643, "a number of them in St. Andrews town." Kirk, *St. Andrews*, 125.

27. Cant, *The University of St. Andrews*, 95.

28. Ibid., 96.

29. That a pattern of shared authority between the university and the town persisted is revealed in the story of a student who went over, along with "a large part of both town and gown," to the Stuart cause. "Arthur Ross, when the rising was nearly quelled, had resolution enough to seize the warrants of the lord lieutenant of Fife, presenting a pistol to the face of an official messenger, at the ford of tiny St. Nicholas burn outside the town; he was sentenced to be whipped *by the professor of Greek*, to be *expelled from St. Leonard's*, and to pay a fine of twelve pounds." Kirk, *St. Andrews*, 150; emphasis added.

30. Cant, *The University of St. Andrews*, 100.

31. Quoted in Kirk, *St. Andrews*, 153.

32. Cant, *The University of St. Andrews*, 111–12.

33. Ibid., 117.

34. This was partly, one suspects, because of "the physical decay of the halls of residence." Kirk, *St. Andrews*, 158.

35. Cant, *The University of St. Andrews*, 119. Consider the case of Duncan Dewar, a student during the period 1819–27: "Like most students of his day, he lived in lodgings in the town, contriving to subsist in reasonable comfort throughout the entire six months' session (from the end of October to the beginning of May) for little more than £14 all found." Ibid., 124.

36. Kirk, *St. Andrews*, 148. "In 1556, St. Andrews burgh had paid £410 as its proportion of the land-tax; by 1695, it paid a mere £72." And it hadn't yet hit bottom. Ibid.

37. Ibid., 157. Cant's lament: "No longer would St Andrews see the brilliant procession to the Butts, the archers splendid in traditional costume, and the more riotous return, volleys of arrows rising about the houses of the patrons and friends of the competitors, and the final junketing in the lodgings of the victor, whose silver medal would shortly hang with its fellows upon the Arrow itself." Ibid., 112.

38. J. B. Jackson, citing Johan Huizinga, says that urban archery typically took place in a consecrated space, "hedged around, hallowed, within which special rules pertain." Jackson, *Landscape in Sight*, 11.

39. Kirk, *St. Andrews*, 149. The definitive source on this bizarre subject is Robert Darnton, *The Great Cat Massacre and Other Episodes in French Cultural History* (New York: Basic Books, 1984).

40. Cant, *The University of St. Andrews*, 142.

41. Kirk, *St. Andrews*, 168.

42. Ibid.

43. Ibid., 181.

44. For example, he "converted East Brun Wynd into Abbey Street, Kirk Wynd into Church Street, Baxter Wynd into Baker Lane, and so on." Ibid., 180.

45. Ibid., 140.

46. Traumas might be more like it. The adoption of professional programs was particularly difficult, for St. Andrews University had always specialized in the arts and sciences and in theology. In fact, one of the most eloquent statements ever made on behalf of liberal education was pronounced at St. Andrews by John Stuart Mill while he was serving as chancellor: "Men are men before they are lawyers, or physicians, or merchants, or manufacturers; and if you make them capable and sensible men, they will make themselves capable and sensible lawyers or physicians." John Stuart Mill, *Inaugural Address Delivered to the University of St. Andrews,* February 1, 1867 (London: Longmans, Green, Reader, and Dyer, 1867), 4.

47. Among the talented young faculty members at Dundee was Patrick (later Sir Patrick) Geddes, the eccentric biologist who became one of the founders of modern urban planning. See Helen Meller, *Patrick Geddes: Social Evolutionist and City Planner* (London: Routledge, 1990). During the 1920s, Geddes was the mentor of the young Lewis Mumford.

48. Cant, *The University of St. Andrews,* 169.

49. Kenneth Dover, *Marginal Comment: A Memoir* (London: Duckworth, 1994), 84.

50. Cant, *The University of St. Andrews,* 180.

51. Dover tells us little of his own role in the development of Andrew Melville Hall except to say that his experience with the architect was "not happy." Dover, *Marginal Comment,* 98. Students seem to loathe the place.

52. Consider, for the sake of comparison, James Howard Kunstler's account of his undergraduate days at SUNY-Brockport, where students "appreciated what life in a real town had to offer. It was scaled to people, not cars. It had the variety that comes from a mixed-use community. Its amenities lay close at hand. . . . We loved our off-campus apartments in the nineteenth-century houses on tree-lined streets or above the shops in the business blocks downtown. We loved rubbing elbows on the streets, meeting friends as we walked or biked to class. We loved the peace and quiet of a small town at night. The campus itself—a miserable island of androidal modernistic brick boxes set in an ocean of parking—was quite secondary to the experience of life in the town." Kunstler, *The Geography of Nowhere,* 14–15.

53. *Prospectus,* 35.

54. Alexander, "A City Is Not a Tree," part 2, 59.

55. By "natural city," Alexander has in mind cities that have "arisen more or less spontaneously" (he mentions Siena and Liverpool, among others). By "artificial city," he has in mind places such as "Levittown, Chandigarh, and the British New Towns." Ibid., part 1, 58.

56. Ibid., part 2, 59.

57. Dover, *Marginal Comment,* 88, 89.

58. Cant, *The University of St. Andrews,* 100.

59. Kirk insists that while "the university failed in the conservative purpose for which it was intended," it "succeeded, for all that, in securing to St. Andrews town some continuity with the Age of Faith—in this effecting a powerful conservative achievement." Kirk, *St. Andrews,* 68.

60. Cant, *The University of St. Andrews,* 69.

61. In the fall of 1997, when the government adopted a policy of charging tuition at British universities, it exempted native Scots attending Scottish universities from one year of tuition. According to the *Chronicle of Higher Education,* the National Union of Students was predicting that this would "devastate universities in Scotland that rely heavily on students from outside," such as St. Andrews. See "Dispatch Case," *Chronicle of Higher Education* 21 (November 21, 1997).

62. Cant, *The University of St. Andrews,* 89.

63. Kirk, *St. Andrews,* 169.

64. As Jackson has written, "the sense of place is reinforced by what might be called a sense of recurring events." John Brinckerhoff Jackson, *A Sense of Place, A Sense of Time* (New Haven: Yale University Press, 1994), 152.

CHAPTER ELEVEN SIMCITY AND OUR TOWN

Portions of this chapter are drawn from Kenneth Kolson, "The Politics of Sim-City," *PS: Political Science & Politics* 29 (March 1996): 43–46.

1. Robert A. Caro, *The Power Broker: Robert Moses and the Fall of New York* (New York: Vintage, 1975).

2. SimCity is the product of a California software firm called Maxis. The 1994 upgrade, called SimCity 2000, has sold millions of copies. An advertisement in the *Washington Post* summarizes the attractions of SimCity as follows: "When kids outgrow Legos and begin to understand that their neighborhoods are fragile and complex ecosystems, it's time for them to explore SimCity. . . . As mayor of a town, a SimCity player is responsible for every facet of a city: planning the buildings, developing infrastructures, deciding on the form of government, designating residential areas, and setting tax regulations. . . . As your children's values and goals get spun into their city, they develop a better idea of who they are and how they fit into the world around them." The most recent upgrade is called SimCity 3000. Sim-City should probably be regarded as another chapter in America's love affair with the machine; see Howard Segal, *Technological Utopianism in American Culture* (Chicago: University of Chicago Press, 1985). See also Peter Bacon Hale's "Meditation II: Two Models for Block 37," in Bob Thall, *The Perfect City* (Baltimore: Johns Hopkins University Press, 1994), 15–31.

3. Michael Bremer, *SimCity for Windows, User Manual* (Orinda, Calif.: Maxis, 1989), 6.

4. Paul Starr, "Seductions of Sim: Policy as a Simulation Game," *The American Prospect,* no. 17 (spring 1994): 25.

5. Johnny L. Wilson, *The SimCity Planning Commission Handbook* (Berkeley: Osborne McGraw-Hill, 1991), 68.

6. Mark Schone, "Building Rome in a Day," review of SimCity 2000, by Will Wright and Fred Haslam, *The Village Voice,* May 31, 1994.

7. Michael Bremer, *SimCity 2000 User Manual* (Orinda, Calif.: Maxis, 1993), 116.

8. Lisa Seaman, "Cancel My Appointments—'til the Year 2000," *Wired* 2 (February 1994): 107.

9. Schone is more blunt: "If you want your Sim citizens to throw you a parade, you'd best push land values up so high that poor folks leave town." Schone, "Building Rome in a Day," 50. Crassly put, but Schone has a point.

10. Robert Dahl, *Who Governs?* (New Haven: Yale University Press, 1961).

11. Schone, "Building Rome in a Day," 50.

12. Starr, "Seductions of Sim," 20.

13. Schone, "Building Rome in a Day," 50.

14. Refuse is conveyed through large-bore steel pipes by an air current traveling at about 20–25 meters per second. See *Kista, Husby, Akall: A Digest for Planners, Politicians, and Critics* (Stockholm: Stockholm Information Board, 1976).

15. See Glaab and Brown, *A History of Urban America;* and Reps, *The Making of Urban America.*

16. Schone, "Building Rome in a Day," 50.

17. It is worth noting, however, that in SimCity 2000 there are riots caused by "heat, crime and unemployment" or by long power blackouts. Bremer, *SimCity 2000 User Manual,* 122. Clearly, the creators of SimCity have rejected Edward C. Banfield's ruminations, in chapter 9 of *The Unheavenly City,* about "rioting mainly for fun and profit."

18. Schone, "Building Rome in a Day," 50.

19. Ibid.

20. Jackson, *A Sense of Place,* 153.

21. Then again, skylines are not uninteresting. See, for example, Spiro Kostof, *The City Shaped: Urban Patterns and Meanings through History* (Boston: Little, Brown and Co., 1991), chap. 5.

22. Mumford, *The City in History,* 277.

23. Witold Rybczynski, "Mysteries of the Mall," review of *A Sense of Place, A Sense of Time,* by J. B. Jackson, *New York Review of Books* 41 (July 14, 1994): 31–32.

24. David Macaulay, *Motel of the Mysteries* (Boston: Houghton Mifflin, 1979).

25. Leonardo Benevolo, *The History of the City* (Cambridge: MIT Press, 1980), 443.

26. Mumford, *The City in History,* 349.

27. Ibid., 348.

28. *The Blue Guides: Northern Italy from the Alps to Rome,* 7th ed., by Alta MacAdam (Chicago: Rand McNally and Co., 1978), 426.

29. Mumford, *The City in History,* 348.

30. R. W. B. Lewis, *The City of Florence,* 129.

31. *The Blue Guides: Northern Italy from the Alps to Rome,* 456.

32. It is significant that, as head of the cathedral's architectural workshop, Arnolfo was working more for the commune than for the church. For example, he received a lifetime exemption from military duty and municipal taxes. Giotto "was even more clearly an employee of the city." David Friedman, *Florentine New Towns: Urban Design in the Late Middle Ages* (New York and Cambridge: Architectural History Foundation and MIT Press, 1988), 164.

33. Benevolo, *The History of the City,* 446.

34. Mumford, *The City in History,* 238.

SELECT BIBLIOGRAPHY

THE NOTES CONTAIN COMPLETE REFERENCES TO THE PRIMARY AND secondary sources that directly inform the text. The following works are recommended to those wishing to read further in the history and politics of urban form.

Abbott, Carl. *Political Terrain: Washington, D.C., from Tidewater Town to Global Metropolis.* Chapel Hill: University of North Carolina Press, 1999.

Alexander, Christopher, et al. *A Pattern Language: Towns, Buildings, Construction.* New York: Oxford University Press, 1977.

Altshuler, Alan. *The City Planning Process: A Political Analysis.* Ithaca, N.Y.: Cornell University Press, 1965.

Anderson, Martin. *The Federal Bulldozer: A Critical Analysis of Urban Renewal, 1949–1962.* Cambridge: MIT Press, 1964.

Argan, Giulio. *The Renaissance City.* New York: George Braziller, 1969.

Arkes, Hadley. *The Philosopher in the City: The Moral Dimensions of Urban Politics.* Princeton: Princeton University Press, 1983.

Bacon, Edmund N. *Design of Cities.* New York: Viking, 1974.

Banfield, Edward C. *The Unheavenly City Revisited.* Boston: Little, Brown and Co., 1974.

Barnett, Jonathan. *The Elusive City: Five Centuries of Design, Ambition, and Miscalculation.* New York: Harper and Row, 1986.

Bender, Thomas. *Toward an Urban Vision: Ideas and Institutions in Nineteenth-Century America.* Lexington: University Press of Kentucky, 1975.

Benevolo, Leonardo. *The History of the City.* Cambridge: MIT Press, 1980.

Birch, Eugenie Ladner. "Radburn and the American Planning Movement: The Persistence of an Idea." *Journal of the American Planning Association* 46 (October 1980): 424–39.

Blakely, Edward J., and Mary Gail Snyder. *Fortress America: Gated Communities in the United States.* Washington, D.C.: Brookings Institution Press, 1997.

Blau, Judith R, Mark La Gory, and John S. Pipkin, eds. *Professionals and Urban Form.* Albany: State University of New York Press, 1983.

Blowers, Andrew, and Bob Evans, eds. *Town Planning into the Twenty-first Century.* London: Routledge, 1997.

Boyer, M. Christine. *CyberCities: Visual Perception in the Age of Electronic Communication.* New York: Princeton Architectural Press, 1996.

———. *The City of Collective Memory: Its Historical Imagery and Architectural Entertainments.* Cambridge: MIT Press, 1994.

———. *Dreaming the Rational City: The Myth of American City Planning.* Cambridge: MIT Press, 1983.

Braunfels, Wolfgang. *Urban Design in Western Europe: Regime and Architecture, 900–1900.* Translated by Kenneth J. Northcott. Chicago: University of Chicago Press, 1988.

Broadbent, Geoffrey. *Emerging Concepts in Urban Space Design.* London: E & FN Spon, 1990.

Brown, Frank E. *Roman Architecture.* New York: George Braziller, 1976.

Buder, Stanley. *Visionaries and Planners: The Garden City Movement and the Modern Community.* New York: Oxford University Press, 1990.

Burke, Gerald L. *The Making of Dutch Towns: A Study in Urban Development from the Tenth to the Seventeenth Centuries.* London: Cleauer-Hume Press, 1956.

Byington, Margaret F. *Homestead: The Households of a Mill Town.* 1910. Pittsburgh: University Center for International Studies, University of Pittsburgh, 1974.

Calthorpe, Peter. *The Next American Metropolis: Ecology, Community, and the American Dream.* New York: Princeton Architectural Press, 1993.

Caro, Robert A. *The Power Broker: Robert Moses and the Fall of New York.* New York: Vintage, 1975.

Cherry, Gordon. *Cities and Plans.* London: Arnold, 1988.

Choay, Françoise. *The Modern City: Planning in the Nineteenth Century.* New York: George Braziller, 1970.

Collins, George R., ed. *Visionary Drawings of Architecture and Planning.* Cambridge: MIT Press, 1979.

Collins, George R., and Christiane Crasemann Collins. *Camillo Sitte: The Birth of Modern City Planning.* 1889. New York: Rizzoli, 1986.

Coupland, Andy, ed. *Reclaiming the City: Mixed Use Development.* London: E & FN Spon, 1997.

Cronon, William. *Nature's Metropolis: Chicago and the Great West.* New York: W. W. Norton, 1991.

Cullingworth, J. B. *The Political Culture of Planning: American Land Use Planning in Comparative Perspective.* New York: Routledge, 1993.

Daniels, Bruce C. *The Connecticut Town: Growth and Development, 1635–1790.* Middletown, Conn.: Wesleyan University Press, 1979.

de la Croix, Horst. *Military Considerations in City Planning.* New York: George Braziller, 1972.

Duany, Andres, Elizabeth Plater-Zyberk, and Jeff Speck. *Suburban Nation: The Rise of Sprawl and the Decline of the American Dream.* New York: North Point Press, 2000.

Ellin, Nan. *Postmodern Urbanism.* New York: Princeton Architectural Press, 1999.

Fairfield, John D. *The Mysteries of the Great City: The Politics of Urban Design, 1877–1937.* Columbus: Ohio State University Press, 1993.

Faludi, Andreas. *Planning Theory.* Oxford: Pergamon Press, 1973.

Fishman, Robert. *Bourgeois Utopias: The Rise and Fall of Suburbia.* New York: Basic Books, 1989.

———. *Urban Utopias in the Twentieth Century: Ebenezer Howard, Frank Lloyd Wright, and Le Corbusier.* New York: Basic Books, 1977.

Foglesong, Richard E. *Planning the Capitalist City: The Colonial Era to the 1920s.* Princeton: Princeton University Press, 1986.

Forester, J. *Planning in the Face of Power.* Berkeley: University of California Press, 1989.

Fowler, Edmund P. *Building Cities That Work.* Montreal: McGill-Queen's University Press, 1992.

French, Jere Stuart. *Urban Space: A Brief History of the City Square.* Dubuque, Iowa: Kendall/Hunt Publishing Company, 1978.

Friedman, David. *Florentine New Towns: Urban Design in the Late Middle Ages.* New York and Cambridge: Architectural History Foundation and MIT Press, 1988.

Friedmann, J. *Planning in the Public Domain: From Knowledge to Action.* Princeton: Princeton University Press, 1987.

Fustel de Coulanges, Numa Denis. *The Ancient City: A Study on the Religion, Laws, and Institutions of Greece and Rome.* 1864. Baltimore: Johns Hopkins University Press, 1980.

Galatay, Ervin Y. *New Towns: Antiquity to the Present.* New York: Braziller, 1975.

Gans, Herbert J. *People and Plans: Essays on Urban Problems and Solutions.* New York: Basic Books, 1968.

———. *The Levittowners: Ways of Life and Politics in a New Suburban Community.* London: Allen Lane, 1967.

Garreau, Joel. *Edge City: Life on the New Frontier.* New York: Doubleday, 1991.

Geddes, Patrick. *Cities in Evolution: An Introduction to the Town Planning Movement and to the Study of Civics.* 1915. London: Ernest Benn, 1968.

Giedion, Sigfried. *Space, Time, and Architecture: The Growth of a New Tradition.* 5th ed. Cambridge: Harvard University Press, 1967.

Girouard, Mark. *Cities and People: A Social and Architectural History.* New Haven: Yale University Press, 1985.

Glaab, Charles N., and A. Theodore Brown. *A History of Urban America.* 2d ed. New York: Macmillan, 1976.

Glazer, Nathan, and Mark Lilla, eds. *The Public Face of Architecture: Civic Culture and Public Spaces.* New York: Free Press, 1987.

Goodman, Paul, and Percival Goodman. *Communitas: Means of Livelihood and Ways of Life.* New York: Vintage, 1960.

Gratz, Roberta Brandes. *The Living City: How Urban Residents Are Revitalizing America's Neighborhoods and Downtown Shopping Districts by Thinking Small in a Big Way.* New York: Simon and Schuster, 1989.

Greenbie, Barrie B. *Spaces. Dimensions of the Human Landscape.* New Haven: Yale University Press, 1981.

Hall, Peter. *Cities in Civilization.* New York: Pantheon, 1998.

———. *Cities of Tomorrow: An Intellectual History of Urban Planning and Design in the Twentieth Century.* Oxford: Basil Blackwell, 1996.

———. *Great Planning Disasters.* Berkeley: University of California Press, 1982.

———. *The World Cities.* 2d ed. New York: McGraw-Hill, 1977.

Hardoy, Jorge E. *Pre-Columbian Cities.* Translated by Judith Thorne. 1964. New York: Walker and Co., 1973.

Harvey, David. *The Urban Experience.* Baltimore: Johns Hopkins University Press, 1989.

Hayden, Dolores. *The Power of Place: Urban Landscapes as Public History.* Cambridge: MIT Press, 1995.

———. *Seven American Utopias: The Architecture of Communitarian Socialism, 1790–1975.* Cambridge: MIT Press, 1976.

Hegemann, Werner, and Elbert Peets. *The American Vitruvius: An Architect's Handbook of Civic Art.* 1922. New York: Benjamin Blom, 1972.

Hines, Thomas S. *Burnham of Chicago: Architect and Planner.* Chicago: University of Chicago Press, 1979.

Hohenberg, Paul M., and Lynn Hollen Lees. *The Making of Urban Europe, 1000–1950.* Cambridge: Harvard University Press, 1985.

Howard, Ebenezer. *Garden Cities of To-morrow.* Edited by F. J. Osborn, introductory essay by Lewis Mumford. 1898. Cambridge: MIT Press, 1965.

Jackson, John Brinckerhoff. *Landscape in Sight: Looking at America.* Edited by Helen Lefkowitz Horowitz. New Haven: Yale University Press, 1997.

———. *A Sense of Place, A Sense of Time.* New Haven: Yale University Press, 1994.

Jackson, Kenneth T. *Crabgrass Frontier: The Suburbanization of the United States.* New York: Oxford, 1985.

Jacobs, Allan B. *Great Streets.* Cambridge: MIT Press, 1996.

Jacobs, Allan, and Donald Appleyard. "Toward an Urban Design Manifesto." *Journal of the American Planning Association* 53 (winter 1987): 112–20.

Jacobs, Jane. *The Death and Life of Great American Cities.* New York: Vintage, 1961.

Johnston, Norman J. *Cities in the Round.* Seattle: University of Washington Press, 1983.

Josephson, Paul R. *New Atlantis Revisited: Akademgorodok, the Siberian City of Science.* Princeton: Princeton University Press, 1997.

Judd, Dennis R., and Susan S. Fainstein, eds. *The Tourist City.* New Haven: Yale University Press, 1999.

Kirk, Russell. *St. Andrews.* London: B. T. Batsford, 1954.

Kostof, Spiro. *The City Assembled: The Elements of Urban Form through History.* Boston: Little, Brown and Co., 1992.

———. *The City Shaped: Urban Patterns and Meanings through History.* Boston: Little, Brown and Co., 1991.

Krieger, Alex, ed. *Andres Duany and Elizabeth Plater-Zyberk: Towns and Town-Making Principles.* New York: Rizzoli, 1991.

Krueckeberg, Donald A., ed. *Introduction to Planning History in the United States.* New Brunswick, N.J.: Center for Urban Policy Research, Rutgers University, 1983.

Krumholz, Norman. "A Retrospective View of Equity Planning, Cleveland, 1969–1979." *Journal of the American Planning Association* 48 (spring 1982): 163–74.

Krumholz, Norman, and J. Forester. *Making Equity Planning Work: Leadership in the Public Sector.* Philadelphia: Temple University Press, 1990.

Kunstler, James Howard. *The Geography of Nowhere: The Rise and Decline of America's Man-Made Landscape.* New York: Simon and Schuster, 1993.

Langdon, Philip. *A Better Place to Live: Reshaping the American Suburb.* Amherst: University of Massachusetts Press, 1994.

Le Corbusier. *The Radiant City.* 1933. New York: Orion Press, 1967.

———. *The City of To-morrow and Its Planning.* Translated by Frederick Etchells. New York: Payson and Clarke, 1929.

LeGates, Richard T., and Frederic Stout, eds. *The City Reader.* London: Routledge, 1996.

Lewis, R. W. B. *The City of Florence.* New York: Henry Holt and Co., 1995.

Lockridge, Kenneth A. *A New England Town: The First Hundred Years.* New York: W. W. Norton and Co., 1970.

Long, Norton E. "The Local Community as an Ecology of Games." *American Journal of Sociology* 64 (November 1958): 251–61.

Lynch, Kevin. *A Theory of Good City Form*. Cambridge: MIT Press, 1981.

———. *The Image of the City*. Cambridge: Technology Press, 1960.

Meller, Helen. *Towns, Plans, and Society in Modern Britain*. Cambridge: Cambridge University Press, 1997.

———. *Patrick Geddes: Social Evolutionist and City Planner*. London: Routledge, 1990.

Melosi, Martin V. *The Sanitary City: Urban Infrastructure in America from Colonial Times to the Present*. Baltimore: Johns Hopkins University Press, 2000.

Meyerson, Martin, and Edward C. Banfield. *Politics, Planning, and the Public Interest: The Case of Public Housing in Chicago*. Glencoe, Ill.: Free Press, 1955.

Miller, Zane L. *Boss Cox's Cincinnati: Urban Politics in the Progressive Era*. New York: Oxford University Press, 1968.

Mitchell, William J. *City of Bits: Space, Place, and the Infobahn*. Cambridge: MIT Press, 1996.

Moe, Richard, and Carter Wilkie. *Changing Places: Rebuilding Community in the Age of Sprawl*. New York: Henry Holt and Co., 1997.

More, Sir Thomas. *Utopia*. Translated by Robert M. Adams. 1516. New York: Norton, 1991.

Morgan, William N. *Prehistoric Architecture in the Eastern United States*. Cambridge: MIT Press, 1980.

Morris, A. E. J. *History of Urban Form before the Industrial Revolutions*. 3d ed. Harlow: Longman Scientific and Technical, 1994.

Mumford, Lewis. "Home Remedies for Urban Cancer." In *The Urban Prospect*. New York: Harcourt, Brace and World, 1968.

———. *The City in History*. New York: Harcourt, Brace and World, 1961.

Mundy, John H., and Peter Riesenberg, eds. *The Medieval Town*. Princeton: Van Nostrand, 1958.

Nivola, Pietro S. *Laws of the Landscape: How Policies Shape Cities in Europe and America*. Washington, D.C.: Brookings Institution Press, 1999.

O'Brien, Patricia J. "Urbanism, Cahokia and Middle Mississippian." *Archaeology* 25 (1972): 188–97.

Oldenburg, Ray. *The Great Good Place. Cafés, Coffee Shops, Community Centers, Beauty Parlors, General Stores, Bars, Hangouts, and How They Get You through the Day*. New York: Paragon House, 1989.

Olmsted, Frederick Law. *Public Parks and the Enlargement of Towns*. 1870. New York: Arno, 1970.

Olsen, Donald J. *The City as a Work of Art: London, Paris, Vienna*. New Haven: Yale University Press, 1986.

Open Space in Urban Design: A Report Prepared for the Cleveland Development Foundation, sponsored by the Junior League of Cleveland, Inc. Cleveland, 1964.

Packer, James E. *The Forum of Trajan in Rome: A Study of the Monuments*, with architectural reconstructions by Kevin Lee Sarring and James E. Packer, additional artwork by Gilbert Gorski. 5 vols. Berkeley: University of California Press, 1997.

Papadakis, Andreas, and Harriet Watson, eds. *New Classicism: Omnibus Volume*. New York: Rizzoli, 1990.

Peterson, Paul E. *City Limits*. Chicago: University of Chicago Press, 1981.

Pirenne, Henri. *Medieval Cities: Their Origins and the Revival of Trade.* Princeton: Princeton University Press, 1925.

Porter, Paul R., and David C. Sweet, eds. *Rebuilding America's Cities: Roads to Recovery.* New Brunswick, N.J.: Center for Urban Policy Research, 1984.

Rasmussen, Steen Eiler. *Towns and Buildings.* Cambridge: MIT Press, 1969.

Reps, John W. *Monumental Washington: The Planning and Development of the Capital Center.* Princeton: Princeton University Press, 1967.

———. *The Making of Urban America.* Princeton: Princeton University Press, 1965.

Robertson, Donald. *Pre-Columbian Architecture.* New York: George Braziller, 1963.

Rodwin, Lloyd. *Cities and City Planning.* New York: Plenum, 1981.

Rogers, Richard. *Cities for a Small Planet.* London: Faber and Faber, 1997.

Rosenau, Helen. *The Ideal City: Its Architectural Evolution in Europe.* 3d ed. London: Methuen and Co., 1983.

Rubenstein, James M. *The French New Towns.* Baltimore: Johns Hopkins University Press, 1978.

Rybczynski, Witold. *A Clearing in the Distance: Frederick Law Olmsted and America in the Nineteenth Century.* New York: Scribner, 1999.

———. *City Life: Urban Expectations in a New World.* New York: Scribner, 1995.

Rykwert, Joseph. *The Seduction of Place: The City in the Twenty-first Century.* New York: Pantheon, 2000.

Saalman, Howard. *Medieval Cities.* New York: George Braziller, 1968.

Sarin, M. *Urban Planning in the Third World: The Chandigarh Experience.* London: Mansell, 1982.

Scargill, Ian. *Urban France.* London: Croon Helm, 1983.

———. *The Form of Cities.* New York: St. Martin's Press, 1979.

Schaedel, Richard P., Jorge E. Hardoy, and Nora Scott Kinzer, eds. *Urbanization in the Americas: From Its Beginnings to the Present.* The Hague: Mouton Publishers, 1978.

Schaffer, Daniel. *Garden Cities for America: The Radburn Experience.* Philadelphia: Temple University Press, 1982.

———, ed. *Two Centuries of American Planning.* London: Mansell Publishing, 1988.

Schuyler, David. *The New Urban Landscape: The Redefinition of City Form in Nineteenth-Century America.* Baltimore: Johns Hopkins University Press, 1986.

Scott, Mel. *American City Planning since 1890.* Berkeley: University of California Press, 1969.

Scully, Vincent. *Architecture: The Natural and the Manmade.* New York: St. Martin's Press, 1991.

Sennett, Richard. *The Uses of Disorder.* New York: Vintage, 1970.

Spreiregen, Paul D., ed. *On the Art of Designing Cities: Selected Essays of Elbert Peets.* Cambridge: MIT Press, 1968.

Squier, Ephraim G., and Edwin H. Davis. *Ancient Monuments of the Mississippi Valley.* 1848. Washington, D.C.: Smithsonian Institution Press, 1998.

Stein, Clarence S. *Toward New Towns for America.* New York: Reinhold, 1957.

Stephenson, R. Bruce. *Visions of Eden: Environmentalism, Urban Planning, and City Building in St. Petersburg, Florida, 1900–1995.* Columbus: Ohio State University Press, 1997.

Stilgoe, John R. *Borderland: Origins of the American Suburb, 1820–1939*. New Haven: Yale University Press, 1988.

———. *Common Landscape of America, 1580 to 1845*. New Haven: Yale University Press, 1982.

Sucher, David. *City Comforts: How to Build an Urban Village*. Seattle: City Comforts Press, 1995.

Sutcliffe, Anthony. *Towards the Planned City: Germany, Britain, the United States, and France, 1780–1914*. New York: St. Martin's Press, 1981.

———, ed. *Metropolis, 1890–1940*. London: Mansell, 1984.

Tafuri, Manfredo. *Theories and History of Architecture*. New York: Harper and Row, 1976.

Tanghe, Jan, Sieg Vlaeminck, and Jo Berghoef. *Living Cities: A Case for Urbanism and Guidelines for Re-urbanization*. Oxford: Pergamon Press, 1984.

Thomas, Cyrus. *The Circular, Square, and Octagonal Earthworks of Ohio*. Washington, D.C.: Government Printing Office, 1889.

Tod, Ian, and Michael Wheeler. *Utopia*. New York: Harmony Books, 1978.

Tuan, Yi-Fu. *Escapism*. Baltimore: Johns Hopkins University Press, 1998.

———. *Space and Place: The Perspective of Experience*. Minneapolis: University of Minnesota Press, 1977.

Upton, Dell, and John M. Vlach, eds. *Common Places: Readings in American Vernacular Architecture*. Athens: University of Georgia Press, 1986.

van der Wal, Coenraad. *In Praise of Common Sense: Planning the Ordinary: A Physical Planning History of the IJsselmeerpolders*. Rotterdam: 010 Publishers, 1997.

———. *Villages in the IJsselmeerpolders: From Slootdorp to Zeewolde*. Lelystad, Netherlands: IJsselmeerpolders Development Authority, 1985.

Venturi, Robert. *Complexity and Contradiction in Architecture*. 2d ed. New York: Museum of Modern Art, 1977.

Venturi, Robert, Denise Scott Brown, and Steven Izenour. *Learning from Las Vegas: The Forgotten Symbolism of Architectural Form*. Cambridge: MIT Press, 1977.

Vitruvius. *The Ten Books on Architecture*. 1914. New York: Dover, 1960.

Von Eckardt, Wolf. *Back to the Drawing Board!* Washington, D.C.: New Republic Books, 1978.

Ward, Stephen V. *Planning and Urban Change*. London: Paul Chapman Publishing, 1994.

Ward-Perkins, J. B. *Cities of Ancient Greece and Italy*. New York: George Braziller, 1974.

Warner, Sam Bass. *Streetcar Suburbs: The Process of Growth in Boston, 1870–1900*. 2d ed. Cambridge: Harvard University Press, 1978.

Whyte, William H. *City: Rediscovering the Center*. New York: Doubleday, 1988.

———. *The Social Life of Small Urban Spaces*. Washington, D.C.: Conservation Foundation, 1980.

Wilson, James Q., ed. *Urban Renewal: The Record and the Controversy*. Cambridge: MIT Press, 1966.

Wilson, William H. *The City Beautiful Movement*. Baltimore: Johns Hopkins University Press, 1989.

Wojtowicz, Peter. *Lewis Mumford and American Modernism: Eutopian Theories for Architecture and Urban Planning*. Cambridge: Cambridge University Press, 1996.

Wood, Joseph S., with a contribution by Michael P. Steinitz. *The New England Village*. Baltimore: Johns Hopkins University Press, 1997.

Wright, Gwendolyn. *Building the Dream: A Social History of Housing in America.* Cambridge: MIT Press, 1983.

Zucker, Paul. *Town and Square: From the Agora to the Village Green.* New York: Columbia University Press, 1959.

SELECT

BIBLIOGRAPHY

ILLUSTRATION CREDITS

Frontispiece: *Peaceful Shaker Village* (Cleveland: The Van Sweringen Company, 1927), n.p. Courtesy of the Western Reserve Historical Society.

Figure 1: From Braun & Hogenburg, *Civitates Orbis Terrarum*. By permission of the Folger Shakespeare Library. Quote is from *The City of Tomorrow and Its Planning*, trans. Frederick Etchells (New York: Payson and Clark, 1929), 91.

Figure 2: From Wolf Von Eckardt, *Back to the Drawing Board!* (Washington, D.C.: New Republic Books, 1978), p. 67.

Figure 4: From James E. Packer, *The Forum of Trajan in Rome: A Study of the Monuments*, with architectural reconstructions by Kevin Lee Sarring and James E. Packer, additional artwork by Gilbert Gorski, 5 vols. (Berkeley: University of California Press, 1997). Courtesy of Mr. Packer.

Figure 7: Photograph by John Stephens. Copyright © 2000 The J. Paul Getty Trust.

Figure 8: Courtesy of Cahokia Mounds Historic Site.

Figure 9: From William N. Morgan, *Prehistoric Architecture in the Eastern United States* (Cambridge: MIT Press, 1980), p. 114. Courtesy of Mr. Morgan.

Figure 11: From Ephraim G. Squier and Edwin H. Davis, *Ancient Monuments of the Mississippi Valley* (1848, Washington, D.C.: Smithsonian Institution Press, 1998). Courtesy of the Library of Congress.

Figure 12: Drawing by Jon L. Gibson. Courtesy of Mr. Gibson.

Figure 13: Courtesy of Alabama Museum of Natural History, Tuscaloosa.

Figure 14: Courtesy of the Western Reserve Historical Society.

Figure 15: From *The Group Plan of the Public Buildings of the City of Cleveland.* Report made to the Honorable Tom L. Johnson, Mayor, and to the Honorable Board of Public Service by Daniel H. Burnham, John M. Carrere, Arnold W. Brunner, Board of Supervision (New York: Cheltenham Press, 1903). Courtesy of the Western Reserve Historical Society.

Figure 16: Courtesy of the Cleveland Union Terminal Collection, Cleveland State University.

Figure 18: Drawing by Jim Anderson. Courtesy of Anderson Illustration Associates.

Figure 19: From *Peaceful Shaker Village*. Courtesy of the Western Reserve Historical Society.

Figure 20: From *Peaceful Shaker Village*. Courtesy of the Western Reserve Historical Society.

Figure 21: Ernest J. Bohn collection, Department of Special Collections, Kelvin Smith Library, Case Western Reserve University. Courtesy of Case Western Reserve University.

Figure 22: From Le Corbusier, *The City of To-morrow and Its Planning*.

Figure 23: From *Erieview, Cleveland, Ohio, An Urban Renewal Plan for Downtown Cleveland* (New York: I. M. Pei and Associates, 1961). Courtesy of the Western Reserve Historical Society.

Figure 24: From *Erieview, Cleveland, Ohio, An Urban Renewal Plan for Downtown Cleveland*. Courtesy of the Western Reserve Historical Society.

Figure 25: From *Cleveland Policy Planning Report* (Cleveland: City Planning Commission, 1975).

Figure 26: From *Cleveland Policy Planning Report*.

Figure 27: From John T. Howard, *What's Ahead for Cleveland?* (Cleveland: Regional Association of Cleveland, 1941). Courtesy of the Western Reserve Historical Society.

Figure 30: From John T. Howard, *What's Ahead for Cleveland?* Courtesy of the Western Reserve Historical Society.

Figure 32: From John T. Howard, *What's Ahead for Cleveland?* Courtesy of the Western Reserve Historical Society.

Figure 38: Photograph by Richard Sexton, © 2000. Courtesy of Mr. Sexton and Reva Lammers.

Figure 47: LC-BH8233-15. Courtesy of the Library of Congress.

Figure 48: Photograph by John Donat. Courtesy of Mr. Donat.

Figure 49: Photograph by Michael Freeman, © 1998. Courtesy of Mr. Freeman.

Figure 52: Courtesy of Chorley Handford Ltd.

Figure 53: Pen-and-ink drawing by John M. Pearson, from *A Guided Walk round St. Andrews*. Courtesy of Mr. Pearson.

Figure 54: John Geddy, *S Andre sive Andreapolis Scotiae Universitas Metropolitana*, circa 1580. Reproduced by permission of the Trustees of the National Library of Scotland.

Figure 55: Courtesy of the University of St. Andrews.

INDEX

References to illustrations are in italics

61, 77, 79, 83, 106, 122; as generators of urban vitality, 64, 118; natural proliferation of, 61, 211n. 7; as places to play, 2; and traffic congestion, 178. *See also* Jacobs, Jane

Sunnyside Gardens (New York, N.Y.), 105, 110

superblocks, 79, 105, 110, 122

Superior, Wisc., 181

sustainable cities. *See* "smart growth"

Tallmadge, Ohio, 52

Teotihuacán, Mexico, 47, 48

Thatcher, Margaret, 149, 151, 155

Theodoric (emperor), 22

Thermidorean Reaction, 7, 8, 104

Thompson Design Group, 85, 86

Tocqueville, Alexis de, 125

"tourist bubbles," 86, 95

Townsend, Lloyd K., 45, 48

Trajan (emperor), 15, 16, 17, 18, 19, 27; Trajan's Market, 15, *23. See also* Forum of Trajan

Trillin, Calvin, 94

The Truman Show (film), 117

Tugwell, Rexford Guy, 106

"turf," 3, 165. *See also* Jacobs, Jane

Turin, Italy, 3

Turner, Frederick Jackson, 52

Turner, Paul Venable, 167

Tyson's Corner (Va.), 113, 137

University of Cambridge, 173–74

University of Chicago, 165

University of Oxford, 166, 174

University of Paris, 130, 167

University of St. Andrews: the bunks, 171; North Haugh development, 172–73; "not a campus university," 166; origins of, 167; and Perth, 168, 170, 175; pier walk, *175,* 176, 183; St. Leonard's, 168, 169, 171, 174; St. Mary's, 168, 169; St. Salvator's, *167,* 168, 169, 172, 174; University College, Dundee, 172, 174, 175. *See also* St. Andrews, Scotland

Unwin, Sir Raymond, 67, 71, 75, 101, 103, 109

urban growth boundary (UGB), 119–21

urban renewal: as land grab, 79–82; and modernist project of therapeutic cleansing, 93–94; and public housing, 77–79, 82, 88, 89; as radical surgery, 80; and SimCity, 178. *See also* Erieview

urban revolution. *See* Childe, V. Gordon

utopia: and Big Plans, 5, 12, 187; *vs.* the market, 111; and professional planners, 76–77; and the Puritans, 49–50; and SimCity, 178, 181, 182

Van Sweringen, Mantis James, and Oris Paxton Van Sweringen, 65, 66, 67, 68, 69, 70, 71, 72, 73, 75

VDNX (Exhibition of the Achievement of the People's Economy), 10–11

Venice, Italy, 3, 5, 105

Venturi, Robert, 2

Versailles, France, 68, 125, 134

Vienna, Austria, 75

Virgil, 22

Vitruvius, 12, 49

Von Eckardt, Wolf, 8

Walthall, John A., 32

Walzer, Michael, 64

"warning out," 52

Washburn, Layton K., 91

Washington, D.C.: baroque regimentation, 133; as City Beautiful, 59; Georgetown, 61, 137; as government ghetto, 61–62; influence of Paris on, 125, 134; McMillan Commission, 142; Metro, 136–40, *137;* Old Post Office (OPO), 142–45, *144;* Reagan Building, 122, 145; Reagan National Airport, 124; slums, 78; suburbs, 117. *See also* L'Enfant, Major Charles Pierre; slug lines

Watson Brake (La.): public architecture, 42–43; putative urbanism of, 44

Waxman, Sharon, 17, 18, 20

Webb, Clarence H., 41

ABOUT THE AUTHOR

Kenneth Kolson was born in Braddock, Pennsylvania, and educated at Allegheny College and the University of Kentucky. He has taught primarily at Hiram College and the University of Maryland, College Park. In 1998, he was a John Adams Fellow at the University of London and an Eccles Fellow at the British Library. A resident of Alexandria, Virginia, Mr. Kolson is Deputy Director for Research at the National Endowment for the Humanities, Washington, D.C.